THE
LOW MAINTENANCE
GARDEN

GRAHAM ROSE

Published in cooperation with
the New York Botanical Garden Institute of Urban Horticulture

PENGUIN BOOKS

The Low Maintenance Garden
© Frances Lincoln Limited 1983
Text © Graham Rose 1983

The Low Maintenance Garden was
conceived, edited and designed by
Frances Lincoln Limited,
Apollo Works
5 Charlton Kings Road
London NW5 2SB

First published in 1983 by
The Viking Press (A Studio Book)
40 West 23rd Street, New York, N.Y. 10010

Published simultaneously in Canada by
Penguin Books Canada Limited

Reprinted in Penguin Books 1987

ISBN 0 14 046.807 2

(CIP data available)

Set in England
Printed and bound in Yugoslavia
by Mladinska knjiga, Ljubljana

CONTENTS

FOREWORD

For ten years, while converting the grounds of a derelict farmstead into a pleasing garden, my wife and I were obliged to garden at weekends only. The experience taught us a great deal about how much can be accomplished in a garden even with only limited time available. By changing our previously held notions about gardening, we coped quite easily with an acre of land and still had time to go to the races if we chose. But it did mean that we had to abandon over-scrupulous attitudes to garden tidiness, and to give up traditional rituals like raising large numbers of annuals under glass. We also had to make the effort to seek out the latest labor-saving equipment, and to find out as much as possible about modern techniques.

Although, in many cases, the tried and tested approach to gardening probably works the best, it is not always appropriate for busy people, nor is it the sole means of achieving an enjoyable garden. Too many people are discouraged from trying to create an attractive garden because they are led to believe that it takes more time than it does. It is to encourage them, as well as to help those who wish simply to cut down on time spent in their gardens, that this book has been written.

I am, of course, not alone in thinking that gardening can be made much easier and, in writing this book, I have drawn on the knowledge and experience of many like-minded people, to whom I would like to express my appreciation and offer my thanks. For their help in compiling or checking the lists of suitable low maintenance plants, I am indebted to: Dr Bill Klein, Paul Meyer and Bill Graham of the Morris Arboretum, Don Evemy and Leo Pemberton, Dorothy Sheffield and Elizabeth McLean, Mary Taylor and Mrs Michael Thompson, Gary Goldbach, Max Sestili Jnr, Stirling (Bill) Macoboy, Charles Nelson, Beth Chatto, Charles Notcutt, Philippe Bonduel and Arnaud Descat. For their general advice, I would like to single out Xenia Field, Geoff Hamilton, Peter Seabrook, Roy Lancaster, Richard Carter-Jonas, Imogen Tucker, Tony Colmer, Niek Roozen, Henriette Shattuck, Robert Ferec, Pierre Benet, Gerard Mathet and Louisette Marty.

A special debt of gratitude is owed to Hedley Thomas, Malcolm Hamilton, Fred Dorn, Graham Sturgess, Edward Bals, Steve Kenward and Jimmy Studer for information on some of the latest techniques and equipment.

Finally, I would like to thank Felicia Joseph who made a wonderful job of turning my messy manuscript into typed copy, and the team of people at Frances Lincoln Limited who were responsible for putting this book together, in particular Susan Berry, Caroline Hillier and Louise Tucker, as well as the artists who produced the splendid illustrations.

My special thanks are reserved for Frances Lincoln, whose idea it was that I should write this book, and for Grace, Doff and Liesi who tolerated the chaos that it created.

CREATING A LOW MAINTENANCE GARDEN

PRINCIPLES AND PLANNING

If you crave the peace and pleasures of a garden as a foil to the stresses of modern life, but lack the time, money or opportunity to maintain it in the traditional manner, the concept of a beautiful garden that looks after itself is irresistible. But is it really possible? As the achievements of good modern designers demonstrate, exciting low maintenance gardens can be created: colorful, fragrant and visually splendid, they require only a fraction of the effort normally associated with the traditional garden, as a result of the tremendous strides that have been made in gardening science and technology in recent years. Hardier, more disease-resistant varieties of some of the most exquisite plants have been bred; cheaper and surer ways of propagating them have been developed, and the previously time-consuming task of feeding and watering has been reduced to a minimum, with the introduction of highly concentrated slow-release fertilizers and the development of auto-

matically controlled drip-watering systems. Nowadays, large numbers of plants can be bought containerized from the growing ranks of nurseries and garden stores, giving the gardener a wide range of well-grown plants that not only provide a garden with an almost instant feeling of maturity but remove the need for time-consuming attention during the troublesome period of the plant's early development. Add to this the advances in the understanding of chemical pesticides and weed-killers which have led to much safer methods of weed and pest control, and you have an almost revolutionary change in previously held notions of gardening.

When these improvements are used to reduce the maintenance of a sensitively designed and intelligently planted garden, the would-be low maintenance gardener will find himself or herself in possession of a garden that is as satisfying to look at as it is easy to run. The image of the low maintenance garden of the past, with all the

Left *A stretch of water reflects the sky, breaking the uniformity of a formally paved area, and providing a home for a wonderful selection of aquatics. As the plants require no attention after they have been thinned out in early summer, a water feature is a surprisingly easy option in a low maintenance garden.*

Right *A fully paved, virtually maintenance-free garden can look delightful when its contours are softened by a few architectural plants in raised beds, with plenty of foliage on the walls. Plants like geraniums that are not frost-hardy can be over-wintered in a porch, and brought out again after the danger of frost is past to enrich the summer planting. Self-watering containers or a drip irrigation system can be used to avoid the chore of watering.*

PENGUIN HANDBOOKS

THE
LOW MAINTENANCE GARDEN

Graham Rose is the Gardening Correspondent of the *Sunday Times*. An entomologist by training, he worked in Africa and the Middle East for many years before returning to England in 1968 to write for a living. Since then, mainly through his work as a journalist, he has continued to travel widely, visiting gardens in many countries and meeting a large number of gardening experts both abroad, and in England.

sepulchral gloom of a cemetery, has been replaced by some of the most exciting and attractive gardens in the world, designed specifically to be more or less maintenance-free. Marshaled rows of dahlias and formal beds of annuals have been replaced by a much more relaxed approach to planting, where all that is best in nature has been allied to the technological advantages of the 20th century.

The wide variety of choice open to the low maintenance gardener today permits a range of styles that will complement the architecture and environment of most houses and match individual needs and varied circumstances. From the small formal patio with its striking plants of architectural character to the soft evergreen leaves of ground cover plants, or a wildflower meadow studded with patches of brilliant color, the low maintenance gardener can take his pick.

ANALYSING YOUR NEEDS

The elements of low maintenance are simple enough to grasp; putting them into practice is more complex. There is a myriad of solutions to the problem of reducing gardening effort. Much of your success in achieving a garden that is appropriate for your needs lies in striking a balance between the raw materials of the land – its assets and drawbacks – and your own preferences in terms of garden style.

First, the general factors need careful consideration. The land itself must be closely examined, and the type and condition of the soil, the climatic variations, the exposure to sun and shade, and the drainage carefully noted, so that you can plan within the limits they impose. It is foolish to ignore these constraints since a great deal of the hard work in gardening can be removed if the plants are suited to the local conditions. For example, if the garden is low-lying it is doubtful whether sections of it will ever drain satisfactorily. Rather than try to install an expensive drainage system, why not consider turning the dampest section into a bog garden, capitalizing on the liability? Equally, if the soil is limestone, rather than wasting time and effort trying to grow acid-loving plants, profit from the situation and grow those plants that thrive on limestone soil.

Assessing your time
An equally important factor is the time you are likely to have available. It needs to be estimated as realistically as possible; it is no good believing that somehow you will find time to maintain an ambitious planting design when clearly you will not. Such an approach will lead to an uncontrolled garden and a feeling of harassment similar to that felt by conventional gardeners who try to emulate the standards of a botanic garden on a small suburban plot.

It is not only the amount of time that is important, but when it is available. You must work out whether you are likely to be free during the periods of the year when the greatest activity is demanded by the kind of garden you favor (always bearing in mind that nature does not perform exactly to order). Your life-style will to some extent limit your choices – if you have a vacation cottage, with only a few weeks of the year available to work in it, the choice of design and planting is far more limited than if, for example, you are free to spend a little time every weekend in your garden.

Future needs
The various low maintenance options must be carefully considered to suit your future as well as your current

Below left *Attractive meadow grasses, thickly studded with wild flowers, like poppies and daisies, make an ideal, easy-to-care-for surround to a country cottage, but can be used just as successfully in a town garden, to replace a time-consuming area of mown lawn. A wild-flower meadow can be controlled by a once-yearly topping with a hired string trimmer.*

Below *Well-established shrubs can be left to fend for themselves in a semiwild corner of a large garden. The small area of mown path is both functional and serves to draw the eye deep into the wilder part of the garden.*

Right *A heavily wooded area provides an ideal home for any moisture-loving plants like primroses, celandines and phlox. Thickly planted, they form an attractive carpet of vegetation, demanding no work. If carefully chosen, they will provide enchantment throughout the year, while helping to keep any weeds at bay.*

needs. For example, it is natural enough for proud new parents to plan the requirements of their children into their garden at the planning stage, but understandable though this is, it is an attitude which should be modified after some calm thought. The real demands of space made by small children are fairly minimal and can normally be accommodated by a flexible plan which allows a rough grassed area to be turned eventually into a more formal patio. Once they are school age, their requirements increase dramatically – so much so that few normally scaled private gardens can meet them.

So while it is a good idea to keep very young children in mind when planning a garden – particularly, say, where a water feature is concerned (it might need a babyproof surround) – their needs should not be allowed to dominate, as they will be important for a few years only. The parents, however, are likely to want to obtain real pleasure from their garden for a long time.

Having established any current and future requirements, you must consider your own preferences. Doing what you enjoy most never seems like hard work, so if you have a penchant for pearly new potatoes or frost-crisp lettuce cut straight from the garden, why not have a small intensively planted vegetable plot incorporating as many labor-saving features as possible – such as a drip watering system, close-planting or black plastic sheeting laid over the surface to keep the weeds at bay? If you balance this with an area of the garden that takes very little time – by carpeting an area of the garden with ground cover plants or turning a lawn into wild-flower meadow that needs topping only once a year – you have effectively reduced the time spent, while achieving exactly what you want from the garden. Even on a small scale this approach can be effective. If you love roses, time-consuming though they are, why not substitute shrub roses for the hybrid teas? They look just as beautiful but are much easier to grow.

The organic approach
Although chemicals are often advocated as a principal means of cutting down work in the garden, particularly for weed suppression or pest and disease control, controversy rages over the wisdom of applying them;

Above *Carefully studied lumber-work, prominent moss-clad rock features, minimal planting and patterned gravel give this oriental-style garden a soothing, restful harmony. Designed to be seen, rather than used, in a sheltered or enclosed area, such a garden requires only occasional pruning of shrubs and the removal of leaf debris in fall, together with the fairly frequent raking of the gravel into interesting surface patterns, if wished.*

Right *Again an oriental flavor has been achieved, but with relatively few, easy-to-look-after ingredients. High-quality cobbled paving and brickwork, a few carefully chosen plants and an intriguing boulder reflected in the raised pool give this maintenance-free town garden a quiet symmetry with a strongly sculptural feel, demonstrating how good design can successfully overcome the limitations imposed by hard surfaces and minimal planting.*

many people are justifiably anxious about the effects. On the whole, in a well-organized low maintenance garden, weedkillers should be needed only rarely, mainly to solve any problems that organic methods have failed to overcome.

One of the first priorities in any garden, low maintenance or otherwise, is to clear it of all annual and perennial weeds before it is planted. This can be done in one all-out effort (hiring help if need be) by digging over the land and clearing out every scrap of weed that can be seen. Even if you have no objection to chemicals, you should still dig through the land in the same way, but you can help to insure against reinfestation by dosing the land with one of the newest and safest pre-emergent weedkillers (see pp. 150–51).

Once the ground has been thoroughly cleared, annual weeds can be kept at bay by generous amounts of mulch laid over the unplanted bare soil. A variety of materials can be used for mulching (see pp. 148–50); some of them, such as coarse tree bark, are sufficiently attractive in their own right to make an acceptable final surface and, by preventing light from reaching any weed seeds, the mulch will suppress their growth. Where an organic mulch is used it will enrich the soil, helping to support healthy plant growth. Additional organic fertilizer may be needed, as the better prepared the soil initially, the less effort required in the long term on plant maintenance.

Pests and diseases deserve, on the whole, a more determined approach. Real plagues of insects or infections by disease can rarely be satisfactorily controlled in the garden by relying on natural biological measures. Pest and disease attacks will either have to be accepted as inevitable by the organic school (and compensated for by the preservation of the natural system) or more effective immediate control measures will have to be sought. Today, modern chemicals and up-to-date equipment can do this relatively safely, provided that they are used with caution. As in most controversial issues, a balanced attitude is probably the best one to adopt. Except in cases where notoriously susceptible plants are inevitably going to be stricken with damaging diseases (and by rights these plants have no place in the low

maintenance garden), it is sensible to confine chemical controls to a 'fire brigade' operation, using them only when it is obvious that plants are going to be seriously damaged or even lost without them.

TACKLING THE WORK

One of the most important factors in a low maintenance garden is the way in which the investment of time and money is made, particularly when planning a garden on a bare plot. Normally, in a traditional garden, the gardener makes the planning decisions, as well as the input of cash and energy, in a piecemeal fashion, tackling one particular section of the garden each year. Over a long period of time, a considerable amount of money and a great deal of effort is expended; indeed, for many people, much of the pleasure of gardening is derived from this continual planning and reworking. The low maintenance gardener, however, will probably benefit from the line 'pay now, enjoy later'. If you can afford it, most of the plants should be bought at a fairly advanced stage of growth. While it is undoubtedly expensive, it has the advantage that large areas of the garden will achieve maturity quickly, cutting down on interim maintenance. In addition, a good proportion of the soil will have to be covered immediately with an easy-to-care-for surface – either hard materials, ground cover plants or wild flowers and grasses. To provide visual

interest in a garden with a fair amount of hard surface, some remodeling of the landscape may be needed, and that, too, will add to the initial expense and effort.

Where an established garden exists, perhaps entailing far more work than a new owner is prepared to carry out, a gradual approach to the alterations is usually the most sensible. In many cases, the garden will become much more interesting as a result, retaining the benefit of the more attractive elements of the original planting so that

it is mature enough to offer a great deal of charm while considerably less fussy in appearance.

The best approach to transforming a traditional garden into a low maintenance type is to determine which areas require the greatest amount of work and then to remove or reduce them one by one, in keeping with your preferences: turning a lawn that needs mowing into a wild-flower meadow, for example, or a border of mixed annuals and perennials into a shrubbery; widen-

Right *A melée of tall, narrow-leaved plants, with colorful perennials rampaging at their feet, has been partially tamed by the inclusion of a narrow path with its stepping stones of circular slabs, leading the eye through the jungle of plants out of the garden.*

Left *The formality of high-quality paving has been beautifully balanced with an equal area of densely planted ground covers to form an attractive outdoor saloon. The contrasting tones of the foliage and the variety of its forms cleverly counteract any feeling of monotony that a static design of this nature might induce.*

ing paths to take equipment more easily; or creating terraces on a sloping garden to lessen uphill work. If wished, a reduced area of border could be retained, with modified perennial planting, and with areas of bare soil covered with heavy-duty black plastic sheeting masked with gravel to cut down on weeding.

Attitudes to planting

Anyone who wants a garden that will more or less look after itself, particularly if they have previously gardened in a more traditional manner, will have to be prepared to adopt a different approach to the plants themselves. Many gardeners are still influenced by a hangover from the 19th-century fashion for growing wonderful blooms at the expense of the overall charm of the garden. Many (although not all) of the best, most natural-looking low maintenance gardens achieve their feeling of enchantment from the general impression they create, rather than from the eye-catching effects of particular plants. Small imperfections in the planting can often be ignored if the general impression is harmonious. Therefore, good design plays a crucial role in determining the success of a low maintenance garden.

GARDEN DESIGN

The principal goal in any low maintenance garden is to reduce potentially time-consuming chores to a minimum, and to build these factors into your design. The gardens illustrated on pp. 19–25 show how the concept of a garden that almost looks after itself can be created in a wide range of styles. When planning your own garden, whether making small changes to areas of the garden or a new design on a bare plot, you should first make a scale plan of the area showing the relationship of the plot to the sun and to any major features, such as buildings, a fine view or mature trees, that might influence the design. Then consider carefully the component parts of the plan and how they will help to reduce work in the garden, while providing a balanced and harmonious overall impression. (For information on more detailed planning of planting see pp. 42–45.)

Although many books have been written about garden design, amateurs *can* create good-looking gardens without much difficulty. There are a few points that should be borne in mind.

To obtain a greater feeling of space, narrow plots may have to be 'widened' and short plots 'lengthened' artificially by playing perspective tricks, such as leading the eye across the plot to make a narrow area look deceptively wide. Lines leading down the garden away from the eye will give an impression of greater length. This can be heightened by reducing the width of such features as terraces, paths or beds as they run down the garden. A similar effect can be obtained by diminishing the height of hedges, fences, trellises, pergolas or the size of trees and shrubs of the same type.

In nature, the intensity of color diminishes with distance and this feature, too, can be used to deceive the eye if, say, bold reds are used in foreground planting and progressively paler shades (through to the most delicate pinks) are used the further they are planted down the garden.

Since the major feature to limit a garden's length is an obvious end wall, many gardeners choose to mask it completely with hedges of foliage or promontories of shrubbery projecting well into the lower end of the garden from its margins. Archways can be made or gaps left between foliage to lead the eye through a screen of plants, giving the impression of acres more of delightful garden beyond.

These simple perspective tricks work remarkably well and are very easy to contrive. And the likelihood of wanting to play them should be borne in mind by low maintenance gardeners with rather small gardens. Just because a garden is small, and requires little work, there is no reason why it should feel cramped and oppressive.

Although garden design may seem frighteningly abstract, all that is required is a little confidence, a moderate amount of research coupled with some time spent thinking about the problem before acting, and a grasp of the basic principles.

Surrounding the low maintenance garden

Frequently gardeners have to accept the boundary barriers that were established before they arrived.

Left *The thick green drapery of trailing ivy has been used to turn a boundary wall into an asset, instead of allowing it to become a restricting barrier to vision. Easy to look after, it nevertheless allows observers to feel that they are peering into the dim margins of an enchanted forest, with the promise of a more exotic garden beyond.*

Below *Low masonry walls, composed of impressive lumps of rock that seem to have tumbled into place by accident, have been backed by thick evergreen vegetation to make an excellent division between neighboring plots. Durable and attention-free, its loose composition distracts the eye effectively from the fact that it is a frontier.*

Where these are ugly they can be covered with quick-growing evergreen plants. But, generally speaking, any garden benefits if the boundary lines are softened or obscured. New brick, simulated stonework or wooden fencing is far better hidden behind a screen of shrubs and trees. However, if you have inherited a particularly attractive brick or stone wall, particularly when it supports good-looking vegetation, it is sufficient compensation for any barrier to vision.

Masonry used for boundary walls has the advantage of being virtually maintenance-free during the likely lifespan of its builder, but it can be costly. Well-weathered wood, which is much cheaper (provided it is protected against wood rot at the outset), ought to last for a decade without the need for any major repairs. Even then, it is only the supporting posts that decay; their replacement is much easier if they are sunk into

metal post holders, driven well into the ground. If the budget permits, posts made of more expensive, mature, treated hardwood will give much longer service.

Many gardeners who wish to adopt a low maintenance approach may have inherited an already well-grown formal hedge which they are reluctant to lose. Left unclipped to grow as it pleases, this hedging will develop an unpleasing shape. Radical pruning can be used to remodel it, cutting out additional stems at ground level to leave two or three main ones. As the plants recover and thicken naturally, they will develop a much more attractive shape and will need only occasional clipping to keep them within bounds.

For new hedges, the hedging plants recommended in the plants section (see p. 63) have been chosen because they require very little clipping to keep them compact.

Paths

In established gardens, considerable alterations may be needed to both pathways and steps to provide easy access to different areas of the garden – a factor which must not be forgotten when planning a garden on a virgin site. The golden rule is to remember that no matter what your planned layout may be for the paths, the shortest route will always be taken from one point to the next. It pays to think hard about the location of the main areas of activity or work in the garden, and to ensure that they are connected by direct paths of sufficient width to allow large wheelbarrows and other machines to pass easily. Where changes in level are involved, steps should be shallow enough to allow wide planks to be used to bridge the steps, or adjacent ramps provided, to allow the passage of wheeled equipment, or of wheelchairs for disabled gardeners.

Wild-flower meadows and ground cover

No moderate-sized low maintenance garden should contain more than a small area of lawn that needs regular mowing. A patch just large enough for a few people to sit on or lie about on in comfort is sufficient. Even with the smallest lawn, it pays to surround the grass with mowing stones laid below the level of the grass, removing the need for laborious edging.

Natural and relaxed, this style of garden is ideal for someone who wishes to turn a more traditional garden into one that is a great deal less time-consuming, while preserving much of the softness of the planting. The lawn nearest the house had been reduced to a small sitting area, while the far end has been turned into a semiwild meadow, planted with grasses, bulbs and wild flowers. A couple of fruit trees have been retained to permit some of the joys of a productive garden to be savored; soft fruit can also be grown in one of the far hedges, if required. The lawn edging stones, and the stepping-stone path, have been laid below the surface of the mown grass to remove the need for laborious edge trimming. The formal borders have been replaced with perennials and ground cover plants, such as heathers, and clad with gravel.

Scale ├──── 3m / 10ft

An evergreen shrub border on the north-facing side of the plot makes the best of a less favorable position. A few herbs have been grown near the house and the part of the garden closest to the house and likely to receive the most wear has been paved.

1 Compact, easy-to-maintain trees planted along the north and east margins act as a windbreak protecting more tender plants.
2 Flower meadow which requires topping only once a year with a hired portable string trimmer. The meadow includes grasses like timothy and crested dog's tail, and bulbs that naturalize easily, as well as a wide selection of wild flowers that reseed themselves.
3 The mown lawn has been reduced to a small glade sown with slow-growing fine grasses, and can be cut in about half an hour with a rotary mower.
4 Beds have been thickly clad with gravel to provide a low maintenance home for compact plants.
5 A wall receiving full sun provides an ideal home for wall shrubs like *Fremontodendron californicum*.
6 Hardier evergreens, like *Lonicera japonica* 'Aureoreticulata' and *Camellia* 'Inspiration' have been grown on a north-facing wall.
7 Shrubs that provide vigorous ground cover have been used to suppress weeds. A thick layer of coarse ground bark is normally put down around them until the plants are established.

WILD-FLOWER MEADOW GARDEN

N◄────

With a bigger garden, a large grassed area may be the only reasonably cheap solution to surface cover. If you do not enjoy mowing, and live in the country, the best approach is to convert quite a large area of the garden into a semiwild area by sowing a meadow lawn which needs only once-a-year attention (see also p. 37). It is best sited some distance from the house, where an air of romantic seclusion can be maintained; too close to the house, it will create a feeling of desolation and neglect.

An alternative is to carpet a large area with ground cover plants. There are many plants that will rapidly cover the ground, providing a lush and attractive surface. If the plants are well-chosen, from low-growing, mat-forming subjects, they can provide a similar effect to that of a traditional lawn with only a fraction of the effort required in maintenance. They can also be used effectively in shady corners of the garden, or in climates that are too hot or too dry to support a traditional fine lawn.

Shrubs and perennials

A shrubbery usually demands a great deal less work than a herbaceous border provided the trees and shrubs are selected with care so that they require little attention, while offering something of value all the year round. As far as possible, they should be evergreen, not only to provide leaf interest throughout the year, but also because most evergreens are less subject to pests and diseases than deciduous plants. If well chosen, they can provide an enchanting sequence of blossoms and fragrance, as well as exciting architectural shapes.

The plants should be selected from those that can grow to their full height without the need for constant lopping and pruning as they age. If only those that are well adapted to the soil, the climate and the position (sun or shade) are chosen, they will require a lot less effort in terms of feeding, soil improvement or protection from frost. Once established, they will need very little effort to keep them looking good, particularly if the soil around the shrubs is well-mulched with an attractive organic substance such as coarse ground bark. Some of the low-growing shrubs, such as the heathers, can be used to create a border that provides color and interest

When designing a garden from a bare plot, a mixture of hard surfaces and permanent planting provides one of the best low maintenance options. By contouring the land, as here, you can give a less heavily planted garden much visual interest, without adding to the maintenance required. The more versatile the design, the more likely it will be to suit your future, as well as your current, needs. Here, the large planted area near the house has been covered with close ground cover, such as *Arenaria balearica*, which provides a showy carpet of starry flowers in spring. It could easily be grassed over with fine, slow-growing grass seed, as could the graveled, circular area at the top of the garden, if more time was available. The stones set slightly below the surface round the margins of each area would allow edge trimming to be avoided in each case.

The small water feature makes a pleasant contrast to the paved area surrounding it, but if the garden is to be used by small children, this area could be turned into a sunken sandpit or play space.

The contouring of the garden has been carefully organized so that any raised beds and terraces have been created from the soil removed from the sunken areas, like the pool (see p. 122). Although the design involves expense initially, the garden will require little upkeep once it is mature since the planting is permanent, with bold architectural evergreens like *Fatsia japonica* and *Camellia*.

1 More or less maintenance-free paving and gravel covers one third of the garden.
2 Ground cover, such as *Arenaria balearica*, requires no upkeep but provides a similar effect to a formal lawn.
3 Permanent planting provides interesting foliage shapes and flower color while demanding little work.
4 Tall shrubs have been under-planted with alpines set in gravel to cut down on weeding.
5 Raised beds cut down on any bending and stretching.
6 The small formal pond is deep enough to keep the water fresh, helped by a recirculating pump.
7 Changes in level are very gradual making it easy to move any wheeled equipment around the garden.
8 Mowing stones have been set around the open spaces of the garden to permit a lawn to be sown, if required in future.

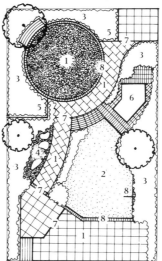

Scale ├── 3m / 10ft ──┤

CONTOURED SHRUBBERY GARDEN

N

in the winter months, and which cover the ground so well that they are virtually maintenance-free.

Small areas of herbaceous planting can still be retained to provide splashes of color in the garden. If the plants are contained in raised beds, they will demand much less bending and stretching. They should be chosen from those that are largely resistant to pests and disease, and that need no staking or dividing. A few annuals can be included in a small section of the garden where appropriate, either from those that are self-seeding or from those that can be pregerminated indoors and sown *in situ* afterward, to ensure a good display of color at the appointed time (see p. 145).

Hard surfaces

Areas of ground near the house, which are usually subject to considerable wear and tear, are often best covered with a hard surface. The materials available range from cheap coarse sands or gravels through middle-priced bricks and tiles, to the most expensive high-quality natural stone pavings. No matter how attractive these materials may be in themselves, they might lose their charm if used unrelieved over large areas of the garden, but if this is the only alternative, try to contour the land on which the surface is laid, to create visual interest. On well-drained flat land this can be accomplished by creating dry, sunken areas and using the soil recovered to establish mounds or terraces elsewhere (see pp. 122–4). On poorly drained flat land, excavations would not be a good idea and earth or other ballast will have to be brought in to create any raised areas. However, much the same effect can be achieved by using a change of surface, such as crushed gravel, beach pebbles, wooden decking or natural stone, to provide visual interest. The planting can, if wished, be fairly minimal, making the garden very easy to run since it demands so little attention.

Scree gardens

A 19th-century low maintenance garden concept – the scree garden – is currently enjoying a revival in popularity. It consists of an area of land thickly topped with fairly fine gravel or crushed stone in which mound-

This garden was designed for a warm, coastal climate, making it an ideal choice of style for a vacation home. A large area of the garden has been covered with stone paving, gravel, pebbles and boulders to create a virtually maintenance-free surface. The planting has been selected for its ability to withstand a dry climate, but the incorporation of a drip-watering system, linked to an automatic clock, would ensure that the plants never suffered from drought in the owner's absence. By using weed-suppressing black plastic sheeting under the gravel-clad area near the house, weeding is reduced to a minimum, while much needed moisture is retained.

The high-quality natural stone walls surrounding the garden and the tough, timber decking of the veranda, while

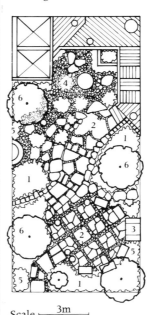

Scale ├─── 3m ───┤
          10ft

expensive initially, require very little maintenance or future expense.

The provision of shaded and sunny sitting areas has been created: the veranda can be covered with a canvas canopy in the hotter months, while the circular paved area at the foot of the garden provides a sheltered sunbathing area. If required, it could be used to incorporate a small swimming pool.

1 Shrubs and perennials that thrive in dry conditions have been chosen, such as *Convolvulus cneorum*, *Phormium tenax*, *Cistus* and *Yucca recurvifolia*.
2 The predominantly paved surface of the garden is more or less maintenance-free.
3 The barbecue area is sited away from the plants, thus avoiding any likelihood of the surrounding trees and shrubs being scorched.
4 The gravel-clad area near the house has been laid over black plastic sheeting to cut down on weeding and to reduce moisture loss.
5 The stone walls of the garden have been used to provide support and protection for easy-to-look-after climbers and wall shrubs like *Jasminum officinale*, *Clematis* and *Camellia* 'Inspiration'.
6 The shade provided by the trees has been used for ground cover plants, to soften the harshness of the large amount of paving, and to suppress weed growth.

MEDITERRANEAN–STYLE SEASIDE GARDEN

N

forming plants are established. Prior to laying the gravel, the ground is well dug, all scraps of weed removed, and it is then enriched with organic fertilizer. Heavy-duty plastic sheeting is used to cover the surface, and the planting holes created in the topsoil by cutting small holes in the plastic, which is then covered with a thick layer of crushed stone or gravel. In general, alpines look best planted in this way as the soft texture and bright colours of the flowers and foliage contrast brilliantly with the harder stone to provide a fine substitute for the conventional herbaceous border. The smaller saxifrages, geraniums, phlox, primulas and thymes and sedums, for example, make excellent subjects for the scree garden.

Water features

A water feature, even on a large scale, takes up far less time than a traditional lawn, and can be used successfully to reduce the harshness of mineral surfaces. It requires only a few hours of intensive, if messy, effort in early summer each year.

There is something quintessential about the best water feature in a garden. It can add a vital animated diversion by reflecting the changing colors and moods of the sky, the temper of the breeze or the bolder characteristics of the vegetation that surrounds it. The sound of water when nudged by the wind or made to tumble over a weir provides relief for perceptions dulled by urban life. Its fluid nature, never quite still nor fully comprehended by the eye, contrasts pleasingly with the solid phlegmatism of the earth. Used properly in a garden design, water can do something for the soul, particularly because it can play host to a range of specially exquisite plants.

Wildlife, too, will soon discover its presence. And even tiny ponds attract their share of frogs, newts and aquatic insects to liven the interest. Goldfish (the initial bonus) soon cede their place as attention rousers to their wilder brothers. However, when contrived badly, a water feature can rapidly turn into a stagnant puddle. The inclusion of a high proportion of moving, shallow water in the system is one way of avoiding the worst of the water garden problems (see pp. 130–31).

This type of garden is a good choice for anyone who wishes to spend more time looking at their garden than using it. It would not, of course, be suitable for a household with young children since the pond, and the veranda, might be hazardous, and there is little play space, but it would make an excellent, virtually maintenance-free, small town garden. The work demanded is minimal once the ground-hugging, carpeting plants and the shrubs have become established, although they would need mulching to suppress weed growth at the outset. The garden has relatively little planting and the shrubs and trees would need only an hour or so a year to keep them tidy. Small stones and pebbles have been used as a permanent mulch around the shrubs, and have been laid over black plastic sheeting to suppress weed growth.

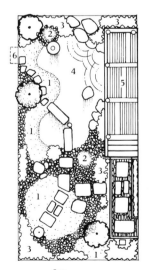

Scale ⊢—— 3m ——⊣
          10ft

The pool is large enough to balance the harsher, pebbled surfaces and is easy to look after, requiring only a once-a-year effort thinning out any aquatics that have grown too vigorously the previous season.

The false half-moon gate facing the veranda has a slightly angled mirror-backing so that it reflects the water, giving an illusion of greater space while involving no extra work in the garden.

1 Ground-hugging, carpeting plants, like *Arenaria balearica* and *Minuartia* have been used to provide a lawn substitute that needs no mowing.
2 Small stones and pebbles, laid over black plastic, make a moisture-retaining mulch. Since the ground is level, the water will not be deflected away from the plants.
3 Evergreen shrubs, which do not shed their leaves, have been chosen for their form as well as foliage, to give the garden an oriental flavor. Subjects chosen, like *Arundinaria, Mahonia* and *Euonymus*, require no pruning.
4 The water area, although large, contains plenty of oxygenating plants to keep it fresh, and a submersible pump will recirculate the water, preventing it from becoming stagnant.
5 The hardwood from which the veranda is constructed ages well without any need for maintenance.
6 The mirror facing the veranda is a useful device in a small low maintenance garden, enlarging its apparent size while introducing no more work.

ORIENTAL-STYLE WATER GARDEN

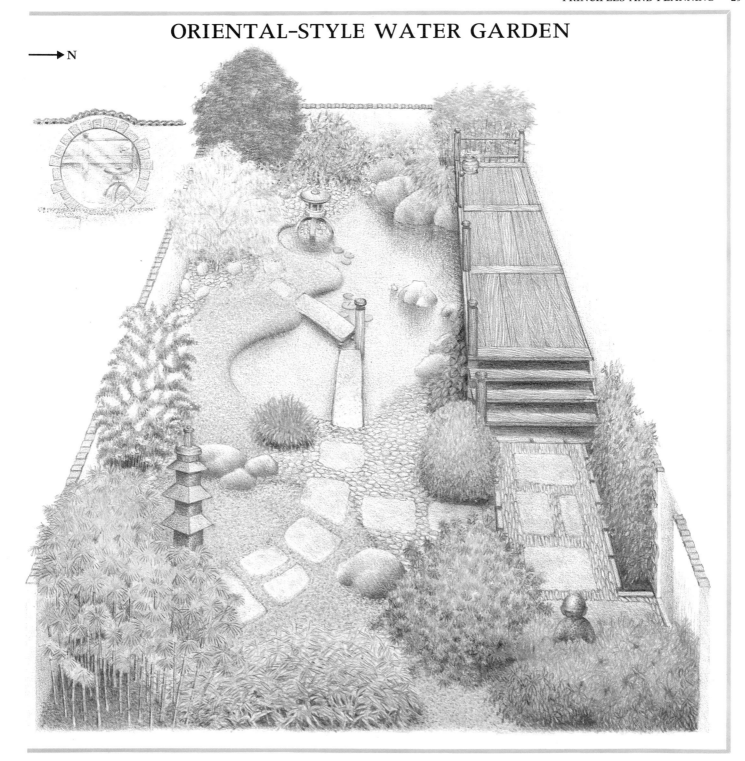

N

SURFACE TREATMENTS

Your choice of ground covering – paving or planting – will be determined partly by taste and partly by such practical considerations as the way you use your garden, the ease of upkeep, and cost. Many paving materials, for example, are far from cheap although none of the initial costs will recur. Such a surface should last for a long time, provided the materials are sensibly chosen and carefully laid. The alternatives – planting a large area with ground cover plants or grass seed (wild or formal) can cost less, but may well take more time to establish and maintain. Often, the most sensible solution is to mix hard and planted surfaces, siting the more durable surfaces where the wear on them is likely to be the greatest.

HARD SURFACES

The aesthetics of hard surfaces are governed by few firm rules, but it is important to consider the overall effect that you are trying to achieve when making your choice of material, and to ensure that it is in keeping with the style of your house: for example, the formality of of well-laid, cut-stone terraces and steps or wood decking will suit most small gardens, while the more loosely textured surfaces, such as gravel and stone chippings, harmonize better with the spirit of a larger, less formal garden. But rules are made to be broken: many people have produced enchanting postage stamp-sized jungles in very small yards. Equally, an area of formal paving with a stone seat, placed deep in a wild garden, where you come across it almost by accident, can convey the exciting impression that it is the relic of a lost civilization.

As a general rule, it is more satisfactory if a formally treated area is laid down close to the house, with successively less formal treatments further away from it. The judicious mixing of materials can provide a welcome decorative element when large areas are to be paved, but it must be handled with care. The juxtaposition of formal paving slabs and rock chippings, crushed from the same stone, would offer a satisfying feeling of harmony, with the textural difference alone provoking interest. The transition from one type of surface to another, even without variety of planting, can provide great visual stimulation.

When required, a more dramatic effect can be created by choosing surfaces that contrast strongly: a formal pattern of dark gray granite setts (cobble stones with a slightly rounded upper surface), for example, could be thrown into relief by an area surfaced with light-colored gravel or crushed stone. But, on the whole, the more calm and natural-looking the garden, the more satisfying it will be. This means that the number of visual changes should be limited to prevent the overall effect from becoming too busy. Should any bright materials be used to clad a prominent ground surface, they will look best if confined to a fairly small and well-defined area, framed by a more sober material.

A good way of reducing unnecessary fussiness, as well as cutting down the chances of materials clashing badly, is to reduce the amount of freestanding garden furniture to a minimum. Instead, it can be incorporated into the general garden design – with a little forethought, stone or wooden benches, 'chairs' and even 'tables', as well as barbecues, can be built in at the time that the terraces or decks are created.

The practical considerations

Before deciding which particular hard surface, or surfaces, to adopt, it pays to find out what materials are available locally at a reasonable price. It is usually possible to obtain natural or simulated stone, formally cut or cast in slabs, or shattered in pieces ready to be laid as crazy paving. Equally, there are few places where locally produced or imported bricks or clay tiles cannot be found; lumber, whether for log sections, duckboards or raised wooden decking, for example, is also easily available.

However, some special materials such as granite setts, large beach pebbles, crushed stone, and gravel, grit or sand of particular grades and colors, can be restricted

Right *The careful choice of surface materials that blend with the surrounding walls has given visual harmony to a garden that requires remarkably little attention. The evergreen ground covers have a softening effect, even in the winter months.*

to certain localities and may be harder to obtain. It also pays to be aware of what, if any, industrial activity there is in your region, as there are some by-products that make unexpectedly good surfacing materials. For example, ashes from furnaces and smelting plants, crushed residues from glassmaking, and even coarse coal dust, can make interesting and attractive surfaces.

Given ample choice, decisions about which material to use will be governed by the architecture of your house, by the effect you are seeking and by the color or textural contributions the surfaces might bring to the overall design. Practical considerations are just as important: as the roots of large trees develop, they can buckle and distort even the most carefully laid sidewalk so the area round mature trees might best be planted with ground cover. Loose materials, like grits, sand and some gravels, can produce mud in wet weather and it is wisest to ensure that there is a harder, more stable surface between them and the house.

If the ground is not well compacted or has recently been made up, caution must be exercised in the type of surface used and, in general, provision made for a much firmer and deeper base than normal.

Some consideration needs to be given to the materials that are suitable for the local climate. Hard surfaces, such as tiles or stone slabs, are clearly a better choice than soft materials like coarse sands in areas frequently subjected to high rainfall. In colder regions, where hard frosts often occur, only tiles, bricks or stone slabs that are genuinely frost-resistant should be used.

Since some surfaces are more trouble-free than others, their future use will help to determine the selection. It is much easier to clear up rubbish from hard surfaces than from loose gravels. While they can be very attractive, loose gravels or coarse sands can easily be kicked about, and where foot traffic is likely to be heavy a solid surface may be more practical.

Paving
If the materials are selected and laid carefully enough, both real and simulated stone provides the noblest substitute for a planted area, but if it is used thoughtlessly the garden will feel harsh and unnatural. Any

paved area must be properly laid on an appropriate base (see pp. 126–8). A poorly constructed terrace, regardless of the quality of the materials, will soon become a puddled, uneven deathtrap.

Wherever possible, you should use local stone since it will blend more harmoniously with the surrounding environment than will stone quarried from other areas. Unfortunately, however, many sedimentary rocks are too soft and will not wear sufficiently well for a formal paving. You can compensate for the lack of durability by setting irregularly shaped pieces of this stone in hard cement to form a crazy paving, but if this effect is not compatible with the rest of the garden landscape, a harder stone may have to be imported from elsewhere. Try to find a variety that echoes the texture and color of the locally available stone.

Left *Different combinations of paving material can provide a satisfying variation where planting is limited. By mixing bricks in a random pattern with formally cut stone slabs, repairs to the latter are easily and cheaply carried out using brick pieces. The low mound-forming plants incorporated in the gaps between the paving stones add texture and charm to the surface.*

Right *Even large areas of the same surfacing material need not be dull. Water, when used imaginately, not only provides a home for striking aquatic plants but also offers a fascinating contrast to a hard surface, particularly where subtle changes of contour have also been incorporated in the design, as shown here.*

A formally cut stone pavement is an asset that will last a lifetime, as it is one of the most durable forms of garden surface. Even if the planting in the garden is neglected to some extent, the quality of the natural stone paving will compensate for it.

Although natural stone, when cut into formal shapes of matching thickness, is the most costly form of paving in terms of materials, it is relatively easy to lay, so the reduced labor costs will help to offset the initial outlay. Irregular fragments of natural stone can usually be bought for about half the cost of the formally cut stone slabs. However, it takes much longer to lay crazy paving than regular stone slabs, so the labor costs will be higher. Also, unless the pieces are fairly large, a much firmer base will need to be provided to prevent them from moving or heaving.

For gardeners working to a tighter budget, a simulated stone paving makes an effective substitute. Most simulated stone is based on cement which is then packed out with anything from crushed natural stone to pebbles of varying colors and sizes, pottery fragments or even seashells. The dimensions of the slabs are very precise since they are cast in factory molds, and they are therefore very easy to lay. Again, they often look more attractive if used in conjunction with other materials: a few cement-based slabs can be laid in an area of gravel, for example, to provide stepping stones. Generally, simulated stone slabs will cost about one sixth of the price of those in natural stone. Competent 'do-it-yourselfers' could provide an even cheaper alternative by casting the cement slabs themselves. In fact, circular molded slabs laid in a well-mulched woodland garden make a good path.

Tiles

Tiles can provide a satisfactory, and cheaper, substitute for a terrace than formally cut stone. A danger for the unwary lies in the wide and exciting range of colors and patterns in which they can be purchased. Intriguing though these can look in the showroom, they may well clash horribly with the subtleties of nature in your garden. Usually the best tiles to choose for a garden setting are those of baked clay, manufactured in slightly varying sizes and shapes, so that they more closely resemble handmade ones. They must be laid with fairly wide separations to accommodate the unevenness in size – normally at least 12mm/$\frac{1}{2}$in apart. If not, the lack of overall symmetry in the terrace will become irritating visually. In areas where hard frosts are likely, make sure that any you buy are frost-proof, or they may crack in icy weather.

To ensure that their surface remains flat, the tiles should always be laid on a concrete screed, and stuck down and grouted with the special cement recommended by the tile suppliers (see p. 128). Good materials can be wasted on a tiled terrace if the grouting is not considered carefully. Both the width and color of the grout used to separate the tiles will contribute to the overall effect. Frequently, a fairly narrow grouting of the same color and tone as the tiles will harmonize very well. Where thin, genuine marble tiles are used, they should be laid so that they butt closely together with no grouting at all between them.

Bricks

Whenever possible, old bricks, rather than new ones, should be used for terraces and garden walls, as they have a more weathered and attractive appearance. However, no matter how tempting a cheap or free supply of bricks may be, if they are to be used to surface well-trodden areas it is vital to ensure that they are sufficiently hard-baked to withstand the wear they will receive and to resist being broken up by frost. If sound old bricks cannot be found, it is better to use one of the new, interestingly surfaced, decorative types of brick that are produced in the kilns these days.

To make the surface more interesting, the bricks can be laid in a multitude of different patterns, exploiting not only the differences in the way they are used, whether laid flat or on their ends or sides, but also in the way in which they are arranged – in herringbone patterns or in squares for example. People seeking an

Right *Clever mixing of materials has been used to create a garden which achieves much of its enchantment from the juxta-position of varied surfaces. A very small area of mown grass has been included to soften the overall design.*

effortless solution to gardening will grout between the bricks to prevent any weed growth between them whereas gardeners with a little more time can allow a small amount of weed growth between the bricks to develop (particularly the mosses and small plants like the stone crops), controlling it with chemical or a little hand weeding from time to time.

Occasional bricks can be missed from terracing to allow room for more deliberate planting of low-growing paving plants – in this case the rubble on which the bricks should be laid will have to be dug out in places to allow the plant roots access to the soil below.

Grouting is unnecessary if the new interlocking, angular bricks are used as a terrace topping. Once they have been firmly tamped down into place, they will remain quite flat. A machine called a tamper can be hired to do this work very effectively, providing a firm, level surface. Coarse grit is brushed into any slight gaps between the bricks.

Granite setts and beach cobbles
The term 'cobbles' embraces both the lumps of granite used for street paving, known as granite setts, and the large rounded stones taken from beaches. While granite setts should be closely set, tamped flat, and then grouted by packing a dry sand/cement mixture between them to make an attractive, even terrace surface, beach cobbles are better used for creating a change of texture in areas not usually trodden on. Although the latter can look attractive – particularly if arranged according to size and color – they are very uncomfortable to walk on in thin shoes, and make an uneven base for furniture.

Beach cobbles should be set in wet cement on a level, hard surface that has been previously topped with a layer of hardened concrete; the upper half of each stone should be set slightly above the cement. Very small stones will provide a smoother surface, but laying them well is a laborious job. Possibly the best place for large beach pebbles is in a seaside garden where the supply is readily available.

Gravel, crushed stones, grits and sand

These are the cheapest and easiest hard-surfacing materials to obtain and lay. Their only disadvantages are that until they become well-compacted and bedded down, some form of weed control will be needed (see p. 151), children may throw the materials around, and since their surface will be softened by heavy rain, they can be trodden into their own version of mud which may be carried into the house.

If sufficiently coarse angular materials are chosen, once they are well tamped down, they will remain stable on even quite steep banks and will also make an attractive base for a scree garden.

To introduce variety into horizontal surfaces covered with these loose materials, two or three different types can be used in the same design. Interesting shapes can be created on the surface by separating the materials with wood, brick or iron bands, or large areas of gravel can be raked into different patterns, to create a formal, Japanese-style garden. Provided the surface is in an enclosed, sheltered area that is not walked upon frequently, the patterns will remain for several weeks before needing re-raking.

Left *Contrasting natural materials, like light-colored beach cobbles and planed dark timber, can often be used to create satisfying ground patterns that need little attention, while providing an excellent back-ground for foliage and flowers.*

Far left *Widely grouted formal dark brick paving makes an* excellent surface for a sitting area, enlivened by containers of plants.

Above *A heavy mulch of gravel can be used to create an easy-to-care-for, attractive scree garden, in which plants like* Bergenia, Sedum album *and* Viola tricolor *provide exciting splashes of color.*

Wood

The disadvantages of wood are: that it is subject to rot, and must therefore be treated regularly with a preservative, and the surface will act as a host for algae, lichens and moss growth which can be very slippery in damp weather. This, too, must be controlled, by treatment with a combined moss killer and algicide.

These handicaps should not prevent wood, with its wonderfully natural allure, being used in the garden. Where it is required for major structural elements, the more durable hardwoods, such as oak or chestnut, should be chosen instead of the cheaper pines. And most lumberyards can supply lumber that has been specially treated against fungus rots and boring insects. There are some very sophisticated fluids available, containing colored stains as well as chemical preservatives, which can be sprayed or brushed on very easily. Similarly, there is a wide range of easy-to-apply chemicals which will suppress moss, algae or lichen growth on wood.

Raised masonry terraces can sometimes look too dominant in a small garden, and wood may be a more suitable material. It will present less of a barrier to vision

Above *Cut logs make attractive stepping stones in a gravel surface planted with low-growing evergreens, bringing a woodland element into a more formal town garden.*

Left *Wood and water combine beautifully when used to provide ground surfaces. Since water will quickly rot the wood, it must be separated from it by a damp-proof layer. Here, the water provides a form of moat between the formality of the house and the wild, marshy garden that surrounds it.*

since the eye can wander through the framework; the decking itself is usually made of duckboarding through which light and water can pass. Wood can be used, too, to relieve the monotony of ground level terraces. Parallel-faced cut logs of the same size (see p. 127), set in cement and surrounded by a loose sand or gravel grouting or an organic mulch, can look most attractive, as can duckboards laid on a concrete base, in designs where a 'timbered look' is allowed to dominate.

PLANTED SURFACES

Grasses and ground covers are your principal choices if you want to cover a large area of your garden with planting. Grass is the most resistant to human traffic but a lawn involves a surprising amount of work during the growing season, particularly in dry climates, although this can be reduced if it is properly planned and prepared. A wild-flower meadow may be a better option for covering a large expanse of ground since it requires only a once-a-season topping with a hired string trimmer. Ground cover plants whose leaves form carpets or canopies so dense that they smother any emergent weeds vary in scale from the creeping thymes and chamomiles to full-sized shrubs. Their uses vary accordingly. They can provide a low, spreading carpet of greenery that resembles a traditional lawn in appearance; they can be substituted for grass in difficult conditions – under trees, for example, or on sloping banks – or they can be used to plant, or underplant, beds of shrubs.

Lawns

If you lay a traditional lawn, the main points to bear in mind are that the ground must be level, that only suitable grass seed should be used and that, wherever possible, mowing stones should surround the grassed area to cut down on laborious edge trimming.

You will need a tough, hard-wearing turf that does not require constant rehabilitation after heavy use, and which remains lush and green throughout the season, without growing so vigorously that it needs frequent cutting – identical requirements to those of groundsmen tending public grass pitches at sports grounds. In fact,

grass breeders have had much success in recent years in developing types of seed that meet these demands, but unfortunately the new varieties of hard-wearing, slow-growing, fine lawn grasses tend not to be stocked by retail outlets. You may have to contact a wholesale agricultural seed merchant to track down a supplier. Among the best varieties to seek are 'Manhattan' and 'Pencross', but there are many other newer types available.

To produce its best effect, and to cut down on maintenance, all new grass seed must be sown in early spring or late summer (that is, at the start of the period when showers can be expected) on well-prepared, free-draining, level land that has been thoroughly cleared of all weeds (see p. 147). A thin layer of peat, about 12mm/$\frac{1}{2}$in thick, should be scattered over the surface of the area to be grassed, and then raked flat. The soil must be well-compacted before the seed is sown – one solution is to hold a party and persuade the guests to trample over the area, treading it down well! Afterward, any raised areas or small hollows must be raked smooth – you can use a plank laid on its edge to detect any minor fluctuations in level. The soil should then be well-compressed again, and given a liberal dose of garden fertilizer containing 5 per cent nitrogen, 10 per cent phosphate and 8 per cent potash, spread at a rate of 100g per sq m/3oz per sq yd, and gently raked into the surface. The seed can then be sown at the rate of 70g per sq m/2oz per sq yd, incorporated into the soil by light raking. You will find it easier to obtain an even spread of both fertilizer and seed if the total quantity is divided into two parts: the first part should be broadcast while walking up and down the area at 1.8m/6ft intervals, and the second part broadcast similarly, walking at right angles to the previous pattern.

After six weeks (provided there has been light rainfall) the young grass should be about 7.5–10cm/3–4in tall, ready for its first topping. The mower – a small, lightweight electric rotary model is ideal – should have the blade raised about 5cm/2in from the surface of the ground for the first topping; the height can be reduced for each subsequent mowing, down to a minimum of 24mm/1in above the soil surface. The work involved will be less arduous, and the appearance of the lawn better, if it is mown frequently. Provided you have laid the lawn carefully, you can mow a small lawn in less than half an hour a week.

If you wish to avoid extra work, you can leave the clippings to wither on the ground, where they will provide an enriching green mulch. If the lawn has been surrounded with mowing stones, the surface of which is 24mm/1in below that of the grass, you can run the mower over them, avoiding the need for time-consuming edge trimming.

Once it is well-established, the mown lawn should need only a few ounces of fertilizer every couple of years to keep it in good condition. If weeds become too dominant, an occasional treatment with weedkiller may be necessary (see p. 150).

Wild-flower meadows

Nothing in nature is more romantic than an old meadow, containing a few attractive trees and shrubs, and packed with bulbs and wild flowers – nodding grasses studded throughout the season with a sequence of traditional flowers like harebells, cowslips, moon daisies and small vetches. A large proportion of the garden could be left semiwild in this way; undisturbed, it would quickly turn into a haven for wildlife, even near the center of a town. The curious seasonal antics of small mammals, the crescendo of evening birdsong and the majestic delicacy of a multitude of butterflies could soon provide you with a garden that is not only easy to look after but also plays a part in helping to preserve the cherished heritage of wild flowers. For apart from its almost pre-Raphaelite attractiveness, this unsophisticated meadow requires

Left *Cornflowers, marguerites, lupins and poppies, mingling with grasses, make a fine flower meadow on a garden margin. Rampaging roses, allowed to ramble freely, provide one of the most delightful screens to blur the garden frontier.*

Right *Low-growing ground-covering plants soon make attractive fillers for the gaps between crazy paving, erasing any feeling of harshness that the stone may introduce. Old walls of dry stone can provide a wonderful home for hosts of plants growing both in the masonry and behind its shelter.*

very little attention. All it will need is a single topping every year in the summer with a hired string trimmer (see p. 157).

It is now quite easy to find seed mixtures that produce a wonderful mixture of meadow grasses and wild flowers, largely as a result of the efforts of the growing lobby of conservationists and environmentalists. However, it is important to choose the right types of plant for your region. It will pay, therefore, to approach a local environmental group for advice or to contact the New York Botanical Garden Institute of Urban Horticulture, Bronx, NY 10458. There are, unfortunately, some unscrupulous and irresponsible suppliers who will offer seed mixtures containing plants that may upset the ecological balance – for example, species from overseas which, while nonaggressive in their natural habitat,

may well run riot in another climate and dominate, if not oust, the native plants.

Although a meadow lawn is easy to look after, it must first be properly laid. The ground should be well-prepared, as for a traditional lawn – that is, cleared of weeds, compacted, leveled and fertilized. However, the seeds of the wild grasses and flowers are so tiny that they need to be mixed with their own volume of damp sand before being broadcast in order to achieve an even spread.

No other special treatment is necessary and the plants will germinate and survive as they do in the wild. By the end of the first fall, the meadow should be topped to a height of 10cm/4in with a hired string trimmer and the hay removed – it makes fine compost or food for the neighbor's rabbit. From the second season onward a single topping in high summer will usually suffice to keep the meadow tidy and attractive.

It is easy to convert a previously mown traditional lawn into a flower meadow. Puncture the surface of the lawn, and its underlying thatch of dead grass, with a hired spiking machine, running over the surface several times. The meadow grass mixture can then be broadcast over the existing surface and raked in hard. The recovery of the lawn grass will be accompanied by the germination of the meadow mixture, and as the more vigorous wild plants mature and reseed themselves, they will begin to dominate the area.

Ground cover

Large areas of planting provide one of the most attractive and natural means of covering the ground in a low maintenance garden, and there is a wide choice of plants that will perform this role in almost any situation, from full shade to full sun, while requiring only minimum upkeep. They provide a marvellous source of greenery and color in the garden and will rapidly produce a thick, weed-smothering mat of evergreen stem and foliage, if they are suitable for the conditions.

In practice, ground cover plants are likely to be used in two distinctly different ways. They can be a feature in their own right, providing a living carpet to the ground, or they can serve a valuable role as weed-

Above *Alpines and wild violets have been used to soften the edge of stone steps, and to produce a ground cover that needs little attention.*

Left *A convincing demonstration of the value of ivy as one of the best weed-smothering ground covers available. It looks particularly good when used in this way to soften the effect of a stepped gravel path; the gravel itself harmonizes well with trees and shrubs.*

Right *Easily curbed when necessary, lady's mantle* (Alchemilla mollis) *can provide a thick ground-covering canopy extremely quickly. Even in the dullest weather, its luxuriant, fresh green foliage is encouragingly bright, contrasting well with the dark stone.*

suppressors in borders or shrubberies, or in awkward corners of the garden – a steeply sloping, sunny bank or a shaded corner. While the tiny plants like *Arenaria balearica*, for example, make excellent lawn substitutes, the larger, low-growing, spreading shrubs like *Hypericum* and *Erica carnea* can be used for a ground cover feature. Even a few climbing plants, such as some of the rambling roses and species clematis, will sprawl horizontally over a sunny slope, producing a mass of color in spring and summer.

The term 'ground cover' is a loose one: most shrubs will provide some form of cover as their leaf canopies knit together, preventing light from reaching the ground beneath them, but the low-growing, mound-forming shrubs and perennials make the best subjects. Shrubs that are many times as broad as they are tall – the horizontal junipers are a good example – can be used successfully as ground cover, but need to be well spaced out for their forms to develop satisfactorily. Initially, the weeds will have to be controlled in the areas around them. The soil can be heavily mulched or smaller, faster-growing, ground cover plants can be planted amongst them. Sun-loving subjects can be used for this role: as the primary shrubs compete more and more strongly

for the available food and light, the secondary plants will simply lose vigor and dwindle away.

Alternatively, groups of plants that spread by forming thicker and thicker clumps of dense foliage can be used – *Erica carnea*, for example – as can those that spread by putting out underground suckers from which new plants emerge or by extending long runners that produce adventitious roots from which new daughter plants are created.

Whichever forms of ground cover you choose, the plants must be given as much help as possible to accomplish this weed-smothering task. When planting, make a generous-sized planting hole for each one and incorporate a good dollop of well-rotted organic matter into the soil at the base of the hole, together with a spoonful of slow-release fertilizers. In dry climates, some form of irrigation system should be provided unless the plants chosen are drought-resistant.

Once the plants are under way, an annual dressing of fertilizer will help to ensure continued fast growth until the desired dense canopy is produced. Complete ground cover will be achieved more quickly if you plant the smaller clump-formers and creepers more densely than normal. Those like *Hypericum* should be planted for this work at 30cm/12in intervals and even fast creepers, like *Vinca* and the ivies, ought never to be separated by more than 90cm/36in, even though their reach is much longer.

Within reason, the more ground cover plants that are established per square yard the better, as you will be able to cease worrying about weeds earlier. To create a successful chamomile lawn, the plants must be put in at 10–15cm/4–6in intervals and well-watered until they are established. However, once their roots have really taken hold the plants can be walked on without any permanent damage; when squashed underfoot, they give off an attractive fragrance on warm days.

It would be too much to hope that no annual weeds, or even the odd perennial, will germinate between ground cover plants, but removal is made much easier if the soil surface is heavily mulched – coarse ground bark is ideal. The mulch will not prevent the creeping ground covers from making effective adventitious roots, but its loose

Left *When well-established, ground cover roses can compete very successfully with weeds to make an attractive alternative to grass or paving. They have the advantage of evolving through the season, parading new foliage, flowers and bright hips in turn. Few plants provide such good value for money, and few people ever attempt to cross the barrier which they create.*

Below *It pays to persist with heathers as ground covers because once they have become well established and their foliage has fused together, the soil blanket is complete and weeds find it almost impossible to obtain space, making it a maintenance-free area. While the winter flowers are the most attractive feature of heathers, the foliage changes color to maintain interest throughout the year.*

nature will allow any weeds to be gently pulled out by hand, as the roots have little to cling to.

By really pampering the ground cover plants initially, weeds should cease to be a problem after two full growing seasons, but life would be too easy if the ground cover solution to low maintenance did not entrain a few minor problems. No one seeking rapid ground cover would choose very slow-growing plants, but it is precisely the vigor of the best ground covers that can prove a nuisance. Having spread over the ground as asked, they then tend to creep into other areas, or even to climb the shrubs they were supposed to be protecting from weed competition. Provided the land has been well-prepared and the soil is loose-textured, rampaging stems can be uprooted and snipped back within bounds surprisingly easily. A good morning's work once a year in late fall, plus a couple of hours in midsummer, ought to be enough to keep the ground cover plants under reasonable control in an average-sized garden.

MINIMUM-CARE PLANTS

INTRODUCTION

The selection of plants is the single most creative act in gardening, as well as being the most rewarding, and will therefore justify the greatest share of your time and effort.

As plants develop, the way in which they have been chosen and sited will determine the character of the garden. In a low maintenance design, where the planted area is often deliberately reduced, each plant will assume greater importance than usual, and any mistakes in selection or location will be more obvious. Although small shrubs and perennials can be moved to rectify any initial weaknesses in your planting design, bolder subjects such as trees and large shrubs will not normally tolerate replanting, so make sure that they are sited in the right place. Although experienced gardeners may be able to suggest remedial measures for planting errors, at best these will only patch over the cracks, so think twice before you grab a spade.

Design considerations
Before plants are chosen and planted, several factors, such as the shape of the plot and the light it receives, the prevailing wind and the type of soil, must be considered. Some of the factors may be so dominant that they more or less dictate the choice to you, but this discipline adds strength and logic to a design, making the selection of other subjects easier.

Most gardeners would agree that their aim is to allow the maximum available sunlight into their plot, which makes it important to ensure that the sun is not cut out by trees and shrubs with large leaf canopies. But if your garden is exposed to strong winds, taller evergreens should be stationed along the windward margins to provide a screen, even at the expense of losing some light.

The eventual size of larger subjects is another important consideration: there is no point in planting big trees where their spreading limbs will be cramped and stunted by competition from other plants or by a solid barrier such as a wall, or where their roots may disrupt an area of paving.

Some plants – clumps of bamboo or the bold-leaved *Fatsia japonica* for example – have a very positive architectural quality that demands attention. There is no point in planting such prima donnas where their qualities cannot be fully displayed. Other plants, such as lilac, while providing colorful flowers and agreeable fragrance, have a fairly indefinite form and can be used to best advantage when closely grouped with similar subjects to play a 'chorus' role, with the taller plants at the back of the bed or shrubbery and the smaller ones in the foreground.

Not only the shape of the plants, but also the color of their bark, foliage and flowers, plays a crucial role in determining where they should be sited. An increased sense of distance can be achieved by arranging those plants with the least intense colors furthest away. If you wished to lead the eye quickly to a distant sector of the garden, you could use a boldly colored subject in the background. It also makes good sense to site most of the fragrant subjects near the house, where you can have the full benefit of their perfume as it floats in through your windows, but one or two such plants might be placed well away from the house to provide an exciting element of surprise when, say, strolling in the garden on a balmy summer's night.

Because you will have to rely upon fewer than normal plants in a low maintenance garden, they must be chosen with great care to provide maximum value in terms of form and color throughout the year. And, of course, they must require the least pruning, clipping, staking or general tidying. A high proportion of evergreens will help to provide interest in the winter months while at the same time creating less work in terms of clearing up dead leaves. Deciduous plants are best chosen from the ranks of those that die back elegantly in fall and winter, leaving some attractive relics of the last season's growth.

Wherever possible you should try to arrange that each section of the garden has a selection of plants that produce their best effects at different times of the year. Heather borders, for example, provide useful winter color and are virtually maintenance-free, reducing the need for weeding.

As a general rule, you should identify the type of soil in your garden (see p. 122) and then try to choose plants that are well suited to it. There is no point in trying to grow lime-hating plants on very alkaline soils or in planting fragile specimens in gardens frequently exposed to tempestuous winds. It would be just as foolish to plant moisture-loving shrubs, such as rhododendrons, in the rain shadow of a high wall. The better suited your plants are to the environment, the less work you will have to do in the way of feeding, watering or spraying against pests and diseases.

Planning a planted area

It is difficult to ensure a satisfactory layout of plants when faced with a patch of well-prepared soil and a box of plants from a nursery. It pays, therefore, to design the proposed planting initially on paper. If the outline of the bed is drawn to scale on graphpaper, circles can be drawn with a compass to represent the spread of each plant. To ensure quick ground cover, you should either make the diameter of the circle for each plant slightly less than the average spread given for each one, or overlap the circles. Remember that the height and spread of any plant will vary according to the type of soil and the local climate – good soil and a warm, moist climate encourage the best plant growth.

Having made a preliminary choice of plants, check that they are suitable for the situation – whether an exposed or sheltered site, a sunny or shaded position, whether spring-, summer-, fall- or winter-flowering. To make sure tall subjects do not mask the shorter ones, mark the plants to indicate their height, and key their flowering seasons with 'E', 'M' or 'L' to denote early, mid- or late season.

Once you are satisfied with the plan, wrap it in clear plastic film to preserve it, so that it can be handled without becoming obliterated by muddy finger marks. If the plants are positioned in their allotted places before being dug in, you can assess the plan and make good any defects before the planting is made permanent.

Right *When carefully chosen and well-established, a closely planted bed of trees and shrubs and mixed perennials can look as colorful and exciting as any garden feature, particularly when, as here, the land on which they are planted is interestingly inclined. Evergreen pines, as well as shrubs like common thyme and broom, help to keep the area looking interesting in winter. In summer, rampaging clump-formers like* Geranium *and* Salvia *flare with color and grow so prolifically that weeds have little chance of becoming established beneath them.*

Containerized plants

No matter how carefully you work out a planting design, it will come to naught if the plants you buy do not thrive. Sadly, many nurseries and garden stores do not select and look after their plants properly, and you must therefore choose very fastidiously, buying only those that are sufficiently well-established to provide an immediate effect and to grow on quickly.

If the nursery objects to your making a detailed examination of the plants on offer (on the grounds that you are not supposed to handle the goods before you have bought them) then you would be better advised to shop elsewhere – a reputable establishment should let you inspect the plants as closely as you want. An indication of a poorly run nursery can be seen in the condition of the soil in the containers: large numbers of weed seedlings indicate neglect, and the plants themselves will probably have suffered similarly.

Faced with a number of containerized plants of the same variety, how do you choose the best? The golden rule is to look at each one carefully: do not grab the tallest – it may simply have put out one long, spindly shoot in an effort to reach the light from an over-crowded position in the nursery. Instead, look for one with three or four shorter, thicker shoots – it will make the best-shaped shrub when transplanted into your garden. Examine the shoots closely: on trees and shrubs, the bark and leaves should have a good, fresh color with no obvious blemishes that could be symptoms of previous pest or disease attack.

If the plant appears to be superficially satisfactory and you have every intention of buying it, do not hesitate to knock it out of the container. Unfortunately, some less reputable nurseries and garden stores rip field-grown shrubs out of the ground and cram them into pots or tubs, selling them a few days later as 'container-grown' specimens. Such plants will not survive transplanting well unless a prolonged rainy season can be expected. To check the condition of the plant, hold it firmly by the stem and invert it, striking the base of the container firmly several times, to release the root ball from the pot. If all the soil in the container falls out as a result and you are left holding a shrub with a small root ball, there is every justification for pointing out to the sales clerk that the shrub or plant was not fit for sale! Nor will the clerk be in a position to argue with you, since you will be holding the evidence.

Any good containerized plant should have a well developed root system, permeating and holding onto much of the potting mix when knocked out of the pot. It should not, however, have spent so long in the container that it has become pot-bound, with the roots having wound themselves around between the potting mix and the pot wall. If there is no alternative to buying such a plant, always tease the root ball out gently before planting. Some plants, however, are so pot-bound that they run dangerously short of water because there is insufficient organic matter in the container to act as a reservoir. In this case, the leaves will have started to wilt and yellow, and the root system will be yellowish-brown. Under no circumstances should you buy a plant in this condition.

Suitability for climate

All the factors mentioned above were carefully considered when selecting the plants listed in this section. Many of them, but not all, should grow well in your area. Plants from cool, moist temperate climates that would normally wither in drier, warmer areas can probably survive satisfactorily in hotter, drier places if a drip irrigation system is used to overcome drought. It is more difficult to get plants that are native to warm regions to thrive in areas exposed to winter frost. Because, although the plants are categorized here by zone (see p. 159), hardiness is not an absolute phenomenon. A shrub that would be hardy following a warm, dry summer and a cool, dry fall (perfect conditions for the woody stems to ripen) may well succumb to a slight degree of frost after a wet summer and a warm, wet fall.

In areas where heavy frosts are habitual, or even infrequent but possible, selections of plants should be made with care. If in any doubt, ask experienced local gardeners or nurserymen about the wisdom of including a particular plant in your garden, and look around to see if there are any examples of the species that have grown in the neighborhood for some years.

Nevertheless, half the fun in gardening is derived from getting away with the impossible. Statements about hardiness are based upon very small samples of experience, and gardens that contain an atypically sheltered corner may well provide a successful home for a plant that is not generally considered to be suitable for the region.

Attempts to ignore the plant hardiness classifications will, of course, remain a gamble and adventurous gardeners would be well advised to restrict their gambling impulses to areas of the garden where losses will not ruin the overall design.

Plant information

The list of recommended plants in this section is divided into the following categories of plant: trees; shrubs; climbing plants and wall shrubs; perennials; annuals; bulbs, corms and tubers; and aquatic and marsh plants. There is also a short chapter on easy-to-grow vegetables, herbs and fruit.

Where classification is debatable, the plant has been listed in the group amongst which it is most likely to feature. For example, *Buddleia alternifolia* appears in the section on trees rather than shrubs since it is more likely to perform the function of a tree. If in any doubt about where to look up a particular plant, consult the index on pp.163–7.

Nowadays most of the trees, shrubs and perennial plants available from garden stores or nurseries are containerized, permitting planting at virtually any time of the year, although the dormant period is normally considered most suitable as it will give the plant the best opportunity to establish itself. Planting details are not included in the plant descriptions unless the plant has some special need. Preferred position and soil are given where this information is likely to affect the plant's chances of survival.

The plants recommended in this section are deemed to be those most suitable for a low maintenance garden, offering the best flowers, fragrance or foliage with the least amount of work but there are, of course, many more which might be suitable. If a particular species or cultivar recommended here is not readily available, ask a reputable nursery or garden store to suggest an alternative. However, since other species, and even other cultivars within a species, may have markedly different characteristics, beware of making substitutions without first checking that they are suitable.

ORGANIZATION OF ENTRIES

The plant entries in this section follow a broadly similar pattern. Each entry is headed by the botanical name of the plant, followed by any popular common name. The botanical name usually consists of two elements. The first is that of the genus of the plant, such as *Abies*, and the second is that of the species, such as *koreana*. (Where the nomenclature of the plant has recently changed, the alternative botanical name is given afterward in brackets.) Occasionally several species of one genus are suitable, and these are listed separately under the main genus heading. Distinct forms of the species maintained only in cultivation, known as cultivars, sometimes form the third element of the botanical name. They are written in Roman type inside single quotation marks, thus *Abies koreana* 'Compact Dwarf'. An entry may be concerned with the genus as a whole, one particular species or even one cultivar of a species, if it is considered particularly suitable for a low maintenance garden. Where the entry describes a species alone, suitable cultivars may be given at the end of it.

Where plants are the result of crossbreeding between different species or cultivars within the same genus (known as hybrids) this fact is indicated by a multiplication sign. **Zone** indicates the broad climatic zone in which the plant can be grown. The map on p.159 gives further information on zonal differences. However, it serves only as an approximate guide and much will depend on local conditions. **H:** indicates the average height of the plant. (In the case of trees, after ten years.) **S:** indicates the average spread of the plant and should serve as a rough guide to spacing for planting. Close-planting (see p.95) can be carried out with even closer spacing than the average spread distance given.

All the plants listed are generally fairly easy to grow and maintain: the easiest of all are marked with an *; those without a symbol are generally suitable; and those marked with a † are well worth growing but require a little more effort. It would be unwise, therefore, to include too many plants with a † symbol when choosing subjects for your garden.

TREES

A good many of the trees chosen are evergreen, as strong emphasis must be placed on this characteristic in the selection of all plants for the low maintenance garden. Once established, they have a number of advantages: not only do they make an interesting contribution to the garden in all seasons, but they also provide an effective windbreak even in the bleaker months, and their shelter will help other plants to survive. One of the most important functions of evergreens, however, is to deny light to the ground beneath their intense leaf canopy, thereby effectively suppressing weeds. Evergreens generally need less attention, in terms of pruning and shaping, than their deciduous counterparts, and since they shed their older foliage only gradually, you do not have to spend a lot of time sweeping up fallen leaves in the fall (see p. 156).

Many of the trees listed here are either fairly slow-growing or remain reasonably small when quite mature, so they will not present problems in the foreseeable future to the gardeners who plant them. However, this does mean that to achieve a feeling of maturity quickly, the slow-growing specimens will have to be bought as large, well-grown trees that have already spent several years in a container. Such trees are expensive, and they can sometimes take a while to re-establish themselves when transplanted in the garden. To protect your investment, therefore, conditions must be right when the trees are planted. In particular, irrigation must be established to guarantee that the tree never suffers from lack of water, no matter how hot and dry the weather might be.

During the first summer, before the roots are established, the tree will probably benefit not only from slow-release fertilizers placed around its roots but also from an occasional dose of diluted fertilizer applied to its leaves (see p. 140). Even though it is theoretically possible to plant containerized trees in any season, fall planting will allow the longest possible period for the root system to become established before the tree's first real test in summer. (It is also very important to make sure the tree is properly planted; for details of how to plant a tree, see p. 48.)

Rapid-growing, large trees can be included in a low maintenance garden provided that it is big enough, and that you do not put in too many of them. If you do find that a tree is beginning to dominate the garden, you can always fell it. However, you must anticipate the tree's removal well in advance, and establish another nearby to fill the gap that will be left.

Most of the trees in this list are strong survivors that need little attention, provided the climate suits them, that healthy specimens have been bought, and that they have been properly planted.

Remember that the roots of some trees go deep and spread wide, so do not plant them close to a paved area, a high wall, or the foundations of your house!

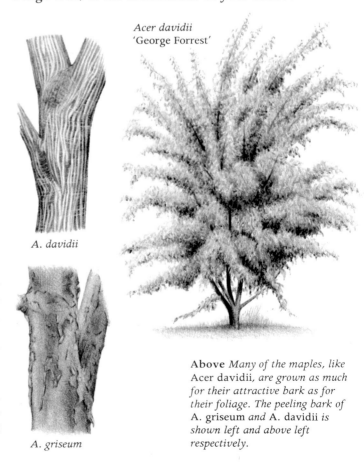

Acer davidii
'George Forrest'

A. davidii

A. griseum

Above *Many of the maples, like* Acer davidii, *are grown as much for their attractive bark as for their foliage. The peeling bark of* A. griseum *and* A. davidii *is shown left and above left respectively.*

ACACIA baileyana

Golden mimosa,
Zones 8–10
H: 7.5m/25ft S: 3.6m/12ft
A small evergreen tree with fine,
shiny, light green leaves and a
fog of bright yellow, globular
flowers in winter and early
spring. A very quick grower, it
prefers a sunny site and neutral
or acid soil. It can be pruned hard
in spring if it becomes too large.

ACER

Maple
A group of trees generally
providing fascinating bark detail
and good leaf color in fall.

A. davidii

Snakebark maple
Zones 6–9   *
H: 4.2m/14ft S: 2.4m/8ft
One of the most attractive
features of this small tree is its
striated green and white bark
offering outstanding value in
winter. It needs cool, moist soil.
'George Forrest': large, dark
green leaves with deep red stalks
and good fall color.

A. griseum

Paperbark maple
Zones 5–9   *
H: 4.2m/14ft S: 3.6m/12ft
An outstanding small tree
offering dark bark that peels back
to reveal cinnamon-orange
beneath. The leaves flare scarlet
before being shed in fall. No
pruning is required except to
ensure the production of a main
stem to a height of about
1.8–2.7m/6–9ft.

ALBIZIA julibrissin

Zones 6–10
H: 4.5m/15ft S: 3.6m/12ft
This small tree, which resembles

mimosa, is grown for its very
delicate, bright green foliage and
the tassel-like pink flowers it
produces in summer. It grows
quickly, given a sunny site. In
colder areas, it flowers only if the
previous season's growth has
been well ripened.
'Rosea': a hardier form with
bright pink flowers.

AMELANCHIER canadensis

June berry
Zones 3–8   *
H and S: 3m/10ft
An attractive small shrubby tree
with midgreen woolly leaves
that turn an attractive color in
fall, A. canadensis bears a
snowstorm of white starry
flowers in midspring, followed
by round, black berries later in
the season. A. canadensis thrives
in any moist garden soil in a
sunny or partially shaded
position.

BETULA

Birch
There are about 50 species of this
graceful deciduous tree. They
thrive in moist sandy soils and
are grown as much for their
attractive bark as for their foliage.

B. papyrifera

Canoe birch, Paper birch
Zones 2–8
H: 6m/20ft S: 2.4m/8ft
An elegant tree, it has slender-
pointed midgreen leaves and
attractive papery white bark
that peels off in large strips.

B. pendula

Silver birch
Zones 5–9
H: 6m/20ft S: 2.4m/8ft
This is a very graceful form of the
birch, with mid-green leaves and
characteristic sparkling silver

Betula pendula

bark and small yellow catkins in
spring.
'Fastigiata': a very erect form,
the leaves of which color a
creamy yellow in fall;
'Tristis': a narrow, weeping
variety.

BUDDLEIA alternifolia

Zones 5–9
H: 2.7m/9ft S: 1.5m/5ft
This tree is noted for its long and
elegant arched stems of thin,
dark green leaves and its
delicately fragrant, lilac-purple
flowers in early summer, which
are a great lure for butterflies and

other nectar-seeking insects. A
vigorous grower, it prefers a
sunny or partially shaded site.
Thinning out old flowering
shoots in late spring will help to
maintain vigor and free
flowering.
'Argentea': leaves with an
attractive silvery sheen.

CARAGANA arborescens

Zones 2–7   *
H: 4.5m/15ft S: 3m/10ft
Grown for its compact habit, this
very slow-growing hardy tree
makes a good windbreak. It has
deciduous leaves and yellow,

pea-like flowers in late spring. It prefers a sunny position and sandy soil.

'Lorbergii': a very graceful form with finely cut leaves.

CHAMAECYPARIS lawsoniana

Lawson cypress
Zones 6–9
H: 6m/20ft   S: 2.4m/8ft
A fast-growing evergreen, this columnar tree will do well in any position. The dark red flowers of the species are profusely borne. Specimens should be selected with care: abnormal, yellowing foliage indicates root infection which could kill the tree, and is untreatable.

'Kilmacurragh': irregular sprays of dark green foliage carried on short, erect branches held tightly in to the main stem.

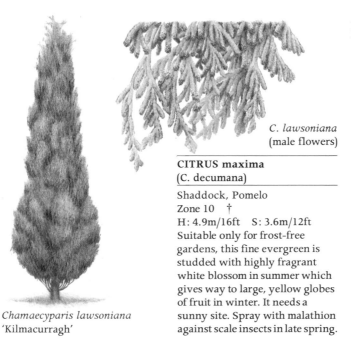

Chamaecyparis lawsoniana 'Kilmacurragh'

C. lawsoniana (male flowers)

CITRUS maxima (C. decumana)

Shaddock, Pomelo
Zone 10   †
H: 4.9m/16ft   S: 3.6m/12ft
Suitable only for frost-free gardens, this fine evergreen is studded with highly fragrant white blossom in summer which gives way to large, yellow globes of fruit in winter. It needs a sunny site. Spray with malathion against scale insects in late spring.

CORNUS florida

Flowering dogwood
Zones 5–9   *
H: 2.4m/8ft   S: 1.8m/6ft
One of the prettiest of all the dogwoods, *C. florida* is grown for the glory of its flowers which have large, elegant white bracts in early summer. It has colorful fall foliage and needs a non-alkaline soil and a lightly shaded position to do well. 'Pendula': drooping branches; 'Rubra' (zones 8–10) pink or rose-colored bracts; 'Welchii': variegated yellow and red leaves.

CRATAEGUS phaenopyrum

Washington thorn
Zones 5–9
H: 45m/15ft   S: 2.7m/9ft
A hardy tree bearing tiny flowers with yellow anthers in

PLANTING A TREE

When planting a tree, make sure that the hole for it is not too big – it should be just large enough to accommodate the root ball comfortably. The tree will have a better chance to thrive if the soil at the bottom of the hole is broken up (to improve drainage), and if plenty of peat and bonemeal, and a good handful of slow-release fertilizers, are mixed with it. A stout stake must be driven into the base of the hole, slightly to one side, to provide support for the tree. Fill the hole after planting with soil in a 2:1 ratio with sphagnum peat, and cram it down well. Check that the tree is firmly anchored, and the tree secured to the stake with straps.

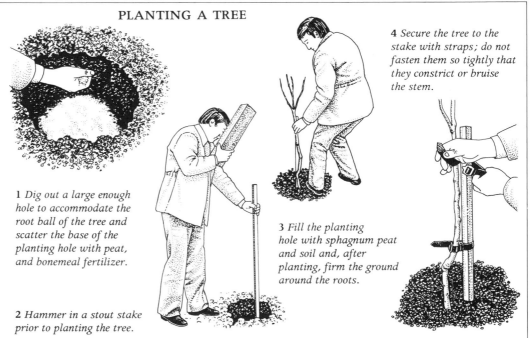

1 Dig out a large enough hole to accommodate the root ball of the tree and scatter the base of the planting hole with peat, and bonemeal fertilizer.

2 Hammer in a stout stake prior to planting the tree.

3 Fill the planting hole with sphagnum peat and soil and, after planting, firm the ground around the roots.

4 Secure the tree to the stake with straps; do not fasten them so tightly that they constrict or bruise the stem.

late spring and bright red, shiny fruit later in the year. It prefers a sunny position and a limestone or rich, loamy soil.
'Fastigiata': columnar form.

ELAEAGNUS angustifolia

Oleaster
Zones 2–8
H and S: 3.6m/12ft
A deciduous, wide-spreading small tree, *E. angustifolia* has narrow, willowlike gray-green leaves. The silvery flowers are followed by edible amber fruits. It will tolerate poor limestone soil but needs full sun.

ERIOBOTRYA japonica

Loquat, Japanese medlar
Zones 7–10
H: 4.2m/14ft   S: 1.8m/6ft
This highly architectural ever-green tree has striking, very long, leathery leaves and clusters of pungent, white hawthorn-

like flowers throughout the winter and late spring. In warm climates, yellow edible fruits follow. In colder areas it does best against a south-facing wall.

EUCALYPTUS niphophila

Snow gum
Zones 7–9   *
H: 10.5m/35ft   S: 4.5m/15ft
As well as a strong eucalyptus fragrance emitted on warmer days, this narrow-leaved gum has a spectacular, mottled bark and clusters of fragrant white flowers in summer. It thrives in a sunny position.

EUCRYPHIA cordifolia

Zones 8–10
H: 3m/10ft   S: 1.8m/6ft
Once established, the thick canopy of heart-shaped leaves of this semievergreen tree provides an excellent wind-break. The white flowers, resembling those of *Hypericum*, appear in late summer. *E. cordifolia* prefers a semishaded position with a nonalkaline soil.

FAGUS sylvatica

European beech
Zones 5–9   *
H: 9m/30ft   S: 4.5m/15ft
This particular beech is one of the most majestic, with its fern-

Eucalyptus niphophila

like deciduous foliage that colors handsomely in fall. It prefers sun or halfshade and a loamy, limestone soil.
'Asplenifolia': very narrow, deeply toothed leaves, giving a very light effect in the landscape. There are numerous other cultivars with colored foliage and an upright habit.

GINKGO biloba

Maidenhair tree
Zones 3–9   *
H: 4.5m/15ft   S: 1.8m/6ft
This lovely conifer has existed virtually unchanged for at least 160 million years, and ought to

be grown as much for its botanical curiosity value as for its beauty. The bright green leaves are simple fans with almost parallel veins, flaring a delightful yellow in fall. In warm climates, do not plant female trees as the fruits become foul-smelling and messy when they fall to the ground. *G. biloba* prefers sun or halfshade.
'Fastigiata': a very narrow, pyramid-shaped variety, suitable for smaller gardens.

Ginkgo biloba

flowers in fall. It prefers a sunny site and a hot, dry summer. 'Rosea': deeper colored flowers than the pink of the species. There are many other hardy, showy cultivars.

MAGNOLIA

Very ornamental trees and shrubs with 80 species, both deciduous and evergreen. Some flower in early spring before the leaves unfold. Most prefer a well-drained loamy, lime-free soil and are easy to grow. Spring-flowering species should be planted in a sheltered spot, to prevent frost damaging the blooms.

M. × loebneri 'Leonard Messel'
Zones 5–9   *
H: 2.4m/8ft   S: 1.5m/5ft
This slow-growing hybrid magnolia produces a sensational display of fragrant lilac-pink flowers in spring before the showy, shiny leaves emerge. A 'prima donna', it deserves a prominent position in the garden.

M. virginiana (M. glauca)
Zones 5–10   *
H: 3m/10ft   S: 1.5m/5ft
A semievergreen whose leaves have shiny green upper surfaces, blue-white underneath, making a fine background for the display of creamy-white, sweetly scented globular flowers that lasts from mid- to late summer. A native of the eastern part of the

GLEDITSIA triacanthos
'Sunburst'

Honey locust
Zone 5   *
H: 4.5m/15ft   S: 1.8m/6ft
A deciduous tree with foliage that is reminiscent of some of the mimosas. It is grown mainly for its showy yellow leaves that lift even the drabbest corner of the garden. Small, insignificant green flowers are carried in mid-summer. It does best in sun or halfshade.

ILEX opaca

Zones 6–9
H: 6m/30ft   S: 3m/10ft
A tough evergreen tree, with short, spreading branches and spiny, glossy-green leaves. It bears bright scarlet-crimson small fruit throughout the winter. *I. opaca* prefers a fertile, well-drained soil and some protection from winter winds and sunshine.

LAGERSTROEMIA indica

Crape myrtle
Zones 7–10
H: 3m/10ft   S: 1.8m/6ft
This elegant tree has an attractively mottled trunk in pink, orange and gray hues. Privetlike, shiny dark green leaves contrast with a froth of crinkly petaled, sugar-pink

Gleditsia triacanthos
'Sunburst'

United States, it was probably the first magnolia to be introduced to Europe.

OLEARIA traversii

Tree aster
Zones 8–10   *
H: 3m/10ft   S: 2.1m/7ft
A small, shrubby tree, it is useful as a windbreak in mild areas, as it produces a dense canopy of shiny evergreen leaves that are white-felted on the undersides. They develop into intriguing loose shapes. *O. traversii* does well in any position or soil.

PINUS

Pine
A large genus of ornamental evergreen trees that provide interesting effects all the year round. They need a sunny position and do not tolerate pollution well.

P. mugo

Mountain pine
Zones 4–8   *
H and S: 4.5m/15ft
This small evergreen tree has a gnarled form, with mid-green needles borne in pairs. There are several low-growing cultivars that are particularly suitable for a low maintenance garden.
'Compacta': dense form;
'Corley's Mat': prostrate and spreading.

P. thunbergiana

Japanese black pine
Zones 5–9   *
H: 3m/10ft   S: 2.4m/8ft
This conifer develops twisted branches from a good straight trunk. Although a slow-growing tree, it will reach a considerable height when mature. The dark, fragrant foliage and bark give the tree its common name. An evergreen, it prefers full sun.

PRUNUS subhirtella
'Autumnalis'

Fall cherry
Zones 5–9   *
H: 6m/20ft   S: 3m/10ft
A real winter winner, this exciting, quick-growing cherry flowers very prolifically in winter. Even when the scented white flowers are ravaged by winter storms, it obligingly offers a further display of blossom in spring. It prefers a sunny site.
'Autumnalis Rosea': rose-colored double flowers. Both forms have a very attractive shape with irregular layers of horizontal branches.

ROBINIA pseudoacacia
'Frisia'

False acacia, Black locust
Zones 3–8   †
H: 6m/20ft   S: 3m/10ft
Grown principally for its showy,

Prunus subhirtella 'Autumnalis Rosea'

buttercup-yellow foliage, this fast-growing deciduous tree offers the bonus of fragrant white flowers in early summer, providing a mecca for bees. The leaves tend to become less yellow and more green with age and the thorny suckers produced by more mature trees should be removed.

SORBUS 'Joseph Rock'

Rowan, Mountain ash
Zones 5–6   *
H: 7.5m/25ft   S: 2.4m/8ft
This very erect form of the rowan is valuable where space is limited. An evergreen, its chirpy, small bright green leaflets flare bright red, orange, copper and even dark purple in fall, enriched by good displays of berries that change from cream to yellow as they mature, persisting well after leaf fall. It prefers sun or half-shade.

THUJA plicata 'Fastigiata'

Western red cedar
Zones 5–9
H 7.5m/25ft   S: 2.4m/8ft
A fast-growing evergreen, this conifer has flat, shiny, rich green leaves; yellow-brown cones are borne on mature trees.
T.p. 'Fastigiata' is a columnar form and does best in a sheltered position with moist soil and in full sun.

Left *A marvellous tree to highlight any corner of the garden,* Robinia pseudoacacia 'Frisia' *looks particularly good when seen against a dark background. Its fairly rapid growth ensures that it contributes quickly to the overall planting design, but it is suitable for small gardens since it reaches no more than medium height.*

SHRUBS

Many of the criteria used for choosing trees can also be applied to shrubs. A high proportion of evergreens has been included in the following list to provide interest in the garden all year round, and to cut down on sweeping up fallen leaves. Nearly all the shrubs chosen have a fairly compact form, allowing them to be packed closely together. This offers the double advantage that not only are you able to have something of interest in the garden at all times of the year, but also weeds will be suppressed in the surrounding areas. They can also be prevented from developing below and between shrubs until their cover is complete if the soil surface in the vicinity is heavily mulched (see pp. 147–8). Alternatively, you can plant smaller, quick-spreading, ground-covering shrubs or perennials below the taller subjects.

Among the shrubs described in this section, the following are most suitable for planting as ground cover: *Cotoneaster congestus, C. horizontalis, Erica carnea, Euonymus fortunei, Genista lydia, Juniperus horizontalis, Rosa gallica, R. × 'Swany', Senecio greyi* and *Vinca minor* and *major*. All of them will tolerate alkaline soil. Other useful ground covers are suggested in the introduction to perennials on p. 74 and the details are given in that chapter. (See also p. 160).

None of the shrubs recommended in this chapter must be pruned, but some of them will definitely benefit from pruning, in terms of increased flower production and general vigor. Some of the strongest-growing specimens may need occasional thinning. If in any doubt about how to prune or thin a shrub, consult a local expert, or the nursery or garden store from which it was purchased.

The method for planting shrubs is similar to that for trees (see p. 48), but the size of the planting hole will depend on the dimensions of the root ball of the shrub. In all cases, it should fit snugly into the hole without rocking about. While some of the taller specimens may need staking, most will survive perfectly well without support.

As a general rule, if a continuous shrub canopy is ultimately required, each shrub should be planted sufficiently far from its neighbor to allow room for its natural spread. The following list gives the average spread for each shrub, but more precise information can be sought from the nursery or garden store when the plant is purchased. Take care to choose only healthy, well-grown specimens that are suitable for the type of soil in your garden.

(For information on suitable plants for hedging, see p. 63. Details of climbing and wall shrubs are given on pp. 67–73.)

ABELIA

A genus of semievergreen and deciduous shrubs that are generally easily grown. In colder areas they will need some protection, such as a sheltered wall.

A. × grandiflora
Zones 7–9   *
H: 1.8m/6ft   S: 1.2m/4ft
Although it has rather unspectacular, small oval leaves, this semievergreen shrub is well worth growing for its clusters of small, tubular pink and white flowers in late summer. It requires a sheltered position in full sun, and benefits from the occasional removal of old branches.

A. triflora
Zones 8–9   *
H: 4.5m/15ft   S: 2.4m/8ft
An erect and graceful shrub, suitable for warmer areas only, *A. triflora* has pink-tinged, white flowers, borne in clusters of three in early summer. They exude a really heady fragrance.

ABIES koreana
'Compact Dwarf'

Dwarf silver fir
Zones 5–7   *
H: 90cm/3ft   S: 1.5m/5ft
Grown principally for the smartness of its evergreen leaves. which are dark green on the upper surface and bright white underneath, this form has no leading stem and slowly spreads horizontally. In warm weather, its foliage smells satisfyingly resinous.
'Prostrata': another low, spreading form.

ABUTILON vitifolium

Tree mallow
Zones 8–9   †
H: 2.4m/8ft   S: 1.5m/5ft
The attractive and unusual vine-shaped gray leaves of this shrub make a fine background for the bell-shaped mauve flowers in late spring. *A. vitifolium* requires a sunny, protected position. After severe winters, dead growths will need to be cut out, often to ground level.
'Album': a white variant to mix with the mauves.

ACACIA drummondii

Wattle
Zones 9–10   *
H and S: 1.5m/5ft
A compact mimosa for the shrubbery, *A. drummondii* carries dense spikes of yellow blossom that contrast well with its small, dark evergreen leaves and shine out beautifully from the shadows in which it prefers to lurk.

Aucuba japonica 'Variegata'

AUCUBA japonica

Japanese laurel
Zones 6–9   *
H: 3m/10ft   S: 1.5m/5ft
This handsome evergreen has glossy leaves; the female plants bear bright red winter berries (if both sexes are grown). *A. japonica* is suitable for all soils and positions, including dense shade.
'Crotonifolia': bright yellow variegations on the leaves, making it a popular plant to brighten up dark corners; 'Goldsport': bright gold variegations. 'Variegata': yellow-spotted leaves.

AZARA lanceolata

Zones 8–10
H: 2.4m/8ft   S: 1.5m/5ft
The narrow, bright green leaves of this evergreen shrub give life to the garden in winter while its mustard-yellow flowers, although unspectacular, fill the air with perfume in spring.

BERBERIS thunbergii

Zones 5–9
H: 1.2m/4ft   S: 1.8m/6ft
A dense, compact shrub with small midgreen leaves that turn brilliant red in fall. Pale yellow flowers are borne in long clusters in early summer, followed by small scarlet berries. It tolerates poor soil and does best in full sun.
'Atropurpurea': purple-red leaves.

CALLISTEMON viridiflorus

Bottle brush
Zones 8–10
H: 1.5m/5ft   S: 75cm/30in
Short, dark green, needle-like evergreen leaves are held on erect stems, making this a very compact plant. It has cylindrical, lime-green flowers in summer. *C. viridiflorus* is unsuitable for shallow limestone soil.

CAMELLIA

These evergreen spring-flowering shrubs need an acid or neutral soil and protection from early morning spring sun which can damage their flowers. If plants become too tall and 'leggy' they can be pruned back hard into the older growth.

C. japonica
Zones 7–9
H and S: 3m/10ft
The hardiest species, with glossy oval leaves and red flowers.

C. sasanqua 'Fragrant Pink Improved'
Zones 8–10
H: 1.5m/5ft   S: 90cm/3ft
Handsome, dark green, shiny foliage and loose, pink, peony-shaped, fragrant flowers from late winter to early spring.

C. × williamsii 'J.C. Williams'
Zones 8–9
H: 1.5m/5ft   S: 90cm/36in
This shrub carries pale pink, medium-sized, simple flowers from late fall to spring.

CASSIA corymbosa

Zones 8–10
H: 3m/10ft   S: 2.4m/8ft
This tropical shrub really needs the shelter of a wall or fence facing the sun, where its finely cut leaves will provide a rewarding background for the golden-yellow fall flowers.

Camellia × williamsii 'J.C. Williams'

CEANOTHUS

Californian lilac
This free-flowering shrub needs full sun and good drainage in any soil except shallow limestone, but evergreen species or hybrids may not survive severe winters.

C. dentatus
Zones 8–10
H and S: 3m/10ft
The tiny-toothed evergreen leaves of this attractive shrub almost disappear in early summer in a haze of bright blue flowers. Although vigorous, it is very easy to keep in check.

C. thyrsiflorus 'Repens'
Zones 6–9
H and S: 1.8m/6ft
A very vigorous evergreen

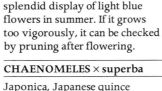

C. × *superba* 'Rowallane'

mound-former, it puts on a splendid display of light blue flowers in summer. If it grows too vigorously, it can be checked by pruning after flowering.

CHAENOMELES × superba

Japonica, Japanese quince
Zones 4–9
H: 1.5m/5ft   S: 1.8m/6ft
Delightful saucer-shaped red flowers appear in very early spring on this adaptable shrub for sun or shade.
'Rowallane': extra large, semi-double crimson flowers followed by large, yellow quince.

CHIMONANTHUS praecox

Wintersweet
Zones 7–10
H: 2.4m/8ft   S: 1.8m/6ft
Strongly scented yellow and purple flowers, borne close to the stems, appear in late winter to provide welcome color in the garden. They are followed by small lanceolate leaves. *C. praecox* prefers full sun and is suitable for all well-drained soils.
'Luteus': large yellow flowers.

Chaenomeles × superba

CHOISYA ternata

Mexican orange
Zones 8–10
H and S: 1.5m/5ft
This wide-spreading shrub has light, shining, evergreen foliage that makes a year-round contribution to the garden. Sweetly scented white flowers are carried in late spring and summer.

CISTUS 'Silver Pink'

Rock rose, Sun rose
Zones 7–10   *
H and S: 90cm/36in
With its exotic, silvery pink, saucer-shaped flowers in mid-summer, this choice evergreen is redolent of much warmer places.

Chimonanthus praecox

C. ' Silver Pink' is a compact form and is tolerant of all soils, even limestone. It grows well in a sunny, sheltered position.

COMPTONIA peregrina

Sweet fern
Zones 2–7
H: 1.2m/4ft   S: 1.5m/5ft
Grown for its highly fragrant, fern-like foliage, it makes a good companion for other ground-covering shrubs like the low-growing junipers. It carries small brown catkins in spring. Semi-evergreen in milder areas, it prefers a sunny, lime-free situation but is sometimes difficult to establish, even on peaty, sandy, acid soils.

Left *A delightful plant for tumbling over walls in warmer areas,* Convolvulus cneorum *will survive any amount of abuse, including long periods of drought.*

fall color before they drop. Insignificant, creamy colored spring flowers are followed by white berries. For best stem effects, prune annually or biennially to ground level. 'Elegantissima' ('Sibirica Variegata'): leaves mottled and margined with white; 'Spaethii': best golden form.

COTINUS coggygria
(Rhus cotinus) 'Purpureus'

Smoke tree
Zones 5–9
H: 1.5m/5ft   S: 1.8m/6ft
The 'smoke' of the common name is provided by wispy pink and purple inflorescences in mid-summer. The very bold purple foliage preserves its fresh look throughout the summer and then flares yellow in fall. Unpruned plants will not produce such a good color.

COTONEASTER

There are both deciduous and evergreen forms of *Cotoneaster*. Most adapt themselves to any soil and situation. The deciduous species have fine fall colors and bright fruit. *C. horizontalis* and *C. microphyllus* 'Thymifolius' make excellent ground cover.

C. congestus
Zones 6–10   *
H: 75cm/30in   S: 1.5m/5ft
This low-growing, evergreen, ground-covering form makes attractive mounds of blue-green foliage that carries small pink flowers in early summer and bright red berries in fall.

CONVOLVULUS cneorum

Zones 8–10   *
H: 75cm/30in   S: 60cm/24in
With its narrow, dark green leaves that have silky hairs on the stems, *C. cneorum* makes handsome mounds, supporting a summer-long sequence of clusters of white trumpet-shaped flowers that emerge from pink buds. It is particularly well suited for a dry, sunny spot.

COPROSMA repens

Looking-glass plant
Zones 9–10   *
H and S: 90cm/36in
A stout, densely branched evergreen, *C. repens* develops a gnarled, picturesque form. It has brilliant green, oval leaves and, although its tiny cream summer flowers are insignificant, the clusters of large orange-scarlet fruit that follow are prominent.

'Argentea': silver-variegated foliage; 'Marginata': yellow-margined leaves; 'Picturata': leaves centrally blotched with yellow.

CORNUS alba

Zones 3–8   †
H and S: 2.4m/8ft
Grown principally for the glory of its brilliant red stems which brighten the winter scene, *C. alba* has light green leaves with good

C. horizontalis
Zones 6–10 *
H: 60cm/24in   S: 2.1m/7ft
(or more)
A good, low subject that will, in time, cover a lot of ground and which does well in a bleak situation. Its foliage, born on fishbonelike branches, colors well in fall before it drops, leaving berries that burn like fiery squibs. It bears pink flowers in early summer.

C. lacteus
Zones 6–10 *
H: 3.6m/12ft   S: 3m/10ft
A distinctly mound-shaped evergreen shrub, its handsome large, dark green, leathery leaves are gray-felted underneath. Creamy white flowers are borne in mid-summer. The red fruits last through the first months of winter.

C. microphyllus 'Thymifolius'
Zones 7–10
H: 90cm/36in   S: 75cm/30in
A small, rounded, delicate evergreen with extremely narrow, small, shining deep green leaves. In fall, they are studded with bright red berries that follow the small white spring flowers.

CYTISUS

Broom
The profuse pea-like flowers that appear in spring on the

Cotoneaster horizontalis

C. microphyllus
'Thymifolius'

Left and above *Two forms of* Cotoneaster. *Left, the deciduous* C. horizontalis *and above, a detail of the evergreen* C. microphyllus 'Thymifolius'

long slender shoots make this a popular garden shrub.

C. maderensis 'Magnifolius'
Zone 10
H: 3m/10ft   S: 2.4m/8ft
One of the most majestic brooms for warmer areas, this evergreen species is grown for its bright yellow flowers with their musky fragrance.

C. × praecox
Warminster broom
Zones 6–10 *
H: 1.2m/4ft   S: 1.5m/5ft
A well-rounded and compact bush for full sun, producing fresh, silky green shoots and a thick crust of creamy-yellow flowers with a pungent odor. 'Albus': white flowers; 'Gold Spear': bright yellow flowers.

Cytisus × praecox

Cotinus coggygria 'Purpureus'

Daphne mezereum

DAPHNE mezereum

Zones 6–9   *
H and S: 90cm/36in
The purple-red flowers are borne on leafless stems and exude an astonishing fresh scent on all but the coldest days in early spring. They are followed by scarlet berries which are poisonous. *D. mezereum* should never be pruned. 'Alba': white flowers and amber fruit; 'Grandiflora': purple fall flowers.

ERICA

Heath, Heather
The needle-like leaves on wiry stems and bell-shaped flowers are characteristic of this low, bushy shrub. Most of them make excellent ground cover, given an acid soil.

E. carnea 'Springwood White'
Zones 6–8   *
H: 25cm/10in   S: 60cm/24in
One of the finest winter-flowering heaths, the tiny white bell-shaped flowers of this prostrate evergreen have chocolate-colored anthers. Its bright green foliage makes

attractive ground cover and it tolerates some alkalinity in the soil.

ESCALLONIA 'C.F. Ball'

Zones 7–10
H: 2.4m/8ft   S: 1.2m/4ft
The dark evergreen leaves of this shrub make a perfect background for the large, tubular, crimson flowers it carries throughout summer and fall. The leaves are highly aromatic when crushed. *E.* 'C.F. Ball' grows well on limey soil and makes a good windbreak in coastal areas.

EUCRYPHIA × nymansensis

Zones 8–10
H: 4.5m/15ft   S: 1.8m/6ft
This erect, evergreen shrub has glossy, dark green leaves and large, single, creamy-white flowers with outstanding yellow stamens in late summer. A quick grower, it prefers semi-shade and a moist, acid soil.

EUONYMUS fortunei
'Emerald 'n' Gold'

Evergreen spindle tree
Zones 5–9   *
H: 60cm/24in   S: 75cm/30in
A good, low, ground-covering evergreen shrub, it forms dense mounds and grows well on most soils. The bright green and gold variegated foliage turns bronze-pink in winter.

FATSIA japonica

Zones 8–10
H and S: 3m/10ft
Grown for its exotic, very large, glossy, palmate evergreen leaves, *F. japonica* also produces heads of globular white flowers at the end of fleshy stems in the fall. It requires shelter in less mild areas.

FUCHSIA magellanica
'Riccartonii'

Zones 7–9   *
H: 1.8m/6ft   S: 1.2m/4ft
One of the larger, hardy fuchsias, it may need protection for the crown in a hard winter. The leaves are in whorls of three, and the flowers, appearing in late summer and fall, have a striking, dark red calyx and violet petals.

GARRYA elliptica

Zones 8–9   *
H: 3m/10ft   S: 2.1m/7ft
This fine, quick-growing evergreen shrub has large, leathery leaves and long, silky catkins of a pale, grayish-green in winter. Female plants bear purple-brown fruits if both sexes are grown. *G. elliptica* prefers a sunny, protected position.

GENISTA lydia

Zones 5–9   *
H: 90cm/36in   S: 1.8m/6ft
A dwarf form of broom, *G. lydia* has arching or prostrate branches covered in bright yellow flowers in late spring and early summer. It makes a good cover for banks, given light soil and full sun.

GRISELINIA littoralis

Zones 8–10   *
H: 3m/10ft   S: 2.4m/8ft
The bold, evergreen, shiny cream and apple-green leaves, packed tightly together, make this a splendid screening plant for milder areas, particularly near the sea. Although it tolerates most conditions, it needs some protection against frost.
'Variegata': nearly as hardy, with white marginal variegations on leaves.

HAMAMELIS mollis

Chinese witch hazel
Zones 5–9   *
H: 4.5m/15ft   S: 3.8m/12ft
Clusters of very tough, highly scented small flowers, with strange, strap-like yellow petals, cling to the bare stems of *H. mollis* in winter. Foliage resembling that of the hazel emerges later, in spring, coloring gold in fall.

Erica carnea 'Springwood White'

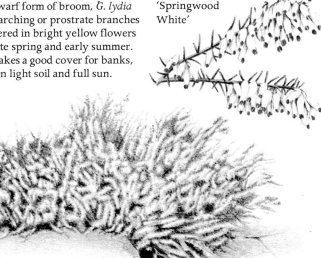

Garrya elliptica

HEBE
Shrubby veronica
This genus of evergreen shrubs offers a wide range of decorative foliage and flowers in a variety of colors and shapes. It is particularly suited to coastal areas.

H. 'Edinensis'
Zones 6–9
H and S: 38cm/15in
A dwarf shrub that looks well in a solo position. It has tiny bright green leaves that overlap and white flowers in summer.

Hibiscus syriacus
'Blue Bird'

H. 'Great Orme'
Zones 8–10
H and S: 75cm/30in
Large, lance-shaped leaves support fuzzy spikes of bright pink flowers from early to midsummer. This very compact shrub makes a good 'spot' plant in borders.

HIBISCUS
These deciduous and evergreen shrubs are renowned for their exotic, showy flowers. *H. syriacus* can be grown in temperate climates. It is very hardy and no protection is needed in most situations.

H. rosa-sinensis
'Pink Glint'
Zones 9–10
H and S: 1.8m/6ft
Pointed, oval, dark green leaves contrast well with the large, loose, pink-petaled summer flowers, that are profuse but short-lived.

H. syriacus
Zones 5–9
H: 2.4m/8ft   S: 1.5m/5ft
These fine, fast-growing shrubs produce glorious, large, single or double flowers in shades from white to purple from midsummer to fall.
'Blue Bird': delicate flowers with violet-blue petals.

HYPERICUM
St John's wort
All the *Hypericum* species are semievergreen and most provide useful ground cover,

Hypericum patulum
'Hidcote'

with profuse, yellow saucer-shaped flowers.

H. patulum
Zones 6–7   *
H and S: 1.2m/4ft
A hardier, well-rounded shrub with golden-yellow flowers throughout the summer.
'Hidcote': larger, more profuse flowers.

H. 'Rowallane'
Zones 8–10
H: 1.2m/4ft   S: 1.5m/5ft (or more)
Given a sheltered site, this is one of the most flamboyant of the genus. It produces particularly large, rich golden-yellow flowers from spring to fall.

Kalmia latifolia

JUNIPERUS horizontalis

Creeping juniper
Zones 3–8   *
H: 30cm/12in   S: 1.8m/6ft (or more)
This creeping shrub provides useful, dense evergreen ground cover. The branches have an attractive, resinous fragrance in warm weather.
'Bar Harbor': steel-blue foliage; 'Blue Rug': 'blue-green foliage.

KALMIA latifolia

Calico bush, Mountain laurel
Zones 5–9
H and S: 2.4m/8ft
One of the most beautiful early-flowering shrubs, it resembles the rhododendron with its glossy, leathery evergreen leaves and its love of acid soil and semishade. Large clusters of bright pink flowers glow out against the darker foliage in spring.

KOLKWITZIA amabilis

Beauty bush
Zones 6–9
H: 3m/10ft   S:2.4m/8ft
An upright shrub with arching branches and matt green leaves, it has pink foxglove-like flowers with a yellow throat. *K. amabilis* prefers well-drained soil and full sun. Remove the older flowering stems occasionally to keep the bush vigorous.

LAVANDULA angustifolia

English lavender
Zones 7–10
H and S: 75cm/30in
A delightful, bushy evergreen for a sunny spot, it has small tubular flowers and narrow spiky leaves, both strongly aromatic. Periodic hard pruning will help to prevent the plant becoming straggly.
'Munstead': dwarf form with deep purple-blue flowers.

MAGNOLIA wilsonii

Zones 8–10
H: 2.1m/7ft   S: 1.5m/5ft
This slow-growing shrub has shiny, deciduous, elliptical leaves and pendulous, saucer-shaped, fragrant flowers in spring and early summer. The crimson stamens contrast with the clear white petals. It prefers halfshade and a moist soil.

MAHONIA × media 'Charity'

Zones 7–10
H: 2.4m/8ft   S: 1.5m/5ft
An upright, stately evergreen with impressive spiny foliage and perfumed yellow winter flowers. It prefers a lightly shaded position and moist soil.

NANDINA domestica

Heavenly bamboo
Zones 7–10
H: 1.5m/5ft   S: 60cm/24in
Grown mainly for its elegant bamboo-like leaves which, although evergreen, turn an attractive reddish-purple in fall. In midsummer, it produces long white flower-heads and, in fall, clusters of scarlet berries. It likes a moist, sunny position.

Below *Lavender and* Santolina *contrast well when planted close together. Both plants thrive when interplanted between paving slabs, helping to reduce the monotony of the hard surface.*

Mahonia × media
'Charity'

NERIUM oleander

Oleander
Zones 9–10
H and S: 3m/10ft (or more)
This quick-growing, sun-loving
evergreen often needs to winter
indoors in more temperate
climates where it can be grown
as a container plant. It has light
green lanceolate leaves and a
froth of pale pink, white or
yellow single or double flowers
from early summer to fall.

OLEARIA × scilloniensis

Daisy bush
Zones 8–10
H and S: 1.5m/5ft
The tough gray, leathery
evergreen leaves are almost lost
beneath a blanket of white
daisy-like flowers in early
summer. It provides an
excellent windbreak for mild
seaside areas.

OSMANTHUS

This genus of graceful, slow-
growing evergreen shrubs
resembles holly, and bears
small, white, scented flowers.

O. delavayi
Zones 7–10   *
H: 1.8m/6ft   S: 1.2m/4ft
This species has small, dark
green leaves and highly
fragrant white flowers,
resembling jasmine, in spring.

O. fragrans
Zones 8–10   *
H: 3m/10ft   S: 1.5m/5ft
A species with lovely, midgreen shiny oval leaves that
look attractive all year, it
bears highly scented white
flowers late in the season.

PAEONIA lutea

Tree peony
Zones 6–9   *
H: 1.5m/5ft   S: 1.2m/4ft
The deeply cut, large leaves
of *P. lutea* have a majestic,
architectural quality matched
by the large buttercup-yellow,
saucer-shaped flowers that
appear in midsummer. *P. lutea*
requires a sunny, well-drained
site with a deep, rich, moist soil.

PHILADELPHUS coronarius

Mock orange
Zones 5–9
H: 2.4m/8ft   S:1.8m/6ft
A dense bushy shrub, it has oval
midgreen leaves and white, cup-
shaped, scented flowers in midsummer. It does best on dry soil
in full sun or partial shade.

PIERIS

A genus of evergreen shrubs
that need a lime-free soil and
prefer a shady position.

P. 'Forest Flame'
Zones 7–9
H and S: 1.5m/5ft
The spectacular, new red leaf
growth turns pink and then
cream before becoming green,
with large, drooping white
flower panicles in late spring.

*Olearia
× scilloniensis*

P. japonica
Zones 5–9
H and S: 2.4m/8ft
The foliage is brilliant red when
young, turning midgreen later.
Drooping white flowers are
borne in terminal clusters in
spring.
'Variegata': yellow-white
edged leaves.

PITTOSPORUM tobira

Zones 8–10   *
H: 2.4m/8ft   S: 1.8m/6ft
A useful hedging plant for
warmer areas, *P. tobira* has
shiny evergreen leaves and
clusters of creamy-white,
fragrant flowers in early
summer, that darken with age.

Pieris 'Forest Flame'

Rhododendron augustinii

Rosa × cantabrigiensis

Rosa rubrifolia

for their attractive flowers. Few are lime-tolerant and most prefer a sheltered site with a high rainfall.

R. augustinii
Zones 7–9
H: 3m/10ft   S: 2.4m/8ft
The light mauve spring flowers of *R. augustinii* make a startling contrast to the small dark evergreen leaves. One of the finest rhododendrons, it prefers halfshade and is a little susceptible to frost.

R. catawbiense
Zones 5–9
H: 3m/10ft   S: 2.4m/8ft
An evergreen, *R. catawbiense* has shiny leathery green leaves and funnel-shaped large lilac flowers with green-spotted throats, borne from later spring to early summer.
'Compactum': dwarf form, up to 60cm/24in tall, with lilac flowers.

ROSA
Rose
Roses offer not only an immense choice of flower size and color, but also cheerful fall and winter hips. Although easy to grow, they do need annual pruning to maintain flowering on larger bushes and are susceptible to black spot in unpolluted areas, where they should be sprayed with benomyl.

R. alba
Zones 5–9
H: 1.5m/5ft   S: 90cm/36in
Large, very fragrant, semi-double flowers appear on the prickly stems in early summer, followed by a heavy crop of scarlet fall hips.

R. 'Canary bird'
Zones 5–9
H and S: 1.5m/5ft
Arching stems of delicate, fresh green leaves support thick clusters of bright yellow flowers with a distinctly oriental appearance. This cultivar flowers repeatedly from early summer to fall.

POTENTILLA fruticosa
Shrubby cinquefoil
Zones 2–8
H and S: 90cm/36in
There are many garden hybrids with flowers varying in color from white to lemon yellow, gold or pink. Occasional pruning will invigorate the plant.
'Veitchii': compact, fresh green foliage and pure white, simple flowers.

PYRACANTHA 'Mojave'
Zones 5–9
H: 1.8m/6ft   S: 1.2m/4ft
An evergreen shrub, it has spiny branches and bright orange-red berries from later summer onwards. It thrives in full sun or partial shade in any fertile, well-drained soil.

RHODODENDRON
A huge genus of ornamental shrubs that are much prized

Right *In as little as two seasons, vigorous plants like* Rosa gallica 'Officinalis' *and* Hosta *will provide excellent ground cover.*

R. × cantabrigiensis
Zones 5–9
H: 1.5m/5ft   S: 90cm/36in
Fragrant, fern-like leaves and soft, yellow summer flowers make this one of the loveliest hybrid roses.

R. gallica 'Officinalis'
Zones 5–9   †
H: 1.2m/4ft   S: 90cm/36in
The crimson petals of the semi-double flowers in summer have a very sweet scent. It benefits from thinning after flowering.

R. rubrifolia
Zones 2–7
H: 1.5m/5ft   S: 90cm/36in
Smooth, reddish, thornless stems carry leaves of shiny purple (in a sunny location) or grayish-green with a mauve cast (in shade). Clear pink summer flowers and red fall hips make this a very ornamental rose. Vigor can be maintained by pruning out any shoots over five years old.

R. × 'Swany'
Zones 5–9
H: 30cm/12in   S: 1.5m/5ft
A vigorous ground cover with stems that form a dense tangle. Small white floribunda-type flowers are carried throughout the summer.

ROSMARINUS officinalis

Rosemary
Zones 7–10   *
H: 1.5m/5ft   S: 1.2m/4ft
One of the finest aromatic shrubs, it has spiky evergreen foliage and pale lavender-blue

CREATING AN INFORMAL HEDGE

Formal clipped hedging is never a maintenance-free choice in the garden, even when the plants are of a type that can be sprayed with growth-suppressant, reducing the need for clipping. But a thick hedge of plants provides a marvellous shelter or windbreak, and acts as a barrier to pollution or noise. For the low maintenance garden, an informal hedge is probably the best choice. It should be left to sprawl naturally, and will require no attention once established. The plants suitable for this treatment have a different form and habit from those used for clipped hedging; good subjects include *Aucuba japonica, Eucryphia × nymansensis, Escallonia, Griselinia littoralis, Mahonia, Olearia, Pyracantha* and *Rosmarinus, Senecio greyi* and *Viburnum tinus.* If you grow a few climbing plants amongst them, such as *Clematis montana, C. flammula* or *Hydrangea petiolaris,* you can create a hedge that offers an exciting decorative feature with splashes of color at different times of the year. Unclipped hedges can become thin at the base; to cure the problem, you should either plant smaller subjects in front of the larger ones or put the hedging plants in a double row.

Senecio greyi

Skimmia japonica

S. j. 'Rubella'

flowers that appear early in the season. It makes a useful informal hedge – any clipping needed can be done in late spring after flowering. 'Fastidiatus': erect habit.

RUBUS biflorus

Ornamental bramble
Zones 7–9
H: 2.1m/7ft   S: 1.5m/5ft
An easy shrub to grow, *R. biflorus* has waxy white stems that brighten up the garden in winter. The leaflets are coated with white felt on the undersides, and the small white summer flowers are followed by edible yellow fruit in fall.

SANTOLINA neapolitana

Cotton lavender
Zones 8–10   *
H: 75cm/30in   S: 1.5m/5ft
The fine, silvery, evergreen foliage supports large numbers of tiny yellow daisy-eye buttons of flowers in summer. It provides good ground cover, needing full sun, looking best against a

background of darker foliage. Hard pruning every two or three years will help the plant to thrive.

SENECIO greyi

Zones 7–10   *
H: 90cm/36in   S: 1.2m/4ft
Oval, silvery-gray, evergreen leaves (which become greener on the upper surface as they mature) form a dense mound. Clusters of neat, yellow, daisy-like flowers appear in abundance throughout summer. Occasional pruning of older wood encourages flowering shoots to emerge. *S. greyi* does well in coastal situations.

SKIMMIA japonica

Zones 6–9   *
H and S: 1.2m/4ft
Glossy, pale evergreen leaves fade to a reddish hue in winter. White, sweetly scented flowers open in spring, followed by bright red fruit on female plants, if both sexes are grown. 'Rubella': male plant with bright red buds in winter.

SPIRAEA thunbergii

Zones 5–9   *
H: 1.5m/5ft   S: 90cm/36in
A twiggy shrub with downy stems and shiny leaves, *S. thunbergii* bears clusters of white flowers that cover the stems in early spring. It likes a sunny spot and benefits if a third of the oldest shoots are removed after flowering.

SYMPHORICARPOS albus

Snowberry
Zones 3–8   *
H: 2.1m/7ft   S: 2.4m/8ft
A shrub grown mainly for its clusters of glistening white berries which stay on the plant throughout the winter. Small pink urn-shaped flowers are borne from mid-summer to early fall.

Viburnum tinus

Right *One of the easiest shrubs,*
Spiraea thunbergii *grows well*
on most soils, providing a welcome
display of pure white blossom early
in the season.

SYRINGA microphylla

Lilac
Zones 5–9
H: 1.8m/6ft   S: 1.2m/4ft
One of the most compact forms
of lilac with small leaves and
rosy-pink fragrant flowers,
appearing intermittently in
dense trusses in late spring and
summer.
'Superba': profuse pink
flowers.

TAMARIX chinensis

Tamarisk
Zones 8–10
H: 3m/10ft   S: 2.4m/8ft
Elegant slender branches,
clothed in very fine, pale
green foliage, bear a host of
tiny, bright pink flowers at
their extremities in late spring.
T. chinensis resists strong, salty
winds but dislikes limestone.

VIBURNUM

A genus of popular ornamental
shrubs bearing white or pinkish
flowers, often fragrant.

V. × bodnantense

Zones 5–9   *
H: 2.1m/7ft   S: 1.2m/4ft
The dense clusters of perfumed
rose-tinted flowers are doubly
welcome on drab winter days.
They resist frost well and bloom
for a long period. The young
leaves are bronze-tinted.

V. tinus

Zones 7–9   *
H. 2.4m/8ft   S: 1.8m/6ft
The thick evergreen foliage of
oval, dark green leaves

contrasts well with clusters of white fragrant flowers in winter and early spring. Indigo-blue berries are borne later. It makes a good hedge for coastal areas, tolerates limestone soil, and withstands urban pollution very well.

Below Vinca minor *is one of the most successful ground covers, seen here at the foot of a white-barked willow tree.*

VINCA major

Greater periwinkle
Zones 6–9
H: 30cm/12in   S: 1.5m/5ft
A rampaging evergreen with purple-blue flowers from spring to early summer, and oval, glossy, mid- to dark green leaves. The stems spread very quickly over the ground, rooting near their tips.
'Elegantissima': variegated pale green and white leaves and bright blue flowers.

V. minor

Lesser periwinkle
Zones 5–9   *
H: 15cm/6in   S: 1.2m/4ft
Similar to *V. major* but with smaller flowers, often continuing into fall. The stems root intermittently over their entire length.
'Alba': white flowers.

YUCCA recurvifolia

Zones 7–10
H: 1.5m/5ft   S: 1.8m/6ft
Long, narrow, strap-shaped leaves form a dense, tall mound from the center of which the flower stalk emerges, bearing creamy-white bell-shaped flowers from late summer to early fall.
Y. recurvifolia does best in poor, sandy soil in full sun.

CLIMBING PLANTS AND WALL SHRUBS

There is no easier or cheaper way of producing a mass of color and interesting foliage in a low maintenance garden than by the judicious use of climbing plants and wall shrubs. In fact, six vigorous climbers, planted in a strip of land 30cm/12in wide by 9m/30ft long will soon provide a froth of foliage and colorful flowers over 56 sq m/600 sq ft of wall. To provide a similar area of color and interest on the ground would require 20 times the area of cultivated land and would need between 100 and 200 times as many herbaceous plants.

All the plants in this section, as well as being generally easy to care for, have some exceptionally attractive features, such as foliage of outstanding character or blooms of great beauty and fragrance. Since many of them are evergreen or hold their leaves for many months, they not only provide color and interest throughout the year but can be used to mask an unsightly wall, even in the cooler months.

Some climbing plants are selfclinging, and will attach themselves to any surface, either by aerial roots or by sticky tendril tips. Others require only some modest form of support in the shape of a trellis or wire around which their stems or leaf tendrils will twine or curl naturally. Most wall shrubs, although they can be induced to climb, will need occasional tying in. It would be wisest therefore to limit the number of these in a low maintenance garden although the work will only take an hour or so two or three times a year during the growing season.

Provided you site climbing plants where they can grow to their full height and spread, pruning is not necessary except to encourage more abundant flowers. The very vigorous species, however, may need thinning after the flowering season is over, to keep them within bounds. If you allow the climbers to grow over a tree, shrub or a low wall, they will generally be more maintenance-free than when grown against a high wall, as they will be able to scramble at will where they please.

Most climbing plants benefit from a well-drained soil and a reasonable supply of water. It pays to include plenty of moisture-holding organic matter in the planting hole, and to cover the root zone with a thick layer of mulch after planting. If the plant is to be grown against a wall, make sure that any support system is strong enough and sufficiently well-secured to bear its weight when mature.

SUPPORTING CLIMBING PLANTS AND WALL SHRUBS

The support system you provide for any climbing plant must be appropriate, and it is therefore important to know whether the plant is self-clinging and will attach itself to any surface, including a bare wall, either by aerial roots or sticky tendril tips, or whether it is of the twining kind, in which case the stems, or the leaf petioles, or the curling tendrils will fasten themselves to any narrow support, such as a trellis or galvanized wires. Wall shrubs can be encouraged to climb, but will need a trellis or wires to which their branches can be tied in when necessary. Freestanding supports, such as pergolas, ropes slung on wooden supports and wigwams of peasticks, are also useful, particularly for rambling roses or *Clematis* for example.

Right *Examples of climbing habit:*
a *the aerial roots of ivy*
b *the tendrils with sucker tips of Virginia creeper*
c *the curling leaf petioles of* Clematis
d *the twining stems of honey-suckle.*

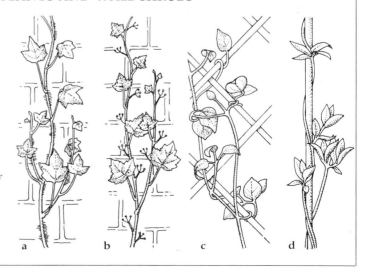

a   b   c   d

Left Campsis grandiflora *is one of the most commanding climbers, providing an exotic feeling rare in climbers that flourish in cooler temperate zones.*

ARISTOLOCHIA macrophylla

Dutchman's pipe
Zones 5–9   *
H and S: 6m/20ft
One of the most arresting, vigorous, twining climbers, it has large, bright green, heart-shaped leaves and pitcher-shaped yellowish-green, brown and purple flowers in early summer. It needs very little support.

BIGNONIA capreolata

Cat's claw, Hug-me-tight
Zones 6–10   †
H and S: 12m/40ft
An evergreen, *B. capreolata* is one of the most vigorous of all climbers. It is self-clinging, clutching at its support with tendrils resembling cat's claws, hence the common name. Brilliant orange-red flowers clothe the plant like a richly colored fleece in early summer. In colder areas, it needs a north- or east-facing wall and therefore some support.

CAMELLIA 'Inspiration'

Zones 7–9
H: 1.8m/6ft   S: 1.5m/5ft
One of the best camellias for training against a wall (it can also be used as a freestanding shrub), it has shiny dark green leaves and large semidouble flowers with deep pink petals in late winter. An evergreen wall shrub, it prefers a shady position on a west wall in colder areas to avoid frost damage, and thrives on an acid or neutral soil.

ABUTILON megapotamicum

Zones 8–10   †
H: 1.8m/6ft   S: 2.4m/8ft
The large, pointed, oval leaves make a perfect foil for the exotic-looking orange-yellow, lantern-shaped flowers in spring and early summer. *A. megapotamicum* needs a sunny spot, in milder areas only, where it may be semi-evergreen. A wall shrub, it needs occasional tying in. 'Kentish Belle'

ACTINIDIA kolomikta

Zones 3–9
H: 4.2m/14ft   S: 1.8m/6ft
A. kolomikta is grown for the glory of its heart-shaped leaves which are green when young, acquiring cream and pink variegations later. A vigorous, twining climber, it has scented white flowers in early summer. It needs some support, and a sunny position on a south-facing wall brings out the leaf variegations well.

AKEBIA quinata

Zones 4–9   *
H: 9m/30ft   S: 6m/20ft
The composite, semievergreen leaves with five long, oval, notched leaflets play host to inconspicuous, fragrant, reddish-purple flowers in spring. In warmer climates, *A. quinata* produces long, purple cylindrical fruit. A vigorous, twining climber, it needs no support if allowed to ramble over hedges and trees.

Abutilon megapotamicum

CAMPSIS

Trumpet vine, Trumpet creeper
There are two species of
Campsis, one of which, *C.
radicans*, is hardy. Both are
self-clinging. *C. grandiflora*
flowers very freely.

Clematis macropetala

C. grandiflora
Zones 8–10
H: 6m/20ft   S: 3.6m/12ft
Composite leaves with seven- to
nine-toothed, glossy leaflets
make this quick-growing self-
clinging vine attractive
throughout the season. It carries
deep orange to red-colored,
trumpet-shaped flowers in late
summer and early fall. In
colder areas, it needs a south-
facing wall and some support.
Annual pruning encourages
maximum flowering.

C. radicans
Zones 5–10
H: 6m/20ft   S: 3.6m/12ft
Very large, composite leaves
with downy undersides marry
perfectly with the large, scarlet
trumpet-shaped flowers borne
freely in late summer. Although
it is self-clinging it needs
additional support when young.
To increase flowering on the
current season's growth, cut
back new growth each spring.
'Flava': larger, rich yellow
flowers.

CEANOTHUS 'Edinburgh'

Californian lilac
Zones 7–9   †
H: 4.2m/14ft   S: 3.6m/12ft
The quite large, ribbed, oval
bright green leaves make
impressive wall color even
before the long sprays of rich
blue flowers appear in early
summer. A fast-growing evergreen wall shrub, it prefers a
sunny position and an acid or
neutral soil, and will need
some support and tying in.

CLEMATIS

The wild *Clematis* species from
which today's more flamboyant
hybrids have been produced
require much less attention. All
Clematis species listed here are
self-clinging, and are
maintenance-free when grown
in a natural setting. They will
need support, such as a trellis,
when grown against a wall.

C. alpina
Zones 3–9   *
H and S: 2.4m/8ft
The deciduous leaves are
composed of nine, thin, oval,
coarsely toothed leaflets. The
flowers are carried on slender
stalks in late spring, and are an
intense violet-blue, with a
central tuft of white staminodes.

C. flammula
Zones 4–9   *
H: 3.9m/13ft   S: 3m/10ft
C. flammula soon forms a dense
tangle of stems with bright
green leaves and carries long
panicles of sweetly scented,
small white flowers in late
summer, followed by silky
seed heads. It grows best with
the roots shaded and the crown
in full sun.

C. macropetala
Zones 2–9   *
H and S: 3.6m/12ft
A slender-stemmed, vigorous
climber with semidouble,
blue flowers in late spring,
followed by fluffy gray seed
heads later. It does well over a
low, sunny wall.

C. montana
Zones 4–9   *
H: 9m/30ft   S: 6m/20ft
One of the most vigorous of all
the clematis, its tangled woody
stems will quickly mask a wall,
even in winter. The dark green,
three-lobed leaves provide a
good contrast to the fragrant,
small white flowers with
twisted sepals that appear in
midsummer.
'Rubens': pale pink flowers;
'Wilsonii': large white scented
flowers that look particularly
attractive against a mellow
brick wall.

Clematis montana

*Fremontodendron
californicum*

C. tangutica
Zones 4–8   *
H: 4.5m/15ft   S: 3m/10ft
Its attractive, sea-green leaves
make *C. tangutica* worthwhile
all season. Rich yellow, lantern-
shaped flowers are produced in
late summer, producing fine,
silken seed heads later. It is
an excellent climber for low
walls, or if allowed to scramble
over large banks.

FREMONTODENDRON
californicum

Zones 7–10   †
H: 3.6m/12ft   S: 2.1m/7ft
This evergreen wall shrub has
smart, palm-shaped leaves that
are underfelted in a rich brown
color. Large yellow flowers
like giant buttercups emerge all
summer. *F. californicum* likes a
south-facing wall and well-
drained soil and will grow
easily on limestone. It does
need training, however.

HEDERA helix

Common ivy
H. helix tolerates most soils
and positions. It provides useful
ground cover for shady
situations, but the cultivars
listed below are a better choice
in terms of improved color,
less rampant growth and
general suitability for the low
maintenance garden. *H.h.*
'Sagittifolia' should not be used
as ground cover.

H.h. 'Buttercup'
Zones 5–9   *
H: 2.8m/9ft   S: 2.4m/8ft
One of the most attractive of
all the self-clinging ivies, it has
small, bright golden leaves that
contrast splendidly with dark
masonry. The full color
of the leaves is produced only
in full sun, so do not grow
H.h. 'Buttercup' as ground
cover in shaded areas.

H.h. 'Hibernica
Irish ivy
Zones 4–9   *
H: 9m/30ft   S: 6m/20ft
The matt, dull green leaves are
five-lobed, with rounded points
curving upward slightly. One
of the quickest growing of all
masking evergreen plants, it
also makes excellent ground
cover, particularly when used
as a backdrop to more brightly
colored plants. Clip it annually
to keep it in check.

H.h. 'Sagittifolia'
Zones 5–9   *
H: 6m/20ft   S: 2.4m/8ft
Darker green than common ivy,
it has slightly smaller,
fascinating, arrow-shaped
leaves that turn a rich purple-
bronze in fall. An ideal
subject for a light-colored

wall, it does not do well as a
ground cover plant.

HYDRANGEA petiolaris

Climbing hydrangea
Zones 4–9   *
H: 10.5m/35ft   S: 4.5m/15ft
Bold, oval, midgreen leaves on
meandering stems form a background to the large corymbs of
greenish-white flowers that
have white florets round the
margin, appearing in early
summer. A vigorous self-
clinging climber, it is ideal for a
north-facing wall.

Below *While often used as a
valuable self-clinging climber,
common ivy* (Hedera helix) *also
makes excellent ground cover as
it puts out new roots from its
spreading stems, rapidly
suppressing weeds in the vicinity.*

Hydrangea petiolaris

JASMINUM

Jasmine
Slender stems and small, often fragrant flowers are the main features of these twining climbers. *J. nudiflorum* provides useful winter color.

J. nudiflorum
Winter jasmine
Zones 5–9   *
H and S: 3.6m/12ft
Bright yellow clusters of small, narrow, trumpet-shaped flowers hug the bare stems throughout winter like bright stars. In summer, the lustrous green leaves make a fine background for other plants. Although technically a wall shrub, it will climb over low walls and hedges unaided but will need support on high walls.

J. officinale
Common jasmine
Zones 7–10   *
H: 7.1m/27ft   S: 6m/20ft
Redolent of the Mediterranean, *J. officinale* has arching, twining stems, lacy foliage and delicate, white, trumpet-shaped flowers in summer that fill the air with the characteristic jasmine perfume.

'Grandiflorum': pink-tinged white petals.

LONICERA

Honeysuckle
Vigorous, scented, flowering, twining climbers that look at their best when allowed to grow in a natural setting. *L. japonica* 'Halliana' is too vigorous for all but poor soils.

L. hildebrandiana
Zones 8–10   *
H: 15m/50ft   S: 9m/30ft
With large, broad, oval, ever-green leaves, creamy-white, scented flowers (which age yellow and orange) and big, shiny red berries, *L. hilde-brandiana* is a spectacular honeysuckle for warmer areas. It needs full sun to flower abundantly and is best grown over a tree.

L. japonica 'Aureoreticulata'
Variegated honeysuckle
Zones 7–9   *
H: 3m/10ft   S: 3.6m/12ft
The major feature of this variety is its small, oval, semi-evergreen leaves with a pronounced, netted, yellow veination. The yellow flowers that appear in summer are insignificant, but produce a fine scent. *L.j.* 'Aureoreticulata' is best grown against a wall in cooler areas, where it will need some tying in.

L.j. 'Halliana'
Zones 7–9   *
H: 6m/20ft   S: 5m/16ft
A vigorous climber over trellis work or in trees, *L.j.* 'Halliana' offers a long season of scented flowers from midsummer to autumn. The flowers change colour from white to yellow,

Lonicera japonica 'Halliana'

Lonicera japonica 'Aureoreticulata'

against a backcloth of simple, oval mid-green leaves.

PARTHENOCISSUS

Virginia creeper
Self-clinging creepers renowned for their vigorous growth and brilliant fall leaf color.

P. henryana
Zones 7–9   *
H: 9m/30ft   S: 4.5m/15ft
The leaves are five-lobed, showing silvery-white veinal variegation before they flare scarlet in fall. It provides a quick-growing mask for an unsightly wall. If the latter is north or north-west facing, it brings out the leaf variegation.

Parthenocissus henryana

Above *A vigorous climber,* Rosa filipes 'Kiftsgate' *is a strong survivor. Its clusters of beacon-bright, small red hips provide welcome winter color, and it can be kept within bounds by once-yearly pruning.*

Rosa 'Madame Grégoire Staechelin'

P. tricuspidata 'Veitchii'
Zones 5–9   *
H. 13.5m/45ft   S: 9m/30ft
The leaves are three-lobed on this rapid-growing creeper, although younger leaves may be composed of three leaflets. It provides excellent color in fall, with small yellow-green flowers in summer.

PLUMBAGO capensis

Zones 9–10   †
H and S: 4.5m/15ft
A wall shrub, *P. capensis* has large clusters of powder-blue, phlox-like flowers that stand above the small-leaved, ever-green foliage for a long period in summer, making it an excellent choice for warm areas.

It can withstand heat and drought, but needs tying in.

PYRACANTHA 'Orange Glow'

Zones 7–9
H: 5m/17ft   S: 2.7m/9ft
Its tidy, evergreen foliage makes *P.* 'Orange Glow' an attractive wall shrub. It bears a mass of creamy-white blossom in summer, followed by bunches of bright orange berries which last into winter. If you prune the new growth after flowering, it will prevent the berries becoming obscured.

ROSA

Rose
A few climbing roses are worth growing for their beauty and fragrance. If allowed to ramble freely over trees and other shrubs, or over fences and low walls, they will require less maintenance than when trained against a high wall.

R. 'Aimée Vibert' ('Bouquet de la Mariée')
Zones 7–9   *
H: 3.6m/12ft   S: 2.7m/9ft
One of the oldest, recurrent-flowering hybrids, *R.* 'Aimée Vibert' is a quick-growing rose, carrying summer-flowering pink buds that open to become medium-large, nearly pure white double blooms.

R. filipes 'Kiftsgate'
Zones 7–9
H: 15m/50ft   S: 9m/30ft
One of the most vigorous roses, *R.f.* 'Kiftsgate' is probably best grown over a tree where it is self-supporting and thus maintenance-free. Once it reaches the top of its support, it flowers freely producing great cascades of yellow-

stamened, simple white flowers with an exquisite perfume in summer. The young foliage is copper-tinged.

R. 'Golden Showers'
Zones 7–9   †
H and S: 2.4m/8ft
An outstanding rose, notable for its strong, self-supporting stems and the polished, mahogany-like appearance of its leaves, that provide a dark, lacquered background for the hosts of golden-yellow flowers that appear over a long season from summer until late fall. It will need some tying in and pruning.

R. 'Madame Grégoire Staechlin'
Zones 7–9   †
H: 4.5m/15ft   S: 3m/10ft
Fine, semiglossy, mildew-free foliage provides a background for the large, deep silvery-pink flowers, splashed with carmine, in midsummer. A rich scent is exuded on warm days. This climbing rose does well on a north-facing wall, where it will need tying in and pruning.

SOLANUM crispum 'Glasnevin'

Chilean potato tree
Zones 7–10   *
H: 5.4m/18ft   S: 4.5m/15ft
S. crispum seems to thrive almost anywhere (it even does well on limestone). Although it needs support on a wall, it will scramble unaided over small fences very quickly. Oval, semievergreen leaves provide a neutral background for the froth of small, rich purple-blue flowers with bright orange stamens that appear in mid-summer and continue through to fall.

TEUCRIUM fruticans

Shrubby germander
Zones 7–10
H and S: 2.1m/7ft
A wall shrub, *T. fruticans* has small, toothed evergreen leaves that are coated with a dense, silvery-white felt. Groups of small, pale-blue flowers appear at the stem ends throughout the summer. *T. fruticans* grows best in a sunny, sheltered position in a light, well-drained soil. It will need tying in, but no pruning.

THUNBERGIA grandiflora

Sky flower
Zones 9–10   *
H: 9m/30ft   S: 6m/20ft
A self-supporting vigorous climber, *T. grandiflora* likes to have its roots in the shade. It has slightly toothed, pointed, evergreen leaves and cascades of large light-blue flowers with yellow eyes. It flowers well into the winter.

TRACHELOSPERMUM jasminoides

Star jasmine
Zones 7–10   *
H and S: 3m/10ft
A twining climber, it has very handsome, dark, oval, evergreen leaves that make a fine contrast to the highly fragrant white flowers that appear from mid- to late summer. Given a protected position in full sun, it will grow vigorously.

VITIS coignetiae

Zones 6–9   *
H: 26m/87ft   S: 9m/30ft
This ornamental vine is a vigorous, self-clinging climber.

Vitis coignetiae

The leaves fade to brilliant orange and crimson shades before dropping in fall. Clusters of green flowers in midsummer give way later to small, purple, grape-like fruit. 'Brandt': larger leaves.

WISTERIA sinensis

Chinese wisteria
Zones 6–10   *
H: 27m/90ft   S: 30m/100ft
This particularly noble twining climber offers glorious pendulous racemes of mauve pea-like flowers in late spring. Attractive light green foliage appears after the flowers to grace the gnarled, woody stems. *W. sinensis* is maintenance-free if allowed to climb over trees.

Solanum crispum 'Glasnevin'

Wisteria sinensis

PERENNIALS

Since the area covered by perennials should be greatly reduced in a low maintenance garden, try to pack as many plants as possible into a small border. (The plants recommended in this section are generally compact forms, requiring no staking). Close-planting will produce foliage that coalesces rapidly to provide an almost complete ground cover, suppressing weed growth quickly. Each square yard of border can carry as many as nine or more plants, offering a fine display for most periods of the year. It is important to plan out the border carefully (see p. 43).

Planting perennials is very easy if the soil is well-prepared first; then use a long-handled trowel or a wrecking bar to dig a hole just large enough to take the roots of each plant comfortably. Fill the hole with water and let it partially drain away before putting the plant in place, and packing the hole with the loose soil. You can let the bed settle overnight, when all the surplus water will have drained away from the root zone, before firming the plants into place with your hands. A sprinkling of slow-release fertilizers will give the plants a good start.

Always try to put in plants that are well suited to the situation, paying particular heed to their preferences for sun or shade, acid or alkaline soil and moist or dry conditions. However, you can also give them some help: for plants like pinks and iris that appreciate a free-draining soil, it is best to mix half a spadeful of coarse grit or pea gravel with the earth, if it is inclined to be heavy, and to plant them on a slight mound. Great moisture-lovers like primulas can have an extra handful of peat mixed with the soil in the bottom of the planting hole, to act as a reservoir in dry weather.

Many perennials make excellent ground cover plants, among them *Ajuga reptans, Alchemilla mollis, Arenaria balearica* and *A. montana, Geranium renardii, Lamium maculatum, Lysimachia nummularia, Mitella breweri, Minuartia verna, Nepeta × faassenii, Pachysandra terminalis* and *Tiarella cordifolia*. Other perennials make attractive subjects for growing over walls or in crevices in a paved area: the best trailing plants include *Arabis caucasica, Aubrieta deltoidea, Ballota pseudodictamnus* and *Impatiens* 'Blitz'; among the subjects most suitable for interplanting are *Arabis caucasica, Aubrieta deltoidea, Campanula carpatica, Dianthus, Hypericum olympicum, Mentha requienii, Sedum spurium* and *Thymus*.

Left *This group of* Bergenia, Hosta, Alchemilla mollis *(lady's mantle) and* Euphorbia *demonstrate how effective plants that are grown principally for their foliage can be when planted together in raised beds. Even the dark green fonds of the paeony, peeping in at the top right of the photograph, make their contribution to an interestingly varied mixture of different leaf forms.*

ADIANTUM pedatum
'Japonicum'

Maidenhair fern
Zones 7–9
H: 45cm/18in   S: 30cm/12in
This fern prefers a shady, moist situation. The copper-colored, tufted fronds are composed of many tiny, finely cut leaflets borne on a purple stalk; they turn bright green in summer. Do not plant too deeply.

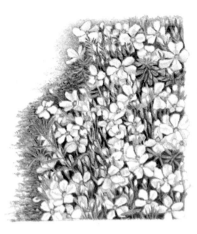

Arenaria montana

AGAPANTHUS
'Headbourne Hybrids'

African lily
Zones 8–10
H: 90cm/36in   S: 45cm/18in
A good feature plant for a
sunny position, *A.* 'Headbourne Hybrids' carries
clusters of very showy flowers
on tall stems in late summer
after the clumps of strap-like
midgreen leaves appear. The
flowers range in color from
pale to dark blue, according to
variety, with some white forms
available.
'Midnight Blue': dark blue
flowers, 60cm/24in tall; '
'African Moon': light blue,
60cm/24in tall; 'Blue Giant':
120cm/48in tall.

AJUGA reptans
'Burgundy Glow'

Zones 5–8   *
H: 10cm/4in   S: 38cm/15in
Grown for its evergreen, rose-
pink and magenta foliage, edged
with cream, *A. reptans* makes
an attractive carpet all winter.
Blue bugle-like flowers on
slender stalks appear in early
summer. It does well on heavy

soil, and prefers a damp site,
tolerating shade. In ideal
conditions, it provides
successful ground cover.

ALCHEMILLA mollis

Lady's mantle
Zones 5–9
H: 45cm/18in   S: 38cm/15in
Grown for its attractive light
green, serrated leaves, *A. mollis*
also produces heads of
yellowish-green flowers from
mid- to late summer. It thrives
in any sunny or partially
shaded position in moist, well-
drained soil, seeding itself
freely to make good ground
cover.

ANEMONE × hybrida
'Bressingham Glow'

Japanese anemone
Zones 6–9   *
H: 90cm/36in   S: 45cm/18in
An excellent plant for providing
flower color from late summer
into fall, it also has elegant
foliage early in the season.
Borne on long stalks above the
crown of the plant, the flowers
are compact with a double row
of deep pink petals and
prominent yellow eyes. No
staking is needed.

ARABIS caucasica
'Flore Pleno'

Wall cress
Zones 6–9   *
H: 25cm/10in   S: 60cm/24in
Trailing mounds of small,
evergreen, gray-green leaves are
complemented by a profusion
of small, double white flowers
from early spring to summer.
An ideal wall or edging plant,
A. caucasica prefers a sunny
site and a rough, limey soil,
but will tolerate any conditions
provided they are dry.

ARENARIA

A genus of low-growing plants
that provide good ground cover.
A. balearica grows best in full
shade, whereas *A. montana*
prefers partial shade.

A. balearica

Zones 8–10
H: 2.5cm/1in   S: 45cm/18in
A. balearica has minute leaves
and star-shaped white flowers
from spring to midsummer.

A. montana

Zones 6–9
H: 15cm/6in   S: 30cm/12in
Mat-forming dark green leaves
form a backdrop to the saucer-
shaped white flowers that
appear in early summer.

ARUNDINARIA

Bamboo
A group of hardy evergreen
perennials. They will spread
rapidly, providing good ground
cover. They prefer moist soil
and a sunny or partially shaded
site, with some shelter from
cold winds.

A. variegata

Variegated bamboo
Zones 7–10   *
H and S: 90cm/36in
An elegant plant for a feature
position, *A. variegata* spreads
easily to make good ground
cover. The leaves are striped
with white.

A. viridistriata

Zones 7–10   *
H: 1.2cm/4ft   S: 90cm/36in
An architectural bamboo with
striking yellow-striped leaves,
A. viridistriata makes a handsome feature plant when
isolated on a stone terrace.

Aster thomsonii 'Nana'

ASTER thomsonii 'Nana'

Zones 4–8   *
H: 38cm/15in   S: 23cm/9in
A fairly loose-petaled, dwarf
form of Michaelmas daisy, it
provides a splash of lavender-
blue from midsummer onward.

ATHYRIUM filix-femina

Lady fern
Zones 4–10   *
H and S: 60cm/24in
An elegant, feathery-leaved
fern, *A. filix-femina* makes an
excellent background
accompaniment to *Hosta*,
Astilbe and primulas. It is at its
best in spring and summer. A
moisture-lover, it prefers a
shaded or semishaded position.

AUBRIETA deltoidea

Zones 7–10   *
H: 10cm/4in   S: 60cm/24in
An evergreen mound-forming
and trailing plant, *A. deltoidea*
produces a crush of light green
foliage with a froth of small,

Bergenia cordifolia

bright mauve flowers for a long period from spring onward. It prefers dry, limey conditions and a sunny site, and is ideal for growing on dry banks, in the front of borders and over walls.

BALLOTA pseudodictamnus

Zones 8–10   †
H: 75cm/30in   S: 45cm/18in
Long, curving stems of small, rounded evergreen leaves are clothed in a gray-white felt. A

Digitalis grandiflora

sun-worshipping plant, it needs well-drained soil. It makes an excellent low hedge for borders and paths, but will need clipping back each spring.

BERGENIA cordifolia

Zones 6–9   *
H and S: 30cm/12in
An excellent ground-covering plant, it will grow and flower on any soil. *B. cordifolia* has large, rounded midgreen leaves and carries heads of lilac-rose bell-shaped flowers in spring. Leave the plants undisturbed unless they get very crowded, in which case they should be divided. Protect from winter sun.

BOLAX gummifera
(Azorella trifurcata)

Zones 4–8
H: 7.5cm/3in   S: 60cm/24in
On a well-drained slope, *B. gummifera* will form dense ground cover. Tiny, three-fingered, palmate leaves pack tightly to form a low, thick, bright green carpet decorated in summer with miniature yellow flowers.

CAMPANULA carpatica

Bellflower
Zones 6–8   *
H: 18cm/7in   S: 30cm/12in
C. carpatica provides good ground cover in the front of a border, for example. Its fresh green, pointed, oval leaves carry a host of small purple or white upturned bells from midsummer to fall.

CHRYSANTHEMUM parthenium

Zones 7–9
H: 30cm/12in   S: 23cm/9in
The lime-green, almost yellow,

leaves form mounds of aromatic foliage, and carry sprays of tiny white daisylike flowers in summer and fall. *C. parthenium* thrives on poor soil in full sun, and seeds itself easily.

DIANTHUS × allwoodii
'Allwoodii Pinks'

Zones 7–10
H: 23cm/9in   S: 38cm/15in
These pinks have very fragrant pink, red or white flowers, and bloom several times in a season. They grow best in well-drained, sandy soil in full sun. They will need to be propagated annually by breaking off pieces from the main stem and inserting them into sandy soil in early fall.

DIGITALIS grandiflora

Foxglove
Zones 7–9   *
H: 60cm/24in   S: 30cm/12in
A compact foxglove that is less likely to dominate a border than larger species. It has velvety, evergreen foliage from which branching stems of soft yellow

flowers emerge in mid- to late summer. It is an adaptable plant, but prefers a moist semishaded position.

DRYOPTERIS dilatata

Broad buckler-fern
Zones 5–10   *
H and S: 60cm/24in
An impressive, graceful fern, with finely divided deciduous leaves, it prefers a moist, shady corner of the garden.

EPIMEDIUM × youngianum
'Niveum'

Barrenwort
Zones 7–9
H and S: 15cm/6in
Grown principally for the astonishing character of its pale chocolate-colored foliage, flushed red in spring and fall, it has a mass of small pure white flowers in spring. It prefers a cool, shady position in which it will remain ever-green. It forms ground cover in the right conditions, and should be divided and replanted after flowering.

Euphorbia griffithii 'Fireglow'

Geranium 'Russell Prichard'

ERYSIMUM alpinum

Alpine wallflower
Zones 5–8   *
H: 15cm/6in   S: 23cm/9in
Thick, low hummocks of small
evergreen leaves are formed,
disappearing in late spring
beneath a show of highly
fragrant, small yellow flowers.

EUPHORBIA griffithii
'Fireglow'

Spurge
Zones 7–9   *
H: 90cm/36in   S: 1.2m/4ft
Spreading slowly by means of
underground rhizomes, *E.g.*

Helleborus niger

'Fireglow' puts up tall stems
carrying narrow green leaves
and heads of glowing apricot-
red flowers in early summer.
Provided the soil is good, it will
tolerate sun and shade.

GERANIUM

Crane's bill
True geraniums are more hardy
than the pelargoniums with
which they are often confused.
G. renardii and *G.* 'Russell
Prichard' both make good
ground cover plants.

G. renardii

Zones 6–9   *
H: 23cm/9in   S: 30cm/12in
A good clump-forming ground
cover plant, with attractive,
sage-colored, scallop-edged
leaves quilted with white hair,
G. renardii has white open, bell-
shaped flowers in early summer,
with an etching of purple veins.

G. 'Russell Prichard'

Zones 8–10   *
H: 23cm/9in   S: 90cm/36in
The deeply divided, gray-green,
semievergreen leaves form
dense mounds of ground cover,
from which emerge long stems
of cupped magenta flowers from
midsummer to the end of
fall.

GYPSOPHILA paniculata
'Rosy Veil'

Zones 7–10   *
H: 25cm/10in   S: 30cm/12in
A low-growing, small-leafed
plant with much-tangled,
twiggy branches, it carries
clouds of small, pale pink
double flowers late in the
season. Although it does well
on free-draining soil in a sunny
position, it is short-lived on
wet soil.

Hosta 'Thomas
    Hogg'

HELICHRYSUM
'Sulphur Light'

Zones 4–9   *
H and S: 45cm/18in
Stems, leaves and buds are clad
with a thick, silvery-white felt,
and provide a slow-spreading,
bright evergreen clump. In late
summer the buds open into
clusters of tiny yellow daisies.

HELLEBORUS niger

Zones 6–9   †
Christmas rose
H and S: 45cm/18in
This hellebore has leathery,
dark green evergreen leaves
and saucer-shaped white
flowers with yellow anthers
that appear in midwinter. It
prefers partial shade and a
moist free-draining soil. In
colder areas, the blooms may
need protection from frost.

HOSTA

Plantain lily
These are excellent foliage
plants for a moist shady
position.

H. tardiflora

Zones 5–10   *
H and S: 30cm/12in
A small species of *Hosta* with
slender, oval leaves of a
beautiful shiny dark green. The
long flower stalks, bearing deep
lilac flowers, emerge in late
summer.

H. 'Thomas Hogg'

Zones 5–10   *
H: 60cm/24in   S: 45cm/18in
A robust plant with generous,
pointed, oval leaves frilled with
cream, it is handsome enough
to be grown for its foliage
alone, although it also produces
slender spikes of lavender-
blue flowers in early summer.

HYPERICUM olympicum

St John's wort
Zones 7–9
H: 15cm/6in   S: 60cm/24in
Masses of bright golden flowers
contrast well with the dense
mounds of evergreen leaves
from midsummer to fall,
making it a good paving plant
in full sun and dry soil.

Lysimachia nummularia

Below *The yellow and orange flowers of Welsh poppies* (Meconopsis cambrica) *add enchantment to any garden in summer, seeding themselves freely.*

HYSSOPUS officinalis

Zones 7–10
H: 45cm/18in   S: 60cm/24in
A semievergreen, *H. officinalis* is grown for its fine leaves. The fragrant, purple-blue flowers are carried during the summer. It needs a dry sandy soil and full sun to thrive.

IMPATIENS 'Blitz'

Busy lizzie
Zone 9–10
H: 30cm/12in   S: 45cm/18in
This fine new plant reputedly has the highest flower to foliage ratio of any *Impatiens* variety. The orange-scarlet blooms have a very long summer season. It grows well in full sun but may need spraying against aphids. It can be treated as a half-hardy annual in colder regions.

IRIS pumila

Zones 7–9
H and S: 15cm/6in
With typical, sword-shaped evergreen leaves, this miniature iris has wonderfully clear, sky-blue flowers. It prefers a sunny position and a neutral soil.

LAMIUM maculatum

Spotted deadnettle
Zones 6–10   *
H: 20cm/8in   S: 60cm/24in
A very fast, ground-covering perennial, with pointed, oval, silver leaves that have a narrow green edging, *L. maculatum* carries small heads of pale reddish-purple tubular flowers throughout much of the summer.

LYSIMACHIA nummularia

Creeping jenny
Zones 6–10   *
H: 3cm/1–2in   S: 60cm/24in
The prostrate meandering stems of small green leaves are covered by a froth of bright yellow flowers in summer. It makes a very good ground cover, but needs plenty of moisture and is therefore also a good bog plant.

MECONOPSIS cambrica

Welsh poppy
Zones 7–9   *
H: 45cm/18in   S: 25cm/10in
The delicate, deeply cut, ferny foliage makes a perfect foil for the trembling, tissue paper-like, thin yellow- or orange-petaled flowers that appear in summer on slender stalks. It prefers a sunny site, and will colonize itself by self-sown seedlings.

MENTHA requienii

Crême de menthe mint
Zones 6–9
H: 10cm/4in   S: 60cm/24in
This semievergreen mint has long self-rooting stems that spread quickly to form dense mats of small, rounded leaves and spikes of pale lilac flowers in summer, giving off a strong aroma of peppermint. Although it can be invasive, it provides good ground cover given a partially shaded position.

MINUARTIA verna

Vernal sandwort
Zones 6–9
H: 15cm/6in   S: 60cm/24in
An excellent ground cover and mound former, *M. verna* has tightly packed, small, thin leaves and a mass of tiny white flowers in late spring.

Right *Evergreen* Pachysandra terminalis *makes a wonderful choice of ground cover. It has the advantage over other good ground cover plants like the ivies that it stands a little taller, making more of a feature, while being just as easy to grow and much less invasive.*

MITELLA breweri

Zones 5–8   *
H: 7.5cm/3in   S: 45cm/18in
A fast ground cover, it thrives in heavy shade, spreading itself by self-sown seeds. It forms a mass of thread-like stems with bright green heart-shaped leaves, carrying minute, very pale green star-shaped flowers in spring. It needs a rich, moist, loamy soil.

NEPETA × faassenii

Cat mint
Zone 5–9
H: 20cm/8in   S: 38cm/15in
A low-growing, mat-forming version of *Nepeta, N. × faassenii* has prominently toothed, grayish foliage on spreading stems, and carries an attractive display of fragrant, lavender-blue flowers for a long period, from early summer to fall.
It needs a well-drained soil in a sunny position. Cut it back in spring to encourage new growth.

PACHYSANDRA terminalis

Zones 6–9
H: 30cm/12in   S: 45cm/18in
P. terminalis is an excellent ground cover plant for shady areas. It has mid- to deep green leaves that make rosette-shaped whorls. Tiny flowers appear in spring.
'Variegata': leaves margined with white.

Paeonia mlokosewitschii

PAEONIA mlokosewitschii

Zones 7–10   †
H and S: 60cm/24in
An outstanding perennial, it needs well-drained soil, and full sun to flower well. The young spring foliage is pinkish-bronze turning to soft gray-green as it matures. Bowl-shaped, acid-yellow flowers open in spring to reveal a forest of golden stamens. If it fails to flower, lift and divide it in fall and replant in rich soil. Once established, leave it un-disturbed.

PELARGONIUM × hortorum

Zones 9–10   †
H and S: 15cm/6in
Even in a low maintenance garden the joy of pelargoniums should not be missed. In colder regions, they can be grown in pots in a warm, sunny position, cut back after flowering and over-wintered in a porch. 'Ringo' cultivars: zonal, ever-green leaves; 'Ringo Snowdon': white flowers; 'Ringo Rose': carmine-red; 'Ringo Picasso': orange eye.

Below *Zonal pelargoniums need little attention once established, making wonderful subjects for containers, thanks also to their resistance to drought.*

Phormium tenax
'Variegatum'

GROWING PLANTS IN CONTAINERS

Provided they are organized carefully, a few containers of plants can make a very successful addition to a low maintenance garden. They are particularly valuable for enlivening hard surfaces, such as patios, but it is important to select a container that is large enough to hold the plants and which is in keeping with its surroundings. Self-watering containers are an ideal choice: they have a reservoir of water (usually under the base of the planter) which, once filled with water, will keep the plant moist for several weeks. A gauge on the side of the planter indicates when the water level inside is dropping. If you wish, you can use ordinary containers, and a drip watering system. The very fine piping is flexible enough to reach

the containers, which can then be watered at the twist of a tap (see p. 141). An automatic clock fitted to the system will take care of the watering while you are absent. Whatever type of container you use, make sure the plant has the right quantity of soil in a suitable mixture (see also p. 134).

Self-watering container

PHORMIUM tenax

New Zealand flax
Zones 8–10　*
H: 1.8m/6ft　S: 1.2m/4ft (leaves)
P. tenax forms impressive evergreen clumps of erect or slightly arching, shiny, sword-blade leaves the dark green upper surfaces of which are strongly striped with orange or red, making it a strongly architectural plant for a feature position. Long panicles of red flowers appear from mid- to late summer. It grows quickly given a sunny site and moist soil but needs protection from frost in cooler areas.
'Variegatum': yellow-striped leaves.

PRIMULA

A large genus of primrose-like plants in an enormous range of colors, they are useful for providing interest in evergreen shrub borders. Many of them make good subjects for bog gardens and waterside planting.

P. denticulata

Zones 6–8
H: 25cm/10in　S: 20cm/8in
The elongated, oval foliage forms a tight evergreen rosette from which the flower stalks emerge to balance aloft flower heads of simple lilac, red or bluish-purple petals with a bright yellow eye from spring to early summer. *P. denticulata* prefers an organic soil and light shade.

P. × 'Garryarde Guinevere'

Zones 6–9　†
H and S: 15cm/6in
Crowded heads of pale lilac, single flowers in spring contrast sharply with very dark bronze,

Primula × 'Garryarde Guinevere'.

evergreen foliage. It grows quickly in a shady position but is prone to bird and aphid damage.

SALVIA officinalis
'Purpurascens'

Purple sage
Zones 7–10
H: 60cm/24in　S: 45cm/18in
This sage fills the garden with a strong, spicy aroma when its grayish-purple, velvety ever-green leaves are warmed by the sun. Its spikes of purple-blue summer flowers match those of many of the popular garden hybrids. It does best on a dry, sunny site and well-drained soil.

SAXIFRAGA

Saxifrage
This family of low-growing evergreen perennials and annuals has starry or saucer-shaped flowers. Most species make good subjects for interplanting or for growing over walls.

S. fortunei 'Rubrifolia'
Zones 7–9
H: 38cm/15in   S: 30cm/12in
Delicate pink stems carrying a
mass of tiny white flowers
in fall emerge from clumps
of highly polished, succulent
bronze-red leaves. An evergreen, it prefers a shady site.

S. × urbium 'Aurea punctata'
London pride
Zones 6–9
H and S: 23cm/9in
Shiny, succulent-looking
leaves, variegated in gold and
green, support sprays of pale
pink flowers in early summer.
An evergreen, it prefers shade.

SEDUM spurium
'Green Mantle'

Zones 6–9
H: 13cm/5in   S: 30cm/12in
Creeping stems, thickly clad
with rosettes of small fleshy
green leaves, form ground-
covering mats, occasionally
carrying small pink flowers in
summer. An evergreen, it does
best in sun or partial shade.

SOLIDAGO hybrida
'Golden Thumb'

Dwarf golden rod
Zones 5–9   *
H and S: 30cm/12in
This miniature version of

golden rod remains tidy, needs
no staking and has plumes of
golden flowers over a long
period from late summer to
fall.

THYMUS serpyllum
'Pink Chintz'

Zones 7–9
H: 15cm/6in   S: 30cm/12in
An evergreen, it produces
cushions of small, woolly leaves
that disappear beneath a haze
of salmon-pink flowers in
summer. It is ideal for interplanting in a terrace, as the
leaves, when crushed underfoot, release the full fragrance
of the plant.

*Tiarella
cordifolia*

TIARELLA cordifolia

Foam flower
Zones 5–9   *
H: 30cm/12in   S: 60cm/24in
This evergreen plant spreads by
underground rhizomes to form
a solid mat. With green foliage
flecked with red, turning
bronze in winter, it supports a
foam of white flower spikes in
spring. It grows well in shade,
forming excellent ground cover.

VERONICA incana

Zones 7–9
H and S: 30cm/12in
The oval leaves are silvery-
white and hairy, borne on
erect stems. An evergreen, it
prefers a sunny, dry situation.
V. incana carries attractive
spikes of deep blue flowers to
provide late summer color.

Left *The tiny mound-forming
plants like the fragrant dwarf
thymes and succulent sedums
make ideal subjects for spreading
across hard surfaces.*

ANNUALS

It may seem contradictory to suggest that you bother to raise annual plants in a low maintenance garden, but their value in introducing color during the 'dead' periods – when summer flowering species are fading and fall flowering plants have not begun to make a show – is undeniable. To obtain this summer bonus, annuals must perform to order; if you simply sow ungerminated seeds in the gaps between the perennial plants the results will probably be disappointing. Unless circumstances after sowing are exceptionally favorable, germination will be slow and irregular, and as so often happens in early summer, conditions may be unfavorable for the early development of annuals. And, as a result, they do not begin to flower until it is too late for them to play their appointed role, their bright kaleidoscope of color lost among the glory of the perennials' fall parade, or clashing harshly with it.

With the hardy annuals, you will increase your chances of success if you pregerminate the seed before sowing it, using the fluid-drilling technique shown on page 145. Prior to sowing the seeds out of doors, loosen the soil and break it into a fine tilth. Give it a light dressing with general garden fertilizer and moisten it well. Indoor sowing helps to guarantee good, regular germination and is an insurance against the irritating failures that can occur when the seed is sown directly into the soil – birds are one of the common causes of loss. Of the plants listed here, *Anchusa capensis* 'Blue Angel', *Calendula officinalis, Dimorphotheca aurantiaca, Eschscholzia caespitosa, Limnanthes douglasii, Nigella damascena, Malcolmia maritima* and *Tropaeolum majus* can be treated as hardy.

With frost-tender annuals, either buy well-established young plants from a reputable nursery or sow a limited range of varieties indoors on the same day in late spring (see p. 144). Once the plants are sufficiently sturdy, they can be put out into the garden at their final spacing on the same afternoon, provided all danger of frost is past.

The whole process need only occupy two short afternoons' work and will provide weeks of pleasure in the summer.

Arctotis stoechadifolia, Dianthus barbatus, Phlox drummondii, Tagetes signata and *Viola × wittrockiana* can be treated as half-hardy annuals. Some of the perennials (see pp. 74–82) native to warmer climates, such as the pelargoniums, can be treated as half-hardy annuals in cooler areas.

Right *Nothing brightens a drab corner more quickly or effectively than a thick cluster of* Dimorphotheca. *They are ideal for easy* indoor sowing, because they could succumb to late frosts if sown directly into flower beds outdoors in spring.

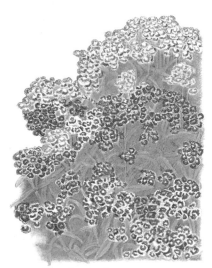

Dianthus barbatus

ANCHUSA capensis

Summer forget-me-not
Zones 3–10   *
H: 45cm/18in   S: 20cm/8in
A grander version of the
ordinary forget-me-not, *A.*

Helichrysum bracteatum

capensis has blue, saucer-
shaped flowers that appear
from mid- to late summer. Sow
in warmth in early spring in a
sunny position, and plant out
in early summer.
'Blue Angel': a more compact,
hardy form with bright blue
flowers, it can be sown *in situ*
from mid- to late spring.

ARCTOTIS stoechadifolia

Zones 5–10   *
H: 60cm/24in   S: 30cm/12in
Large, white daisy-like flowers
with black and gold eyes chirp
out from any border from
midsummer to fall. *A.
stoechadifolia* prefers a sunny
situation. Sow seeds in warmth
in early spring and plant out in
flowering positions in early
summer, in groups.

CALENDULA officinalis

Pot marigold
Zones 3–9   *
H: 45cm/18in   S: 30cm/12in
With typical, large, round,
orange marigold heads, these
vigorous and robust plants will
seed themselves everywhere,
reappearing in successive years.
They flower from summer to
fall, preferring a sunny
spot. Sow *in situ* in spring or,
for spring flowering in zones
7–9, in fall.
'Fiesta Giant': double flowers
in shades from creamy-yellow
to bright orange.

DIANTHUS barbatus

Sweet William
Zones 3–8   *
H: 45cm/18in   S: 30cm/12in
A short-lived, summer
flowering perennial that can be
treated as an annual to obtain
flowers in the year of sowing.
Densely packed flower heads,

in colors ranging from white
to red, appear in midsummer.
D. barbatus prefers a sunny
spot and a neutral or alkaline
soil. Sow in warmth in early
spring and plant out in early
summer.
'Wee Willie': dwarf form,
15cm/6in tall.

DIMORPHOTHECA aurantiaca

Star of the Veldt
Zones 7–10   *
H and S: 30cm/12in
A very free-flowering dark-
eyed daisy. Flowers are borne
from midsummer to early
fall in shades from white to
orange, according to variety.
Sow *in situ* in a sunny position
in midspring.
'Glistening White'

ESCHSCHOLZIA caespitosa
(E. tenuifolia)

Zones 4–8   *
H and S: 23cm/9in
A dwarf annual, it carries
lovely buttercup-yellow four-
petaled flowers from mid- to
late summer, above a mass of
finely divided blue-green

Viola × wittrockiana

Nigella damascena

foliage. *E. caespitosa* will
reseed itself in successive
seasons, and prefers a sandy
soil, and a sunny position. It is
best sown *in situ* when the last
frost is over.

HELICHRYSUM bracteatum
(H. macranthum)

Zones 4–9   *
H: 110cm/42in   S: 30cm/12in
The red, pink, brown, yellow
or white petals contrast with

the green, brown or gold centers, demanding attention from mid- to late summer. *H. bracteatum* is much loved for use as dried flowers. Sow seeds in warmth in early spring and plant out in early summer into well-drained soil in a sunny position.
'Bright Bikini': dwarf mixture, 30cm/12in tall.

LIMNANTHES douglasii

Poached egg flower
Zones 4–8   *
H: 15cm/6in   S: 10cm/4in
Pale, glossy-green foliage pillows a mass of white, open, cup-shaped flowers with gold centers and a fine light perfume. An ideal paving plant, it flowers in midsummer. Sow *in situ* in early spring. It will reseed itself easily.

MALCOLMIA maritima

Virginia stock
Zones 4–9   *
H: 15cm/6in   S: 10cm/4in
The crowded, multicolored display of small, confetti-like, fragrant flowers all summer long makes it well worth including *M. maritima* as an annual. Sow *in situ* in gaps in a border in spring. It will seed itself if the soil is undisturbed.

NIGELLA damascena

Love-in-a-mist
Zones 4–9   *
H: 60cm/24in   S: 23cm/9in
Bright green, fern-like foliage provides a backdrop for the blue and white flowers that are surrounded by a fine ruff of thread-like bracts, from mid- to late summer. Sow *in situ* in midspring.
'Miss Jekyll's Blue': large, bright blue semidouble flowers.

PHLOX drummondii

Zones 4–9
H: 38cm/15in   S: 23cm/9in
Thick mounds of red, pink, purple, buff or white flowers are formed for weeks on end, from summer to fall. Sow seeds in warmth in early spring, and plant out in groups in early summer.
'Nana Compacta': a dwarf, bushy strain, 23cm/9in tall.

TAGETES signata
(T. tenuifolia)

Signet marigold
Zones 4–9
H: 30cm/12in   S: 23cm/9in
Renowned for their scented leaves, these dwarf marigolds have small, single flowers that are less fussy than some of the larger forms. They range in color from yellow to deep orange. Sow in warmth in

spring and plant out in groups in summer. (The flowers may be subject to mold in wet districts.)
'Golden Gem': dwarf variety, 20cm/8in tall, with bright orange petals and a richer colored eye.

TROPAEOLUM majus

Nasturtium
Zones 4–9   *
H: 2.4m/8ft   S: 38cm/15in
A climbing and trailing annual with circular, midgreen leaves and large yellow and orange trumpet-shaped flowers from midsummer to early fall.
The leaves and stems have a pungent smell when crushed. Sow *in situ* in midspring.
'Jewel Mixed': yellow, scarlet and orange flowers, 30cm/12in tall; 'Gleam' cultivars: semi-double orange, yellow and scarlet flowers.

Above *Nasturtiums* (Tropaeolum majus) *tolerate very poor soil to provide a summer-long parade of fresh, bright flowers. They look particularly good against the masonry in a low maintenance garden.*

VIOLA × wittrockiana

Pansy
Zones 4–9
H: 20cm/8in   S: 30cm/12in
Heavily patterned, flat-faced flowers appear repeatedly throughout the year in a multitude of colors: white, yellow, red, purple and bicolored. *V. × wittrockiana* provides the best color value of any garden plant. Sow seeds in warmth in early spring, and plant out in groups in a sunny or partially shaded position in early summer. Guard against slug damage.

BULBS, CORMS AND TUBERS

Bulbs, corms and tubers are an excellent choice for a low maintenance garden because one of their principal characteristics is their dislike of being moved or disturbed. They are a form of perennial in which the plants reproduce themselves by storing food and moisture underground. In a flower meadow, it is important not to mow the area closely, as the leaves of any bulbs must remain to provide the food storage for the following year. To keep bulbs thriving, it is best to give them an annual application of a good general purpose garden fertilizer.

Most bulbs, corms and tubers spread themselves easily, naturalizing either by seed, by producing small offsets (in the case of bulbs) or simply by spreading (in the case of corms and tubers). Where these plants form part of a perennial border, they should be dug up and divided every few years to spread them over a wider area (if wished) and to prevent the clumps becoming too thickly clustered.

It is important when planting bulbs to put them in the right way up (with the pointed end upward). Generally the bulb should be planted at a distance below the soil equal to twice that of its depth, so that a bulb 5cm/2in long should be planted 10cm/4in deep. Although a dibble or trowel can be used for planting bulbs in a prepared bed or border, a bulb-planter or crowbar is a more useful tool for planting in matted grass, such as in a meadow lawn.

To prevent bulbs rotting, make sure the base of each one sits firmly on the soil at the bottom of the planting hole. If it is allowed to lodge in a cone-shaped hole, water collects in the space between the bulb and the soil. Where the soil is inclined to be heavy, it is best to make it more free-draining by adding coarse sand or grit (see p. 133).

The following bulbs will all naturalize well if planted in the right setting. *Colchicum speciosum, Eranthis hyemalis, Fritillaria meleagris, Galanthus nivalis, Muscari armeniacum, Ornithogalum umbellatum* and *Scilla sibirica* will all do well in both woodland and meadow gardens. *Anemone nemorosa, Crocus chrysanthus, Cyclamen coum,* and *Iris reticulata* will naturalize in woodland areas, and *Narcissus* and *Scilla bifolia* will do so in meadow grass. *Nerine bowdenii* will naturalize in a well-drained border.

Anemone blanda

Left *The larger trumpet narcissi look best when they have been allowed to naturalize in a flower meadow. Their taller stems allow the nodding heads to reach well clear of the surrounding coarse grasses.*

ANEMONE

A large group of perennials and tubers. The species given here are all spring-flowering tuberous plants, although *A. coronaria* 'De Caen' will also flower in summer or fall, depending on the time planted. *A. nemorosa* will naturalize well in a woodland setting.

A. blanda
Zones 6–9 *
H: 15cm/6in   S: 10cm/4in
A. blanda provides bright blue flowers from early to midspring. Pale blue, mauve, pink and white forms are also available. Planted in fall in full sun, *A. blanda* does well on limestone soil.

A. coronaria 'De Caen'
Zones 7–9 *
H: 45cm/18in   S: 15cm/6in
Large poppy-like flowers in red, pink, blue and white are displayed amongst attractive frills of foliage, followed by unusually decorative seed heads. Plant in organic soil in midspring for summer flowering, in summer for fall flowering and in fall for an early spring show.

A. nemorosa
Wood anemone
Zones 7–9 *
H and S: 15cm/6in
Among the most enchanting of all woodland plants, *A. nemorosa* is a persistent ground cover plant on any moist soil with a high organic content. It has delicate white flowers that appear in midspring. Plant soon after flowering before the foliage has died down.

BLANDFORDIA nobilis

Christmas bells
Zones 9–10   †
H: 50cm/20in   S: 35cm/14in
Rising in tufts of grass-like leaves, the tall flower stems each bear in midsummer from two to ten tubular, bell-like blooms that are lined orange-scarlet and tipped with yellow. Frequent watering and feeding will encourage *B. nobilis* to flower more freely. Plant in fall.

Colchicum speciosum

BRODIAEA californica

Zones 8–10 †
H: 60cm/24in S: 15cm/6in
A member of the onion family, *B. californica* produces clusters of starry lilac or violet flowers on tall, leafless stems in early summer. It prefers a sunny, sheltered site in well-drained soil and will spread and naturalize in warm climates. Plant the corms in groups in early fall.

CAMASSIA cusickii

Quamash
Zones 6–9 *
H: 90cm/36in S: 30cm/12in
A member of the lily family, *C. cusickii* has large spikes of star-shaped, pale lavender-blue flowers and midgreen, strap-shaped leaves, making an impressive show in midsummer. Plant in moist, heavy soil in fall in full sun.

COLCHICUM speciosum

Fall crocus
Zones 6–9 *
H: 25cm/10in S: 23cm/9in
The mauve trumpet-shaped

flowers resemble those of spring crocus but provide welcome color in fall when numerous other plants are fading. Plant in mid- or late summer, arranged in clumps of six or more. *C. speciosum* naturalizes well in grass, but the massive rosettes of leaves produced in spring must be left to die down naturally.

CRINUM × powellii

Zones 8–10
H: 75cm/30in S: 45cm/18in
Long blade-shaped leaves are surmounted with thick stalks bearing large rose-pink to white flowers from mid- to late summer. Plant in mid- to late spring, preferably against a south-facing wall, and protect from frost.

CROCUS chrysanthus

Zones 6–9
H: 10cm/4in S: 7.5cm/3in
With typical grassy leaves, these dazzling plants hoist their paper chalices in early spring. They do particularly well in pots or tubs. Although neither pest- nor disease-free, and a great temptation to hungry birds, they are well worth growing. Plant in well-drained soil in groups in early fall. 'Cream Beauty': creamy white petals; 'E.A. Bowles': buttercup yellow with bronze feathering; 'Snow Bunting': white with a golden throat; 'Zwanenburg Bronze': dark bronze outside with a deep yellow interior.

CYCLAMEN

A group of tuberous plants with shuttlecock-shaped flowers. *C. coum* will naturalize well and makes a good choice for a shady woodland garden.

Crocus chrysanthus

C. coum

Winter cyclamen
Zones 7–9
H: 7.5cm/3in S: 10cm/4in
Among the most exquisite of plants, this dwarf cyclamen has plain or slightly marbled, leathery, rounded leaves and typical shuttlecock-shaped flower heads with white, pink or carmine colored petals, and a crimson blotch at the base. *C. coum* needs an adequate supply of leaf mold and good drainage. It reproduces itself by seed and corms. Plant in summer.

C. persicum

Zones 9–10
H and S: 20cm/8in
With rounded, brighter green leaves than most cyclamen, this species has a long flowering season from winter to late spring. The fragrant blooms are white to pale bluish-pink with a darker blotch at the base of each petal, borne on tall elegant stems. Plant in summer.

Cyclamen coum

DODECATHEON media

Zones 6–9
H: 40cm/16in   S: 30cm/12in
Rosettes of fresh green long, oval leaves near the ground carry clusters of erect flowering stalks, topped by pink to lilac cyclamen-shaped flowers with yellow anthers from early to midsummer. Plant in fall in shade in moist soil, rich in leaf mold.

ERANTHIS hyemalis

Winter aconite
Zones 5–9
H: 10cm/4in   S: 7.5cm/3in
Deeply cut pale green leaves surround the lemon-yellow flowers that appear in early spring. *E. hyemalis* will naturalize in a moist, loamy soil and does well in partial shade, as underplanting amongst shrubs or in a woodland garden. Plant in late summer.

EREMURUS × 'Shelford'

Foxtail lily
Zones 7–10
H: 1.8m/6ft   S: 60cm/24in
Impressive flower spikes in white, yellow, orange-buff or pink tower in midsummer above clumps of strap-like leaves. Plant in fall in well-draining, loamy soil, preferably in a sunny sheltered spot.

Right *Snowdrops* (Galanthus nivalis) *and winter aconites* (Eranthis hyemalis) *are among the most welcome providers of early spring color in the garden. A few bulbs will soon spread to carpet the ground and, in fact, they look their best when they have been allowed to develop freely into good-sized clumps or thick drifts.*

Fritillaria meleagris

FRITILLARIA meleagris

Snake's head fritillary
Zones 7–9
H: 38cm/15in   S: 15cm/6in
Simple, fleshy, grass-like leaves
each carry stems with one or
two graceful, purple and white
chequered bell-like flowers,

Iris reticulata

from mid- to late spring. *F.
meleagris* naturalizes readily in
grass, making it an ideal choice
for a meadow lawn. Plant
bulbs on their sides in moist
conditions in fall.
'Artemis': purple-grey;
'Charon': deep purple.

GALANTHUS nivalis

Common snowdrop
Zones 4–9
H: 15cm/6in   S: 10cm/4in
In cool, temperate climates,
this is the first harbinger of
spring as its elfin-like white
bell-shaped flowers peep up
through melting snow. Plant
new bulbs just after the
flowering period ends, in a
moist, shaded site, if possible.
G. nivalis will do well in a
wooded setting, or in grass
under trees.

IRIS reticulata

Zones 7–9
H and S: 15cm/6in
A bulbous mini-iris that
provides welcome color with
its blue or purple flowers in
winter. Plant in clumps in
fall, in light limestone.
Good drainage is essential if
the plants are to naturalize and
form large groups.

LEUCOJUM aestivum
'Gravetye Giant'

Summer snowflake
Zones 7–9
H: 60cm/24in   S: 20cm/8in
Once established, each plant
carries clusters of white snow-
drop-like flowers, tipped
attractively with very pale
green, in summer. It will do best
in a sunny position with moist
soil. Plant in late summer or
early fall. *L.a.* 'Gravetye Giant'
is much more robust than the

species, which can be used
instead, if necessary.

MUSCARI armeniacum
'Blue Spike'

Zones 7–9   *
H: 20cm/8in   S: 15cm/6in
From a clump of dark green,
grass-like leaves, small spires
thickly clad with double, bright
blue flowers are put up in
spring. Plant from late summer
to midfall in groups in full
sun. Divide groups every three
to four years.

NARCISSUS

A large genus comprising the
ever-popular daffodils and
narcissi. All are suitable for a
low maintenance garden, but
the species and cultivars given
here are particularly attractive.
Plant in early fall.

N. cyclamineus
Zones 5–8   *
H: 15cm/6in   S: 7.5cm/3in
A dwarf narcissus that
naturalizes in grass, it has
cyclamen-like, rich golden
flowers in early spring. It does
best in moist soil in the open or
in partial shade. It multiplies
both by offsets and seed.

N. 'Dove Wings'
(N. cyclamineus × N. 'Mitylene')
Zones 6–8   *
H: 35cm/14in   S: 20cm/8in
An outstanding hybrid with
swept-back, cyclamen-like
white petals and a cup that
turns white.

N. 'Peeping Tom'
Zones 5–9   *
H: 38cm/15in   S: 25cm/10in
The long bright yellow trumpets
give the long-lasting flowers an
inquisitive look.

Leucojum aestivum

NERINE bowdenii

Zones 8–10   *
H: 60cm/24in   S: 15cm/6in
Clusters of rose-pink trumpet-
shaped flowers are displayed in
fall and the strap-shaped
leaves appear after the flowers.
Plant the bulbs in well-drained
soil in late summer or spring.
N. bowdenii flowers best in a
warm border when it will
reproduce rapidly. Divide every
four to five years.

Scilla sibirica

'Fenwick's Variety': more vigorous and larger than the species, with deeper pink flowers.

ORNITHOGALUM umbellatum

Star of Bethlehem
Zones 6–9   *
H: 20cm/8in   S: 15cm/6in
A good subject for naturalizing in both grass and woodland, *O. umbellatum* carries star-shaped white flowers with green stripes in spring. Plant in fall.

SCILLA

A group of bulbs that have blue flowers and strap-like leaves. They look best grown in a natural setting.

S. bifolia
Zones 7–9   *
H: 15cm/6in   S: 10cm/4in
Flower heads comprising up to eight turquoise-blue bells are carried on each stem in early spring, among the dark green grass-like leaves. *S. bifolia* naturalizes well in grass and is a good subject for a meadow lawn. Plant in moist, well-drained soil in a sunny or partially shaded position in late summer or early fall.

S. sibirica
Zones 3–8   *
H: 15cm/6in   S: 10cm/4in
Small brilliant blue flowers appear in early spring. *S. sibirica* will survive and multiply in both flower meadows and wood-

Right *The tiny* Narcissus cyclamineus *spreads rapidly to provide splashes of color when emerging from the dark green of the surrounding ground cover plants.*

land gardens. Plant in late summer or early fall.

TULIPA

Tulip
A large group of bulbs with bright, waxy flowers. Some species will naturalize but many

are too flamboyant to look attractive in an informal setting.

T. humilis
Zones 8–9
H: 15cm/6in   S: 7.5cm/3in
A tiny pink tulip that appears in early spring. Plant in fall.

T. springeri
Zones 6–9
H: 38cm/15in   S: 15cm/6in
Mahogany-red flowers are produced in late spring. *T. springeri* naturalizes well in an open, sunny border. Plant in fall.

AQUATIC AND MARSH PLANTS

Water gardening is great fun, mainly because aquatic plants are surprisingly easy to grow. The only work needed consists of a few hours of splashy fun in spring when the new plants are put in and any vigorous older ones are cut back and divided, where necessary.

To get the best out of water and marsh plants, you should follow a few simple rules. Firstly, always give the plants the situation they prefer: marsh plants need a permanently moist situation, marginal aquatics can be planted in shallow water up to 7.5–10cm/3–4in deep, and floating or submerged aquatics generally need about 30cm/12in of water. Water lilies, however, like a depth of at least 45cm/18in of still water. Secondly, do not leave the plants out of the water for any length of time between purchasing them and planting them otherwise they will deteriorate rapidly.

Specially designed baskets with perforated sides can be used for planting aquatics. If they are lined with burlap, the baskets will hold the potting mix until the plant roots enmesh with the soil. By that time the burlap will have rotted and the plant roots can penetrate the water through the perforated sides of the baskets. The best potting mix for planting aquatics and marsh plants is derived from well-rotted fibrous turf, but if this is not available, you can use a good garden loam, provided it is uncontaminated by weedkillers or chemicals that might be harmful to pond life. Although aquatic plants need little feeding, they will benefit from an annual dressing of coated slow-release fertilizers in spring, just before the growing season starts.

Pond weeds are a vital feature of any water garden since they liberate oxygen on bright days, which is then passed to the sub-surface aquatic life. Any water feature must include a number of oxygenating plants, such as *Egeria densa, Potamogeton crispus* or *Ranunculus aquatilis*. Free-floating plants generally require no potting mix; anchor the base with a weight to prevent them tangling with other plants.

ASTILBE chinensis 'Pumila'

Zones 7–9   *
H: 45cm/18in   S: 60cm/24in
One of the best marsh plants, it will also provide excellent ground cover in a moist, shaded position. It produces an intricate tracery of ferny midgreen foliage and slender spikes of small rose-lilac flowers from midsummer through to fall. Plant in fall or spring.

CALTHA palustris

Double marsh marigold
Zones 5–9   *
H and S: 30cm/12in
A marsh plant and marginal

Left *One of the most spectacular plants for use in marshy areas and for pond margins,* Lysichiton americanus *will spread rapidly given the damp moist conditions in which it thrives.*

aquatic that has bright yellow double flowers in late spring on stems clad with lush green foliage. Plant in spring or fall.
'Flore Pleno': bright golden yellow large double flowers.

EGERIA densa

Argentinian waterweed
Zones 7–10   *
H and S: 90cm/36in
A submerged aquatic, it produces a mass of meandering fine stems with small bright green leaves and white flowers in summer. It is one of the best oxygenating plants for a water feature, if given plenty of light. Plant in a sandy potting mix.

GLYCERIA aquatica 'Variegata'

Zones 6–9
H: 60cm/24in   S: 45cm/18in
A marginal aquatic, it produces

good-sized clumps of striped, grassy leaves, making a good natural foil for the flowering plants in a water feature. It will need annual thinning if grown in a small pond.

Caltha palustris

IRIS kaempferi

Zones 6–9   *
H: 90cm/36in   S: 45cm/18in
A marsh plant, *I. kaempferi* has slender deciduous foliage and

Myosotis scorpioides

typical rich purple iris flowers in midsummer. It will not tolerate limestone and needs added humus. Plant in moist soil spring or early fall in full sun. 'Variegatus': yellow and green striped leaves.

LYSICHITON americanus

Yellow skunk cabbage
Zones 4–9
H: 90cm/36in   S: 60cm/24in
A marsh plant and marginal aquatic, *L. americanus* forms large clumps of long, leathery bright green oval leaves. The arum-like flowers are deep golden-yellow, borne between early and late spring. It does best in loamy soil and a sunny or partially shaded site.

Nymphaea odorata 'Sulphurea Grandiflora'

MIMULUS luteus

Blotched monkey flower
Zones 6–9   *
H: 38cm/15in   S: 30cm/12in
A marsh plant with light green foliage and snapdragon-like yellow and red spotted flowers, *M. luteus* seeds itself easily. Plant in spring in sun or light shade in moist soil.

MYOSOTIS scorpioides

Water forget-me-not
Zones 6–9   *
H: 23cm/9in   S: 30cm/12in
A quick-growing marginal aquatic and marsh plant, it produces tiny sky-blue flowers in spring. Plant in fall.

NYMPHAEA

Water lily
A group of elegant water plants with large leaves and cup-shaped blooms. The leaves help to prevent the growth of algae.

N. alba

White water lily
Zones 6–9
H: 15cm/6in (above water)
S: variable
A large, vigorous floating aquatic suitable for lakes and large ponds.

It produces pristine, waxy white petals with bright yellow eyes in summer. Plant in spring.

N. odorata 'Sulphurea Grandiflora'

Zones 8–9
H: 30cm/12in   S: 120cm/48in (or more)
A floating aquatic, *N. odorata* is one of the most attractive of all water lilies with the characteristic floating leaves and very large, cup-shaped pale sulphur-yellow fragrant flowers. Plant in midspring or early summer.

PONTEDERIA cordata

Pickerelweed
Zones 7–10   *
H: 60cm/24in   S: 38cm/15in
A marginal aquatic, *P. cordata* has handsome heart-shaped leaves wrapped round stems that develop showy purple-blue spikes of flowers in later summer and early fall. Plant in early spring and protect leaves in winter in colder areas.

POTAMOGETON crispus

Curled pondweed
Zones 5–9
H and S: variable
A submerged aquatic, the thin strands of curly leaves form rafts of foliage that are green in shade and reddish-brown in sunlight. It oxygenates water effectively.

RANUNCULUS aquatilis

Water crowfoot
Zones 4–8   †
H: 60cm/24in   S: 45cm/18in
A floating and submerged aquatic that is useful for fast-running water or larger ponds. It has small white-petaled flowers in spring and summer. It makes a good oxygenating plant, but will need thinning regularly.

Ranunculus aquatilis

SARRACENIA flava

Zones 8–10
H: 75cm/30in   S: 30cm/12in
An unusually elegant insectivorous marsh plant, *S. flava* produces eye-catching yellowish flowers and greenish-yellow erect pitchers in spring. They have a pungent smell.

TYPHA minima

Dwarf reedmace
Zones 7–10   *
H and S: 45cm/18in
A marginal aquatic, it has thick grass-like leaves that bulk quickly into crowns supporting brown mace that resemble those of bulrushes.

VERONICA beccabunga

Brooklime
Zones 7–10   †
H and S: 30cm/12in
A marginal aquatic with elliptical smooth leaves bearing clusters of small blue flowers in summer. It has creeping stems and is liable to be invasive if not cut back regularly.

VEGETABLES, HERBS AND FRUIT

A small kitchen garden is manageable, even if you have only little time available, provided you adopt not only a radical approach to growing crops but also limit your horizons. You will have to be much less ambitious in terms of growing targets and in the range of crops grown than a traditional gardener would be. Nevertheless, there are a number of vegetables that can be grown relatively easily; herbs should present no real problem, but fruit growing should be approached with caution in a low maintenance garden.

VEGETABLES

First of all, even in the largest garden, it is probably best to limit the vegetable plot to about 9m by 4.5m (30ft by 15ft), and it should be sited where it will catch plenty of sun if the crops are to do well. If, rather than trying to grow vegetables in the standard long rows, you divide the plot into blocks of 1.5m by 1.2m (5ft by 4ft), surrounded by 60cm/2ft wide paths, you will save a lot of work. You can tend the plants quite easily from the paths instead of trampling on the soil around the crops. As a result, the ground will not be compacted and the roots of the vegetables will plunge deeply into the earth, finding water more easily than they would normally. You can then plant more closely than normal (known as close-planting), producing higher crop yields per unit area, as evaporation is reduced and the weeds are suppressed by the dense foliage of the plants. Although the vegetables will tend to be smaller than average, they will taste as good, if not better, than their larger counterparts. Also, by close-planting vegetables, you minimize the effects of cold wind and bad weather, as the plants provide protection for each other.

One of the best labor-saving techniques in the vegetable garden is to use heavy-duty black plastic sheeting as a mulch around the plants (see p. 150). It can be used for any vegetables that are grown from immature plants rather than from seed, and will not only suppress weeds, but will retain valuable warmth and moisture. However, it can be laid only on level ground or the plastic will funnel the rainwater away from the plants, depriving them of moisture. A side benefit of the black plastic is that slugs are reluctant to crawl across it, so the vegetables may suffer less pest damage as a result.

Left *The vegetable plot divided into small blocks, rather than rows, to make it easier to tend the plants without compacting the soil. Stone or concrete slabs used for paths between the blocks will also cut down on weeding, as will close-planting the vegetables, or growing them through black plastic sheeting, as shown.*

One method of getting quick returns on the vegetables and avoiding hard work weeding around young seedlings is to grow many of the crops from bought plants rather than from seed. Although they are more expensive to buy than seed, they still represent a saving on shop-bought vegetables, and have a much better flavor.

One task in the low maintenance garden cannot be escaped : really thorough soil preparation. Unfortunately, there are no short cuts. You must clear the land of all weeds, double dig it (below) and add large quantities of well-rotted organic matter, such as spent mushroom compost, spent hops or good refuse compost. No further major digging will be required for about four or five years (since you do not tread on the soil around the plants, it does not get compacted), but a wheelbarrow load of organic matter per square yard should be spread over the plot each year, tickled in lightly with a fork.

To obtain good yields, the plants must have plenty of nutrients, water and sunlight, and no competition from weeds. The close-planting system, together with black plastic sheeting as a mulch, should largely take care of the weeds but the plants will still need regular watering. The easiest method is to install a drip-watering system (see pp. 141–2), with four emitters for each block of vegetables. Once established, the crops will benefit from a dressing of balanced garden fertilizer.

Crop protection
The main causes of poor or damaged crops are cold weather and pests or diseases. If frost is predicted, you may find that it is necessary to provide some form of screening around the plot, and to use covers over the plants. They can be made easily and cheaply, as shown right.

Although the vegetables listed in this section have been selected for their ability to resist most of the more common pests and diseases, no vegetables are ever immune. If you dislike the idea of using chemical controls, you must accept some damage to, or loss of, your crops. Otherwise, the safest general purpose insecticide to use in the vegetable garden is probably permethrin.

The vegetables suggested here include some of the easiest cultivars to grow, but there are, of course, many more, and good ones are being constantly developed. If you concentrate on easy growers, you are more likely to get a good yield and a satisfying return for your effort. Some crops, however, are not worth trying in a low maintenance garden; with peas, for example, it is difficult to obtain a sufficient number of pods at the right stage for picking unless a very large area of ground is planted.

A typical simplified selection of easy vegetables for the low maintenance garden might include: broccoli, perpetual spinach, onions, turnips, beet, radishes, lettuce, corn salad, green beans, zucchini, tomatoes and new potatoes. If you grow early new potatoes and onions from sets, rather than from seed, and the zucchini and tomatoes from young plants, you can plant them through heavy-duty black plastic sheeting, cutting down on weeding, and, in the case of the potatoes, avoiding any earthing up.

Double digging *The soil should be cultivated down to a depth of about 60cm/24in to provide a rich friable soil for your vegetables, enabling you to close-plant them. No further major digging will be needed for several years. Mark each block off into rectangles, 60cm/24in wide by 75cm/30in long. Take the soil out of the first rectangle to a depth of about 30cm/12in, and pile it near the* *last rectangle that will be dug. When you have removed all the soil from the first trench, fork the bottom over to a depth of about 30cm/12in, and incorporate a thick layer of good garden compost. Then remove the soil from the adjoining rectangle, turn it over and remove any weeds, and pile it into the dug trench. Continue in this way over each block.*

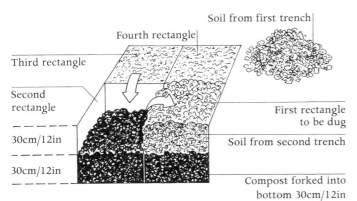

Soil from first trench

Fourth rectangle

Third rectangle

Second rectangle

30cm/12in

30cm/12in

First rectangle to be dug

Soil from second trench

Compost forked into bottom 30cm/12in

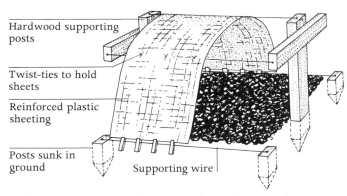

Hardwood supporting posts

Twist-ties to hold sheets

Reinforced plastic sheeting

Posts sunk in ground

Supporting wire

Making a cover *A cover large enough to protect one complete vegetable block can be made quite easily using a hardwood lumber and wire frame, as shown, over which reinforced plastic sheeting is clipped, to form a protecting covering for the vegetables.*

The sprouting broccoli, turnips, beet, perpetual spinach, radishes, lettuce and corn salad can all be grown from seed, and close-planted. If you wish to grow bunching onions from seed, you can treat them in the same way, but growing bulbing onions from seed will involve weeding.

Apart from corn salad and perpetual spinach, the crops are grown through the summer when conditions are most favorable for their growth in terms of protection from cold and bird damage. Winter-grown vegetables are slower-growing and tend to suffer more from pests and diseases. During the winter, when any of the planting blocks are empty, you could cover the surface of each with black plastic fitted to wooden battens to keep weeds at bay.

ALLIUM CEPA/ONION   For bulbing onions, plant onion sets about 10cm/4in apart in the row and between rows in early spring. Harvest them in fall. For bunching onions, sow the seeds thinly in drills about 10cm/4in apart, in succession from early spring. Harvest as required. Suitable cultivars include: for bulbing onions, 'Early Yellow Globe' and 'Stuttgarter'; for bunching onions, 'White Lisbon'.

BETA VULGARIS/BEET   Sow the seeds thinly in drills about 15cm/6in apart and thin to 7.5cm/3in between the plants. It is best to sow them in succession in spring and early summer, harvesting the beet while they are still quite small. Suitable cultivars include: 'Detroit Dark Red' and 'Ruby Queen'.

BETA VULGARIS CICLA/EVERLASTING or PERPETUAL SPINACH   Sow the seeds in drills about 15cm/6in apart in early spring and thin to 15cm/6in between the plants. Harvest by pulling the largest leaves from each plant, which will produce a good crop of new leaves.

BRASSICA OLERACEA ITALICA/BROCCOLI (CALABRESE)   Sow the seeds in rows about 23cm/9in apart in midspring and thin to 15cm/6in between the plants. Harvest when the flower buds are formed. Suitable cultivars include: 'Waltham No. 29' and 'Green Comet F1'.

BRASSICA RAPA/TURNIP   Sow the seeds in drills 15cm/6in apart in succession from midspring. Thin to 7.5cm/3in between the plants and harvest while the roots are still young – not more than 5cm/2in in diameter. Suitable cultivars include: 'Seven Top' and 'Tokyo Cross'.

CUCURBITA PEPO/ZUCCHINI   Sow the seeds indoors in warmth (see p. 144) in early spring. Plant out under a cover, spacing the plants 75cm/30in apart. Remove the covers when the plants have begun to flower, and harvest the fruits when they are about 10cm/4in long. Suitable cultivars for your garden include 'Burpee Golden Zucchini', 'Zucchini' and 'Richgreen Hybrid Zucchini'.

LACTUCA SATIVA/LETTUCE   Sow the seeds in drills 15cm/6in apart in succession from spring, through the summer, and thin to 15cm/6in between the plants. (The thinnings are very good to eat). Suitable cultivars include: 'Summer Bib', 'Buttercrunch', 'Ruby', 'Royal Oak Leaf' and 'Salad Bowl'.

LYCOPERSICON ESCULENTUM / TOMATO   Outdoor bush varieties that require no pinching out or much other attention are ideal for the low maintenance vegetable plot. Plant out young plants through black plastic sheeting in early summer, spaced 40cm/16in apart. Suitable cultivars include: 'Pixie' (early); 'Big Girl' (midseason); 'Ramapo' (late season).

PHASEOLUS VULGARIS/FRENCH or GREEN BEAN   Sow seeds in drills 30cm/12in apart in late spring and thin to 30cm/12in between the plants. Suitable cultivars include: 'Provider', 'Bountiful' and 'Tendercrop'.

RAPHANUS SATIVUS/RADISH Sow seeds in succession from early spring, through summer, in drills 5cm/2in apart, and thin to 3cm/1½in between the plants. Suitable cultivars include: 'Champion' and 'Icicle'.

SOLANUM TUBEROSUM/POTATO Plant early varieties of seed potato through black plastic sheeting in mid-spring, about 12.5cm/5in deep and 30cm/12in apart. They are ready for harvesting after about 12 weeks. The best cultivars to use are the early varieties, such as 'Red McClure', 'White Cobbler' and 'Superior'.

VALERIANELLA LOCUSTA / LAMB'S LETTUCE or CORN SALAD   This provides a useful winter salad crop. Sow the seeds in drills in succession in mid- to late summer, 15cm/6in apart, and thin to 10cm/4in between the plants. Cover the leaves in winter.

HERBS

Since herbs are generally very easy to grow, they deserve a place in any low maintenance garden. They should be sited near the house in a sunny, sheltered position. Perennial herbs can be purchased as container-grown plants from a nursery, but many of them are easy to propagate (see p. 145), if you wish to beg cuttings or roots from a neighbor. The annual herbs, such as parsley or coriander, can be grown from seed using the fluid drilling techniques described on p. 145.

A few herbs, such as mint and tarragon, can be invasive and will colonize the bed if given a chance. By planting them in a square well made out of heavy-duty plastic sheeting you can limit the reach of their roots.

Among the best culinary herbs for the garden are chives (*Allium schoenoprasum*), coriander (*Coriandrum sativum*), tarragon (*Artemisia dracunculus*), basil (*Ocimum basilicum*) – although it is frost-tender, it can be grown as an annual, in pots – parsley (*Petroselinum crispum*), thyme (*Thymus vulgaris*), sage (*Salvia officinalis*), rosemary (*Rosmarinus officinalis*) and marjoram (*Origanum majorana*). Most herbs can be harvested and dried for year-round use. They should be picked on a sunny day and tied in bunches, before being hung to dry in a cool, well-ventilated room.

FRUIT

Adopting low maintenance techniques does not mean that you have to abandon all hopes of fruit production, provided that you realize that the crops will be much lighter than usual and that you may, on occasions, fail to get a crop at all. To produce an abundant supply of fruit, pruning, spraying against pests and diseases and protection from bird damage are normally essential, but even by doing nothing except protecting the young trees from weed competition, you will still normally have the joy of collecting sufficient fruit each year to make a few tarts or pots of jelly and jam. Nor will you have to forgo the pleasures of strolling up the garden on a late summer afternoon and picking the fruit while it is still warm from the sun.

As far as fruit trees are concerned, nurseries have now developed more compact types that can be grown, if need be, in a small raised bed or even in a tub on a terrace. Some of the new dwarf fruit trees are good value in the low maintenance garden, since you will not have to clamber up a ladder to harvest the crop, or reach up to the high branches when it comes to pruning. Among the dwarf trees that are suitable for the low maintenance garden are varieties of apple, pear, cherry and plum.

If you want any soft fruit in the garden, why not consider growing red- and blackcurrants, blueberries and blackberries as part of an informal hedge? Any crop provided will be a bonus. Strawberries grown in one of the specially designed strawberry planters are easy to care for if given a drip-watering system, and will both look attractive and provide an excellent crop. In larger gardens, the small woodland varieties of strawberry make an excellent substitute for purely decorative plants, offering the bonus of good ground cover and of delicious little strawberries in a good year.

Using the new CDA techniques (see p. 153–4) you can spray your fruit trees fortnightly while the fruit are developing, using one of the specially formulated insecticides or fungicides. Those opposed to the use of chemicals in the garden can simply leave the trees and plants alone – after all, the flavor and texture of a good apple is not lost simply because it has a gnarled or scabby skin.

LABOR-SAVING DESIGNS

GARDEN DESIGNS, PLANS AND PLANTING

Gardeners seeking inspiration from living examples of successful low maintenance gardens do not have very far to look these days. In all parts of the world, for identical reasons, there is a growing movement toward creating gardens that require only minimum attention. Professional landscape designers face an increasing number of requests from clients for garden designs that allow them to enjoy all the benefits of a lush and attractively planted garden without the need to become a slave to the plot.

A notable feature of many of these designs is their astonishing diversity. Just because a garden is low maintenance, there is no need for it to become a stereotype. Although the gardens in this section might at first sight seem to bear many of the characteristics of the best traditional gardens, close examination reveals their low maintenance assets. Without exception, they need a great deal less work. Looking after them entails much less mowing, weeding, staking, tying-up, pruning, planting out and dividing than is normally involved in managing the older style of garden that many of these designs resemble.

The gardens included in this section cover a wide range of styles: large-scale gardens with significant areas of grass, intimate small courtyard gardens, a semi-wild rural garden and a variety of treatments for the easiest of all low maintenance choices, hard surfaces. The plans and plant lists have been included so that anyone who so wishes can translate some of the ideas onto their own plot of land.

A GARDEN WITH A LARGE WATER FEATURE

This almost maintenance-free garden is a perfect example of the way in which a clear initial vision and an uncompromising approach toward its execution can provide a deeply satisfying garden that is nevertheless extremely easy to run.

To make such a large area of paving and brickwork feel natural, interest has been created by subtle changes of level and by the creation of easy-to-tend raised beds. The extended water feature makes a marvellous contrast to the hard surfaces, and the long, shallow canal leads the eye away from the house, up to a higher level pond which serves as a raised bed for deeper aquatics.

The lush planting helps to balance any harshness introduced by the large areas of paving, and a high proportion of the greenery is provided by ferns, like *Polypodium vulgare*, that form virtually weed-proof ground cover, and by bamboos. The planting requires very little maintenance, in terms of cutting back, deadheading or staking.

The only work in the garden is the control of the weeds that grow in the cracks between the bricks, but overhead shade has encouraged the growth of moss, reducing the likelihood of weeds, and softening and enhancing the appearance of the hard surfaces.

Above *Small, acid-loving rhododendrons provide a splash of welcome color in front of the easy-to-look-after raised beds.*

Right *Water features combine well with low maintenance paved surfaces, particularly when extended into long canals.*

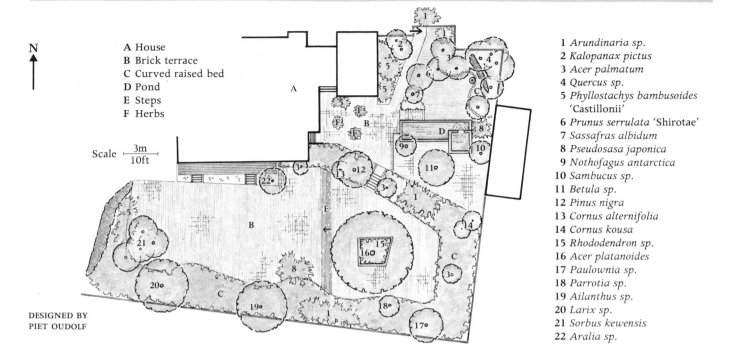

N

A House
B Brick terrace
C Curved raised bed
D Pond
E Steps
F Herbs

Scale $\frac{3m}{10ft}$

DESIGNED BY
PIET OUDOLF

1 *Arundinaria sp.*
2 *Kalopanax pictus*
3 *Acer palmatum*
4 *Quercus sp.*
5 *Phyllostachys bambusoides* 'Castillonii'
6 *Prunus serrulata* 'Shirotae'
7 *Sassafras albidum*
8 *Pseudosasa japonica*
9 *Nothofagus antarctica*
10 *Sambucus sp.*
11 *Betula sp.*
12 *Pinus nigra*
13 *Cornus alternifolia*
14 *Cornus kousa*
15 *Rhododendron sp.*
16 *Acer platanoides*
17 *Paulownia sp.*
18 *Parrotia sp.*
19 *Ailanthus sp.*
20 *Larix sp.*
21 *Sorbus kewensis*
22 *Aralia sp.*

A RECENTLY PLANTED, PAVED TOWN GARDEN

A thorough and uncompromising design demonstrates just how attractive a very low maintenance garden can be if its theme is pursued with determination. A busy person could look after a garden like this in less than an average of one hour per week, and even if he or she was obliged to be absent for several weeks in succession, the garden would not suffer provided it was watered in dry weather.

The design demonstrates how the sensitive use of hard materials like paving and gravel can provide an open area which is nonetheless fascinating. While about half of the ground surface is planted, the borders require practically no work once the shrubs and small trees have grown to fill their allotted spaces. A few herbaceous perennials like *Iberis*, *Bergenia* and *Epimedium* have been cunningly used to give the impression that normal border plants have not been neglected, but the majority of the plants are evergreen shrubs, some of which grow slowly and all of which remain tidy and involve little work, while offering plenty of color and fragrance as the season progresses. A lot of attention has also been given to the choice of plants for their shape, both individually and in juxtaposition with their neighbors.

Since the solid paving and the paths of stepping stones set in gravel (to provide a welcome change of texture), represent approximately half the garden area, they have been used to play geometrical games at ground level, forming circles, semicircles, triangles and rectangles, designed to lead the eye about the garden and draw attention to a variety of short, intriguing vistas. These can also be appreciated when looking down from the house.

On some areas of the higher boundary walls, trellis panels have been provided to support climbing plants whereas other wall areas have been made more visually stimulating by the inclusion of decorative panels of molded highrelief.

Although the garden is on two levels, this fact has been disguised as much as possible by the very gradual slope of the paths joining one level to the other. The elimination of steps allows anything on wheels to be taken easily to any part of the garden.

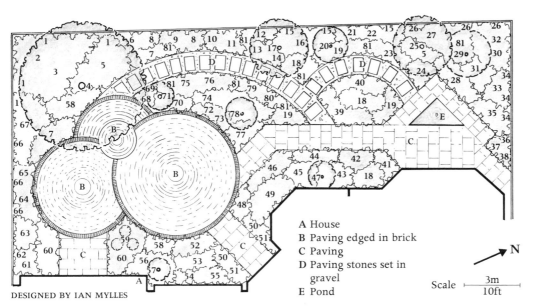

A House
B Paving edged in brick
C Paving
D Paving stones set in gravel
E Pond

N

Scale |—| 3m / 10ft

DESIGNED BY IAN MYLLES

1 *Pyracantha coccinea* 'Lalandei'
2 *Elaeagnus × ebbingei*
3 *Gaultheria shallon*
4 Plane tree
5 *Lonicera nitida*
6 *Cotoneaster salicifolius*
7 *Bergenia cordifolia* 'Sunningdale'
8 *Chaenomeles speciosa*

9 *Prunus laurocerasus* 'Otto Luyken'
10 *Rhododendron* 'Palestrina'
11 *Lilium martagon*
12 *× Fatshedera lizei*
13 *Fuchsia magellanica*
14 *Hebe pinguifolia* 'Pagei'
15 *Hedera canariensis* 'Gloire de Marengo'
16 *Viburnum tinus*

17 Existing poplar tree
18 *Phormium tenax*
19 *Senecio greyi*
20 *Betula papyrifera*
21 *Viburnum rhytidophyllum*
22 *Eremurus bungei*
23 *Helianthemum* 'Wisley Pink'
24 *Thymus vulgaris* 'Aureus'
25 Existing poplar tree
26 *Rosa* 'Mme Grégoire Staechelin'
27 *Rhododendron* 'Pink Pearl'
28 *Santolina neapolitana*
29 *Acer pseudoplatanus* 'Worlei'
30 *Escallonia* 'C.F. Ball'
31 *Cistus ladanifer*
32 *Magnolia grandiflora*
33 *Spartium junceum*
34 *Ceanothus impressus*
35 *Cotoneaster horizontalis*
36 *Jasminum officinale*
37 *Laurus nobilis*
38 *Saxifraga umbrosa*
39 *Salvia officinalis*
40 *Hebe brachysiphon*
41 *Euphorbia robbiae*
42 *Helianthemum* 'Wisley Primrose'
43 *Pieris* 'Forest Flame'

44 *Iberis sempervirens* 'Snowflake'
45 *Camellia × williamsii* 'Donation'
46 *Epimedium perralderanum*
47 *Amelanchier canadensis*
48 *Hebe sp.*
49 *Skimmia japonica*
50 *Rhododendron* 'White Lady'
51 *Philadelphus* 'Bouquet Blanc'
52 *Epimedium macranthum*
53 *Osmanthus delavayi*
54 *Viburnum davidii*
55 *Lilium pardalinum*
56 *Camellia ×* 'Leonard Messel'
57 *Prunus* 'Amanogawa'
58 *Cotoneaster conspicuus*
59 *Buxus sempervirens* (clipped)
60 *Euonymus fortunei* 'Silver Queen'
61 *Fatsia japonica*
62 *Jasminum nudiflorum*
63 *Garrya elliptica*
64 *Camellia japonica* 'Adolphe Audusson'
65 *Vinca minor*
66 *Rosa* 'Guinée'
67 *Mahonia bealii*
68 *Rhododendron* 'Vuyk's Rosy Red'
69 *Lilium rubellum*
70 *Rhododendron yakusimanum*
71 *Philadelphus* 'Belle Etoile'
72 *Rhododendron* 'Hinomayo'
73 *Lilum auratum*
74 *Rhododendron* 'Loder's White'
75 *Fuchsia magellanica* 'Riccartonii'
76 *Daphne odora* 'Aureomarginata'
77 *Bergenia stracheyi* 'Silberlicht'
78 *Magnolia × soulangiana*
79 *Choisya ternata*
80 *Cytisus × beanii*
81 Mixed spring bulbs

Left *Thick gravel and paving slabs combine to provide visual interest, while making a foil for the brightly colored spring bulbs.*

A LARGE INFORMAL GARDEN

Pollarded willows, alders and deep dikes surround this fairly large garden. The owners were anxious to spend as little time as possible on its upkeep, and sought a colorful and attractive leisure area that harmonized with the surrounding landscape. The link between the garden and the countryside around was retained by preserving the existing trees. Maintaining the strange, but characteristic, heads of the pollarded willows is a very simple matter of a couple of hours' amputation every three years.

Since hard surfacing would have looked too bleak over such a big garden, quite a large area has been devoted to rough grass below trees. A lightly-mown version of the misty surrounding meadows, it is merely topped occasionally to prevent it looking unkempt, so that it resembles a well-grazed pasture. The informality of the grass acts as a wonderful foil to the bold stretches of well-laid brick paving, regularly shaped raised beds and broad stretches of gravel near the house where heavy lumber has been used to introduce different hard texture to the ground surface. An attractive feature of this garden is the way in which the hard surfaces 'flow'

in between the planted areas and, as in the case of the wood decking, patches of planting invade the harder surfaces.

The way in which good low maintenance gardeners match the planting to the environmental conditions is displayed in the area alongside the dike where moisture-loving plants, including ferns, have been used, luxuriating in the particularly damp soil. In such circumstances they have prospered well enough to provide an attractive soil cover.

Gardening time has been strictly confined to the central activity area between the house, barn and stables, where sunny and shaded terraces have been provided with restricted borders of colorful herbaceous plants. The use of annuals has been limited to a few pots scattered on the terraces, where they give full value during the summer without any attendant weed control problems.

Dense planting of aquatics in a pond area alongside the dike reinforces the feeling that there is plenty of soft herbaceous material on the site to contrast with the hard surfaces and the islands of largely evergreen shrubs in the raised beds.

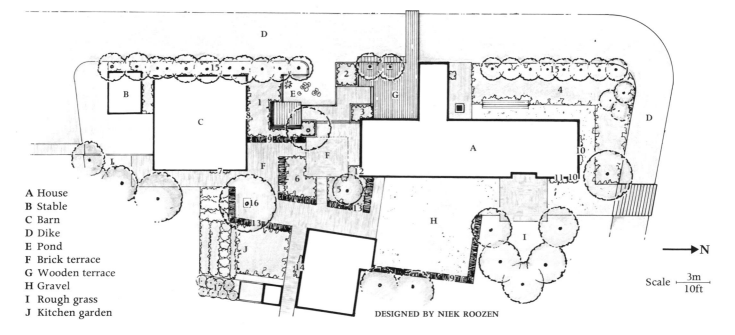

A House
B Stable
C Barn
D Dike
E Pond
F Brick terrace
G Wooden terrace
H Gravel
I Rough grass
J Kitchen garden

DESIGNED BY NIEK ROOZEN

Scale ⊢——⊣ 3m / 10ft

→ N

1 *Aruncus sylvestris*
Spiraea bumalda 'Anthony Waterer'
Geranium grandiflorum 'Johnson's Blue'
Betula sp.
Matteucia struthiopteris
Anemone × hybrida 'Rosea Elegans'
Asperula odorata
Thalictrum dipterocarpum
Dicentra formosa
Hosta sieboldii
Digitalis purpurea
Ligularia dentata 'Othello'
Lythrum salicaria 'Robert'
Lysimachia punctata
Lysimachia nummularia
Myrica gale
Viburnum rhytidophyllum
Mahonia aquifolium 'Atropurpurea'
Philadelphus 'Virginal'
Asarum europaeum

2 *Ligularia przewalskii*
Bergenia cordifolia
Iris sibirica
Polygonum affine 'Superba'
Primula japonica
Primula florindae
Lysimachia nummularia

3 *Aster novi-belgii* 'Professor Kippenburg'
Anaphalis triplinervis
Thymus serpyllum 'Splendens'
Lavandula angustifolia 'Blue Dwarf'
Syringa microphylla 'Superba'
Arundinaria sp.

4 *Rodgersia tabularis*
Ligularia dentata
Matteucia struthiopteris
Primula vulgaris
Vinca minor
Rosa glauca
Rodgersia pinnata 'Superba'
Rosa moyesii 'Geranium'
Ligustrum ovalifolium
Crataegus monogyna
Myrica gale

Alnus glutinosa
Magnolia stellata
Salix alba 'Tristis'

5 *Syringa vulgaris*
Prunus lusitanica
Hydrangea macrophylla
Stachys lanata 'Olympica'
Sedum telephium
Achillea millefolium 'Red Beauty'
Gypsophila paniculata 'Rosy Veil'
Campanula lactiflora
Buddleia davidii 'Empire Blue'

6 *Saponaria ocymoides*
Salvia × superba
Rudbeckia speciosa
Monarda didyma 'Prairie Night'
Oenothera fruticosa
Delphinium 'Blue Emperor'
Helenium autumnale 'Moerheim Beauty'

7 *Rubus phoenicolasius*
8 *Lonicera periclymenum*
9 *Fagus sylvatica*
10 *Hydrangea petiolaris*
11 Roses

12 *Clematis montana* 'Rubens'
13 *Ilex crenata*
14 *Vitis* 'Triomf van Boskoop'
15 Pollarded willows
16 Apple tree
17 Fruit bushes

Above *A pleasing jumble of plants like* Vinca *and ferns at the base of pollarded willows emphasizes the wild feeling in this garden and reduces the need for any weeding in beds.*

A TINY PATIO GARDEN

Although only very small, this town garden conveys an amazing feeling of leafiness and space, helped by the change in direction of the path that leads from the gate to the house door, tempting the eye to travel around the garden. The inclusion of a bed of bold plants situated across the direct sight line also helps to give the impression of greater size and depth.

The high dark brick walls, which might otherwise seem forbidding, have been used to support a number of attractive climbing plants and wall shrubs, some of which, such as the ivies, honeysuckle and pyracantha, retain their foliage in the winter, overcoming any dead-season bleakness.

Interest has been created in the paved area by incorporating an attractive mixture of large and small stones in the gaps left between the paving slabs, to provide a decorative mulch through which the ornamental grasses can emerge.

The planting has been chosen with care, not only to provide good ground cover but also to offer something of interest in terms of color and form throughout the year. Since different conditions, from full shade to full sun, occur in parts of the garden, the planting has been planned accordingly, so that the subjects are suited to the situation.

Particular emphasis has been placed on evergreens with attractive foliage, like *Arundinaria murielae*, *Senecio laxifolius* (whose silver foliage makes a splendid contrast to the dark brickwork), *Euphorbia wulfenii* and *Mahonia*.

Although the apple tree is small, its canopy provides an intriguingly shadowy corner, giving the garden a sense of mystery in summer which is enhanced by the dark ivies masking the boundary wall in that corner, giving the impression of a larger garden beyond.

The garden is, in fact, almost maintenance-free and requires no digging or weeding. The only work needed is the occasional sweeping of the paved area, and some snipping back and tidying of the planting, which is permanent. Coarse bark mulch has been used as a weed-suppressant in areas of the garden where the ground cover is not yet complete.

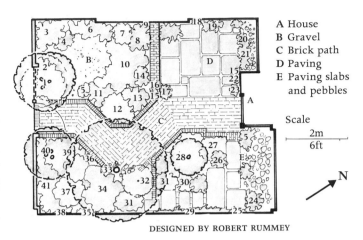

A House
B Gravel
C Brick path
D Paving
E Paving slabs and pebbles

Scale

2m
6ft

N

DESIGNED BY ROBERT RUMMEY

1 Three birch trees
2 *Arundinaria murielae*
3 *Pyracantha spp.*
4 *Euphorbia wulfenii*
5 *Avena candida (Helictotrichon sempervirens)*
6 *Arundinaria nitida*
7 *Hippophae rhamnoides*
8 *Senecio laxifolius*
9 *Actinidia chinensis*
10 *Ruta graveolens*
11 *Hebe subalpina*
12 *Mahonia × media* 'Charity'
13 *Lavandula spica* 'Hidcote'
14 *Helichrysum angustifolium*
15 *Festuca glauca*

16 *Allium christophii*
17 *Miscanthus sinensis* 'Gracillimus'
18 *Jasminum spp.*
19 *Santolina virens*
20 *Sedum spectabile*
21 *Saxifraga × urbium*
22 *Geranium renardii*
23 *Parthenocissus henryana*
24 *Polystichum aculeatum*
25 *Hedera helix*
26 *Bergenia cordifolia*
27 *Crocosmia × crocosmiiflora*
28 *Salix elaeagnos*
29 *Hydrangea petiolaris*
30 *Luzula sylvatica*

Ajuga reptans
31 *Cornus alba* 'Spaethii'
   Euonymus fortunei 'Silver Queen'
32 *Cotoneaster × rothschildianus C. salicifolius*
33 Existing apple tree
34 *Viburnum davidii*
35 *Lonicera japonica* 'Halliana'
36 *Pachysandra terminalis*
37 *Sorbaria aitchisonii*
38 *Hedera spp.*
39 *Polygonatum multiflorum*
40 Existing holly
41 *Hedera helix* 'Hibernica' as ground cover and climber

Below left *Ornamental grasses can look as attractive as any garden plants, and their hardiness and ability to compete with weeds makes them a fine candidate for any low maintenance garden. Striking effects can be obtained if they are set off against dark foliage, as here.*

Below *Ground covering plants have been used to good effect in a corner of this high-walled garden, while the curve of the path gives an illusion of much greater space.*

A CONTOURED, HARD-SURFACE GARDEN

This design, in which the principle of low maintenance has been wholeheartedly embraced, demonstrates how attractive a garden of this type can be if money is not a limiting factor. A very large amount of the ground surface has been clad with work-free hard materials; in effect the design is really a giant masonry relief sculpture, embracing the inclusion of attractive plants as part of the overall composition, and a large area of reflective water, planted with admirable restraint, which is contained at ground level and raised above it, in ponds created in thick shuttered concrete.

In contrast, another large area of ground is paved in carefully patterned granite setts within a framework of rough concrete slabs. The slab motif has been repeated to define the edge of a terrace with a wall that also acts as a built-in bench.

Beautifully designed, substantial wood pergolas have been used to provide support for climbers that require little maintenance, softening the overall effect.

The planted areas are heavily clad with weed-suppressing ground covers from which randomly scattered natural boulders emerge, creating a link between the earth and the cut or reconstituted stone.

All the plants have been chosen for their strong architectural qualities and the way in which the character of their form and foliage either complements, or contrasts strongly with, that of their neighbors, as well as for their ease of upkeep.

1 *Pinus sp.*
2 *Nothofagus antarctica*
3 *Cytisus × praecox* and *C. kewensis*
4 *Liriodendron tulipifera*
5 *Ilex aquifolium*
6 *Hibiscus syriacus*
7 *Picea omorika*
8 *Viburnum plicatum* 'Mariesii'
9 *Liquidambar styraciflua*
10 *Taxus baccata*
11 *Magnolia × soulangiana*
12 *Ginkgo biloba*
13 *Euonymus alatus*
14 *Heracleum mantegazzianum*
15 *Pyracantha coccinea*
16 *Chaenomeles speciosa*
17 *Rhododendron: R. catawbiense* 'Grandiflorum'; *R.* 'Cunningham's White'; *R.* 'Roseum

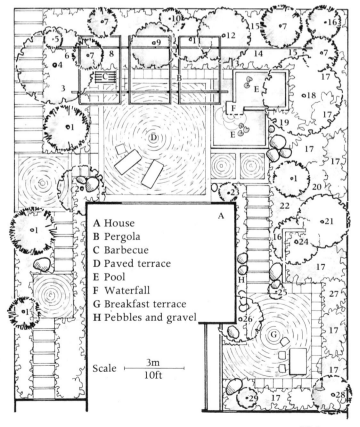

A House
B Pergola
C Barbecue
D Paved terrace
E Pool
F Waterfall
G Breakfast terrace
H Pebbles and gravel

Scale ⊢ 3m / 10ft ⊣

DESIGNED BY VALTIN VON DELIUS

N ⟵

Elegans'; *R. repens* 'Baden-Baden'; *R. impeditum* 'Blue Tit'; *R.* 'Koster's Brilliant Red'; *R.* 'Nancy Waterer'; *R.* 'Knaphill Persil'
18 *Catalpa bignonioides*
19 *Arundinaria murielae*
20 *Buddleia davidii* 'Royal Red'
21 *Laburnum × watereri* 'Vossii'
22 Mixed perennials and roses
23 *Pinus mugo*
24 *Parrotia persica*
25 *Acer palmatum* 'Dissectum'
26 *Aralia elata*
27 *Daphne mezereum*
28 *Chamaecyparis nootkatensis* 'Pendula'
29 *Prunus* 'Amanogawa'

Right *Water provides a home for pleasingly different aquatic plants, all of which demand little work.*

Below left *Formal designs in hard masonry can reduce work at ground level to a minimum and, when offset by carefully selected plants, still provide an attractive, easy-to-care-for garden.*

A LARGE, SEMIWILD RURAL GARDEN

Lying on a steeply sloping site, between a small oak wood and a dashing stream, the perfect low maintenance semiwild garden has been created on a large plot of land in the heart of the countryside. The success of the design comes from the designer's courage in packing the garden with his favorite plants and then simply allowing them, once they are well-established, to compete with nature for survival. The plants selected have either a strongly architectural form, permitting them to stand out well from the surrounding wilder vegetation no matter how exuberant it is, or they have sufficiently bright colors to draw the eye immediately.

A relatively small area of mown grass has been maintained, to prevent the wilder part of the garden from encroaching on the house, but much of the rest of the garden is covered with a natural flowering pasture that needs topping only twice a year.

Features of the garden are the way in which a single color theme has been introduced in areas of the garden to bring a feeling of unity to the design, and the careful selection of plants to suit the varying conditions in different parts of the garden, so that best use is made of the damp, shady areas near the streams, and of the sunny, dry slopes near the house. Ground cover plants have been used to advantage, and the inclusion of a wide range of hardy geraniums – an excellent low maintenance standby as they survive most competition – offers attractive flowers and weed-suppressing foliage.

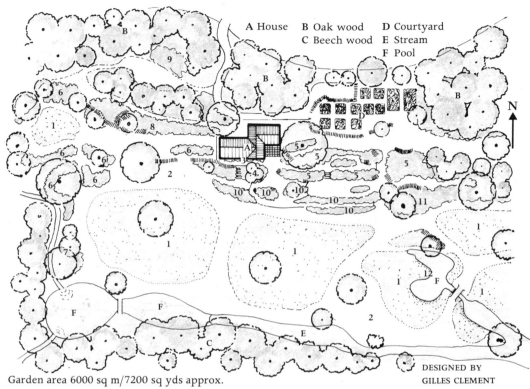

A House B Oak wood D Courtyard
         C Beech wood E Stream
                      F Pool

N

Garden area 6000 sq m/7200 sq yds approx.

DESIGNED BY
GILLES CLEMENT

There are over 250 types of plant in this south-facing garden that lies on a slope leading down to the stream and pools.

Among the main features of the planting are:

1 Wild-flower meadow
2 Rough grass lawn
3 Some of the best plants in this area include spectacular climbers and wall shrubs on the south-facing walls of the house, including *Fremontodendron californicum, Actinidia chinensis, Clematis orientalis* and *Vitis coignetiae*
4 To the south of the house, feature shrubs including *Acer japonicum* 'Aureum', *Abelia × grandiflora, Rhododendron yakusimanum* and *Nandina domestica* hold pride of place.

5 In the dry, sunny area east of the house, various species of *Euphorbia, Ceanothus, Lavandula, Senecio, Thymus, Hebe* and *Geranium* flourish.
6 To the west of the house a pink garden has been created with some eye-catching shrubs like *Cornus kousa, Rosa* 'Albéric Barbier', *R. chinensis* 'Mutabilis' and *Camellia sasanqua* 'Maiden Blush'.
7 On the south-west side of the garden, near the stream, a shrubbery has been created with subjects like *Pieris, Hamamelis,* and *Garrya elliptica.*
8 On the dry, sunny slope above and to the west of the house, trees, shrubs and perennials like *Robinia pseudo-acacia* 'Frisia', *Skimmia japonica* and *Polygonatum multiflorum* flourish.
9 On this dry, rocky slope, various species of *Cistus* do well, as does *Abutilon vitifolium, Yucca gloriosa* and *Olearia.*
10 In the moist, sunny area to the south-east of the house a range of perennials has been planted, including *Allium* and *Helleborus,* as well as shrubs like *Lonicera pileata* and *Abelia.*
11 To the east of the house, an orange garden has been created with azaleas, *Mimulus, Viburnum farreri* and *Photinia × fraseri.*
12 Down near the lake, a bog garden provides a marvelous home for irises, *Caltha palustris, Typha minima* and willows.

Left *Plants like these* Eremurus *are a good choice in a semiwild garden where they will overcome any competition.*

Right *A view of the south-east margin of the more closely planted area near the house.*

A SMALL, HIGH-WALLED GARDEN

This small, town garden owes its charm to a triumphantly successful solution to the daunting problems presented by the site. The garden is almost completely enclosed by darkly forbidding brick walls that are nearly 12m/40ft high, buttressed for much of their length by an ugly concrete thickening at the base. Turning adversity to advantage, the designer has converted the top of the buttress into a high terrace garden, its vertical face clad with a wafer of attractive brick. Bold white pergola and trellis work has been used both to mask much of the rest of the unattractive brickwork, or distract the eye from it.

To create a feeling of unity between the two levels of the garden and to allow easy access to both, a feature has been made of the attractive linking staircase; its simple, round-topped arch support (which looks lighter than solid masonry) is backed with a heavy-duty mirror that doubles the apparent size of the garden. Most dramatically, it reflects the foliage surrounding and growing in the pond in front of it, lightening the garden by reflecting the brightness of the sky. (The black pond lining helps to increase the reflectiveness of the water surface.) The hexagonal shape of the pond is repeated in the panels of light-colored paving slabs, the color of which was chosen to draw more light into the garden.

The constriction of the vertical walls has been used to advantage to support a host of climbing and trailing plants such as *Clematis*, ivies and honeysuckle which, while softening its bleakness, are also easy to maintain.

Much of the rest of the planting is in raised beds to avoid stooping, and mulches have been used to reduce weeding. To avoid the need for mowing a lawn substitute – closely planted *Arenaria balearica* – has been used to surface quite a large area of the high terrace. In addition to a thick carpet of foliage, it offers the bonus of tiny white star-shaped flowers in spring.

To obtain the maximum feeling of leafiness, much of the planting is in bold architectural subjects like *Fatsia japonica*, camellias and ferns which do well in low light and require virtually no attention.

1 *Acer platanoides*
2 *Pieris formosa* 'Forrestii'
3 *Rhododendron kiusianum*
4 *Camellia × williamsii* 'Donation'
5 *Chamaecyparis lawsoniana* 'Ellwoodii'
6 *Sambucus racemosa*
7 *Plumosa aurea*
8 Birch
9 *Rhododendron* 'Blue Tit'
10 *Hedera canariensis*
11 *Rhododendron* 'Hinomayo'
12 *Rosa* 'Albertine' *R.* 'Mermaid', etc.
13 *Viburnum × burkwoodii*
14 *Rhododendron* 'Cecile'
15 *Rhododendron* 'Blue Bird'
16 Shield fern
17 *Thuja occidentalis* 'Rheingold'
18 *Lavandula sp.*
19 *Clematis montana*
20 Weeping birch
21 *Cornus alba* 'Elegantissima'
22 Magnolia stellata

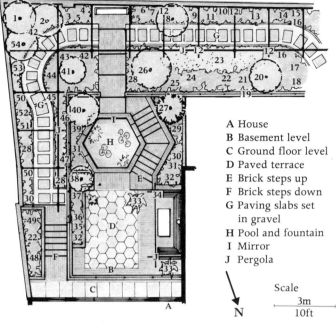

A House
B Basement level
C Ground floor level
D Paved terrace
E Brick steps up
F Brick steps down
G Paving slabs set
   in gravel
H Pool and fountain
I Mirror
J Pergola

Scale

3m

10ft

N

DESIGNED BY ROBIN WILLIAMS FOR THESAURUS

23 *Arenaria balearica*
24 *Cytisus × praecox*
25 *Juniperus* 'Gray Owl'
26 *Prunus sargentii*
27 *Thuja sp.*
28 *Mahonia japonica*
29 *Hypericum patulum* 'Hidcote'
30 *Fatsia japonica*
31 *Aucuba japonica* 'Picturata'
32 Bedding plants
33 *Trachycarpus fortunei*
34 *Rosa* 'Dorothy Perkins'
35 *Hedera colchica*
36 *Arundinaria pumila*
37 Ferns
38 *Amelanchier canadensis*
39 *Arundinaria nitida*
40 *Rhus typhina*
41 *Alnus incana* 'Aurea'
42 *Euonymus fortunei* 'Emerald
   Gaiety'
43 *Skimmia japonica*
44 *Viburnum × bodnantense*
   'Dawn'
45 *Viburnum tinus*

46 *Lonicera japonica* 'Halliana'
47 *Ceanothus ×* 'Cascade'
48 *Juniperus prostrata*
49 *Cytisus × beanii*
50 *Escallonia sp.*
51 *Thuja plicata*
52 *Hebe marjorie*
53 *Chamaecyparis lawsoniana*
   'Allumii'
54 *Prunus sp.*

Far left *Masonry dominates this
high-walled garden but attention
focuses on bold-leaved evergreens and on the tumbling
climbers that soften its outlines.*

Above right *The walkways on
the higher terrace are clad in
virtually maintenance-free
paving and gravel.*

Right *A cleverly angled mirror
behind the pond gives the illusion
of a much larger garden.*

A COASTAL GARDEN FOR A WARM CLIMATE

At this landscape architect's own seaside home, most of the ground surface is covered either with handsome formal paving or evergreen ground covering plants that require very little work – a treatment that is both agreeable and effective.

To suppress weed growth while the ground covers are becoming established, a thick mulch of ground tree bark has been used. It looks attractive and is coarse enough not to blow about, while allowing those weeds that might float in on the breeze to be tweaked out easily.

Since weeds do not usually present too much of a problem when plants are established in walls, the tall vertical surfaces have been cleverly used to enrich the area with foliage and flower cover, without increasing the work load.

Subjects like bamboos, when established in large containers, can provide a tall and attractive leaf cover while occupying only a relatively small ground area. They have also been used successfully to provide a junglelike feeling to balance the preponderance of masonry, and demonstrate that you need not confine container growing to small subjects.

In the front garden, giant boulders, impressive walls of rough-hewn rock, high-quality semiformal stone paving and a very subtle curved brick path and set of steps have been arranged to create an exciting front garden, even before the inclusion of a single plant, illustrating how satisfying a low maintenance garden can be when the hard ingredients are chosen and placed with care. Planting can then be confined in most areas to attractive ground-hugging plants which quickly blanket the soil and suppress weed growth. If the plants are chosen carefully enough and sited thoughtfully, even with a limited list to choose from, you can produce the impression that the species are as varied and numerous as those of a more conventional garden.

A few horizontal junipers and other evergreens, and a single splendid cut-leafed maple spreading over the margin of a small pond, when seen clearly against light-colored masonry can catch the eye more successfully than fifty different subjects all vying for attention in a grand herbaceous bed.

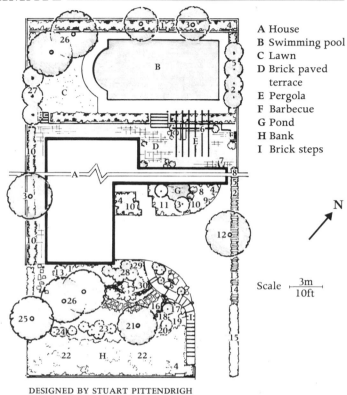

A House
B Swimming pool
C Lawn
D Brick paved terrace
E Pergola
F Barbecue
G Pond
H Bank
I Brick steps

N

Scale $\frac{3m}{10ft}$

DESIGNED BY STUART PITTENDRIGH

Below *Climbers and ground covers make an easy-to-look-after surface, an attractive contrast to the brick walls and stone paving.*

Above right *Black-stemmed bamboos and hanging baskets of plants soften the contours of the brick-paved patio and its pergola.*

1 *Gardenia augusta*
2 *Rhododendron sp.*
3 *Acer palmatum*
4 *Dicksonia antarctica*
5 *Camellia sasanqua*
6 *Celsima sp.*
7 *Black-stemmed bamboo*
8 *Viola hederacea*
9 *Cissus sp.*
10 *Nandina domestica*
11 *Juniperus conferta*
12 *Betula pendula*
13 *Plumbago capensis*
14 *Grevillea × 'Robyn Gordon'*
15 *Sabina vulgaris*
16 *Erigeron sp.*
17 *Ajuga reptans*
18 *Iris sp.*
19 *Thymus sp.*
20 *Cotoneaster horizontalis*
21 *Sapium sebiferum*
22 *Trachelospermum jasminoides*
23 *Russelia equisetiformis*
24 *Bauera rubioides*
25 *Gordonia axillaris*
26 *Eucalyptus sp.*
27 *Banksia leptospermum*
28 *Murraya paniculata*
29 *Sabinea vulgaris*
30 *Agapanthus sp.*

A MEDIUM-SIZED GARDEN WITH MIXED HARD SURFACES

In this medium-sized garden, which has a strong low maintenance appeal, one of the most attractive features of the design is that it offers several different vistas, thereby not revealing all its secrets at once.

A large proportion of the ground is covered with an interesting mixture of materials, such as wood, brick and concrete. Each different type of covering has been used over a sufficient area to make its presence felt, without one single surface being allowed to dominate. Wherever the brick paving might have appeared too monotonous, it has been punctuated with an informal studding of cut-log sections. Shallow steps and the bold margins of railroad ties have been used extremely effectively to create acceptable transitions from one type of surface to another, or between different levels.

The rest of the ground surface has been cleverly planted with bold subjects that make a very positive contribution to the overall scene and are vigorous enough to look after themselves once established. Their arrangement has been carefully considered to ensure that their characteristics can be expressed to maximum effect: bright colors have been used to contrast well with dark backgrounds, and plants with feathery foliage have been used against subjects with dark leaves.

The very bold pond feature can be glimpsed from any part of the garden, its reflective surface acting as a wonderful foil to the masonry, while creating a bright, easy-to-look-after heart to the garden.

1 *Gleditsia triacanthos*
  'Sunburst'
  Robinia 'Bessoniana'
  Kitchen garden
2 *Viburnum × bodnantense*
3 *Sorbus aucuparia*
4 *Lavatera trimestris*
5 *Agapanthus sp.*
  Hypericum sp.
  Bergenia sp.
6 Fruit trees and strawberries
7 *Betula papyrifera*
  Pinus nigra
  Crataegus 'Paul's Scarlet'
  Pinus mugo
  Corylopsis pauciflora
  Genista lydia
  Campanula persicifolia
  Campanula garganica
  Achillea sp.
  Geranium endressii
  Salvia sp.
  Aquilegia 'Mrs Scott-Elliott's
   strain'

Thymus vulgaris
Veronica gentianoides
Digitalis
Lavandula
Verbascum nigrum
Malva alcea
8 *Lysimachia punctata*
  Lysimachia nummularia
  Geum sp.
  Iris sibirica
  Gynerium argenteum
  (*Cortaderia selloana*)
9 *Prunus serrulata*
  Viburnum plicatum
  tomentosum
  Geum 'Juliana'
  Tiarella cordifolia
  Asperula odorata (*Galium*
  odoratum)
10 *Miscanthus sinensis*
   'Giganteus'
   Alchemilla mollis
   Rhus glabra
   Matteuccia struthiopteris

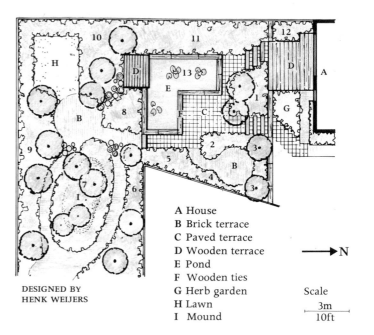

**DESIGNED BY
HENK WEIJERS**

A House
B Brick terrace
C Paved terrace
D Wooden terrace
E Pond
F Wooden ties
G Herb garden
H Lawn
I Mound

→N

Scale
3m
10ft

11 *Miscanthus sinensis*
   'Giganteus'
   Arundinaria murielae
   Symphytum peregrinum
   Ligularia dentata 'Othello'
   Lysimachia punctata
   Geranium platypetalum
   Trollius europaeus
   Euphorbia polychroma
12 *Prunus laurocerasus*
13 *Nymphaea* 'James Brydon'
   Pontederia cordata
   Butomus umbellatus
   Sagittaria sagittifolia
   Iris pseudacorus
   Acorus gramineus 'Variegatus'
   Caltha palustris
   Myosotis sp.

Left *Plants crowd together to form
a jungle that more or less looks
after itself.*

Right *A water garden needs little
maintenance yet the plant forms
add variety to any garden.*

A BRICK-PAVED TOWN GARDEN WITH AN ORCHARD

This is an excellent example of a design where most of the features of a good traditional garden have been preserved without the need for much work. Its real triumph is the way in which it manages to preserve a casual and natural feeling while incorporating much formally treated surface, although, by contrast, an area of the garden has been devoted to an orchard which needs only occasional mowing, and a snip now and again with the shears to keep it tidy.

Much of the paving is of old London-stock bricks laid on edge. They have been used very successfully to clad the gentle gradient where the ground changes level, cleverly avoiding the work problems associated with mown or planted slopes. Several varieties of ivy, the roots of which enjoy the moisture beneath the bricks, have been used to relieve the harshness of the hard covering, while patches of large cobbles surrounding the shrub and tree stems, and stretches of gravel and stone paving, have been used to provide an alternative texture to the brick.

Much of the summer color in the garden is provided by climbers, such as splendid roses like 'New Dawn', 'Mermaid' and 'Albertine', and by *Hydrangea petiolaris*, *Clematis montana* and *Vitis coignetiae*. Wall shrubs, like *Magnolia grandiflora*, and plants in small raised beds and pots, which require no weeding, make their contribution to the summer parade.

Great care has been taken in the choice of freestanding shrubs and trees to place the emphasis on evergreen subjects, in order to keep the garden looking good throughout the winter and to provide a good variety of both fine and bold-leaved forms, which compensate for the absence of colorful but work-intensive borders.

The willow trees that were planted prior to the house being built act as a gentle foil to its uncompromising but attractive lines. The resulting shade conditions in the courtyard to the east of the plot have been taken into consideration in the choice of plants, whereas the open orchard area to the west of the plot has provided an ideal home for sun-loving specimens.

1 *Rhododendron ponticum*
2 *Petasites japonicus* 'Giganteus'
3 *Rheum palmatum*
4 *Hedera helix* 'Sagittifolia'
5 *Lonicera periclymenum*
6 *Polygonum baldschuanicum*
7 *Dryopteris filix-mas*
8 *Salix × chrysocoma*
9 *Ficus carica*
10 *Fatsia japonica*
11 *Saxifraga × urbium*
12 *Pinus strobus*
13 *Arundinaria japonica*
14 *Hosta sieboldiana*
15 *Vitis coignetiae*
16 *Iris foetidissima*
17 *Viburnum tinus*
18 *Viola sp.*
19 *Pulmonaria saccharata*
20 *Choisya ternata*
21 *Ilex sp.*
22 *Prunus laurocerasus*
23 *Skimmia japonica*
24 *Rosa* 'Albertine'

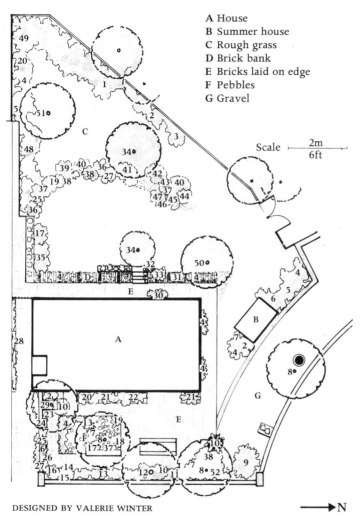

A House
B Summer house
C Rough grass
D Brick bank
E Bricks laid on edge
F Pebbles
G Gravel

Scale ⊢——⊣ 2m
            6ft

DESIGNED BY VALERIE WINTER

→ N

25 *Symphytum orientale*
26 *Asarum europaeum*
27 *Alchemilla mollis*
28 *Rhododendron ponticum*
   Dryopteris filix-mas
   Symphytum orientale
   Hedera helix
   'Sagittifolia'
   Choisya ternata
   Fatsia japonica
   Lonicera sp.
29 *Prunus avium*
30 *Magnolia grandiflora*

31 *Helxine soleirolii*
32 *Clematis sp.*
   Rosa 'Iceberg'
33 *Viburnum plicatum* 'Mariesii'
34 Apple tree
35 *Buddleia sp.*
35 *Sophora japonica*
36 *Pentaglottis sempervirens*
37 *Euphorbia wulfenii*
38 *Lamium maculatum*
39 *Ligularia dentata*
40 *Cynara cardunculus*
41 *Cornus alba*

42 *Echinops ritro*
43 *Digitalis sp.*
44 *Chrysanthemum maximum*
45 *Paeonia sp.*
46 *Delphinium sp.*
47 *Heuchera sp.*
48 *Hydrangea petiolaris*
49 *Garrya elliptica*
50 Greengage tree
51 *Epimedium sp.*
52 *Galanthus nivalis*
   Mahonia aquifolium
   Betula pendula

Far left *The foliage overhanging part of this paved area can introduce interesting light effects. The areas of sun and shade can be used to accommodate plants with different needs.*

Above *Ground covering ivies are allowed to wander onto the paving to soften its effect, while a dramatic* Fatsia japonica *catches the eye.*

A GARDEN WITH SITTING AREAS IN SHADE AND SUN

This garden comprises two circular terraced sitting areas, one in shade and the other in sun, linked by a bridge over a pool. The design demonstrates how even a rigid brief can be turned to good advantage, its constraints providing the garden with a pleasing feeling of unity, integrity and strength.

The designer's solution to providing visual interest has been to link the circular forms of the brick-surfaced areas with a curving asymmetrical water feature, bringing reflected light, and some exotic plant forms, right into the heart of the garden. The water not only offers the opportunity of introducing an exciting variation in the planting and a gentle contrast to the hard surfaces, but it is also very easy to maintain.

The brick used for the circular terraces might have appeared too dominant if its effect had not been softened by the introduction of a simple wooden bridge, cleverly arranged at an angle between the two areas, so that the eye moves across the garden rather than directly down it.

Bold plants in containers have been used to enliven the hard surfaces and to introduce more vegetation than the limited planting area would otherwise have allowed. The only real effort demanded by the garden is in the occasional sweeping of the terraces.

A House
B Circular brick terrace in shade
C Circular brick terrace in sun
D Wooden log surround
E Pond **F** Wooden bridge

Scale 2m / 6ft N

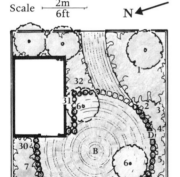

DESIGNED BY DICK HUIGENS

1 Mixed planting of *Betula*, *Hedera helix*, *Luzula sylvatica*, *Carex morrowii* 'Variegata' and *Deschampsia caespitosa*
2 *Carex pendula*
3 *Aruncus dioicus*
4 *Campanula latifolia* 'Macrantha'
5 *Ligularia przewalskii*
6 *Robinia hispida* 'Macrophylla'
7 *Heracleum mantegazzianum*
8 *Rhus typhina* 'Dissecta'
9 *Ajuga reptans*
10 *Iris sibirica*
11 *Thalictrum aquilegifolium*
12 *Hemerocallis spp.*
13 *Lythrum salicaria*
14 *Hosta sieboldiana* 'Elegans'
15 *Aralia elata*
16 *Miscanthus sinensis* 'Giganteus'
17 *Echinops humilis* 'Taplow Blue'
18 *Macleaya cordata*
19 *Stachys grandiflora* 'Superba'
20 *Hosta ventricosa*
21 *Festuca scoparia*
22 *Brunnera macrophylla*
23 *Cotoneaster salicifolius*
24 *Ligularia dentata* 'Othello'
25 *Waldsteinia ternata*
26 *Tradescantia* 'Zwanenburg Blue'
27 *Aesculus parviflora*
28 *Rodgersia aesculifolia*
29 *Filipendula rubra* 'Venusta'
30 *Eupatorium purpureum*
31 *Clematis montana* 'Rubens'
32 *Anemone × hybrida*
33 *Myosotis scorpioides*
34 *Typha minima*
35 *Alisma plantago-aquatica*
36 *Ceratophyllum demersum*
37 *Hydrocharis morsus-ranae*
38 Container plants

Below *Really bold foliage, coupled with reflective water and contrasting natural wood, transforms a bare low maintenance garden into an enchanting glade.*

LOW MAINTENANCE TECHNIQUES

SCULPTING THE LAND

If you cover a large part of your garden with a hard surface, you will probably need to introduce interest to the design by making significant changes in contour, as well as in types of surface. Terraces and sunken sections, mounds and steps, and maybe a water feature, will all help to provide visual variety. If several types of soil cover are used, the perimeter of each contour can serve satisfactorily as the point at which the surface varies. For example, a formally paved terrace, its mass of earth held in place by a stone or brick wall, could stand above an area clad with attractive crushed rock or gravel.

Low maintenance though hard surfaces are, they can involve a great deal of work initially, and shifting the earth to making telling contour changes with primitive aids such as a pick, shovel and wheelbarrow is a long, arduous business. Hired help can prove expensive and it may well be more economical to use some of the large machinery now available. In a few hours it can accomplish work that would take months with hand tools, and can usually be hired relatively cheaply and easily.

Some of the larger earth-moving machines, such as the big backhoes, are best operated by an expert. Although the machinery can sometimes be hired on a self-drive basis, it takes years of practice to handle it with precision. An experienced operator, however, has such control over the bucket that he can use it to push a cork into a a champagne bottle. It may therefore work out less expensive to hire the operator as well as the machine.

When planning to make fairly major changes of level in your garden, the rule should be to use the largest capacity machine available: it will carry out the work fastest and most cheaply. The tractor-mounted backhoes of the type you see working on building sites can be used in a fairly large garden, provided access is not restricted. Even then it is still possible to use a large backhoe, by hiring a mobile crane to lift it over the house roof if you cannot get it into the garden any other way. Be prepared to adopt a somewhat cavalier attitude towards notions of permanence: it may well be more economical in the long term to hire a big backhoe and knock down a section of your garden wall or fence to let it through, rather than to use smaller-scale

CREATING CHANGES OF LEVEL
A three-dimensional drawing of a largely paved and gravel-clad garden showing variations in surfaces and levels (see also p. 21). None of the changes of level is higher than 90cm/36in in any single step. The terrace at the south end of the plot is level with the ground floor of the house, and the garden slopes away gradually on the east side, rising equally gradually on the west side. The plan of work is shown in the diagram opposite.

machinery or a large labor force. The extra capacity of the big machine could more than make up for the inconvenience of knocking down and rebuilding part of a wall. Any gardener who is irritatingly timid in this respect deserves the mediocre garden that will probably result.

On small sites and on those with restricted access, or where only a small amount of earth moving is required, a scaled-down version of the big backhoe is probably the most practical solution. It can be hired with an operator and, despite its small size, will shift a large amount of earth in a very short time. It is narrow enough to be trailed behind a car to the site and, with its wheels removed, is light enough to be mounted on a dolly and small enough to pass through a space about 1m/3ft 3in wide – the average width of the passageway between two town houses.

To get the very best results from a backhoe you need a carefully worked out plan, right, so that you shift the earth in the most economical way. The backhoe will operate only when stationary, however, so care must be taken in planning the program of work to make sure that the least number of changes of position are made. (It has a total reach of about 8.4m/28ft.)

Various other machines can be hired to ease the work of contouring the land. Dump trucks can move the spoil from one area of the garden to another, and a machine like a small tractor, running on caterpillar tracks, can be used to level the land with a large steel blade. With one of these machines, an experienced operator is able to level great mounds of soil evenly over the ground as easily as soft butter can be spread on toast, saving much tiresome work for you, and leaving the ground as smooth as a bowling green.

Useful though all these large machines are, some caution must be exercised when using or hiring them. First, with all heavy machinery, the site must be dry. If the soil is wet, it will compact under the weight of the machine and disrupt any natural or man-made drainage. If in any doubt, seek professional advice. While major earth-moving work should be undertaken only in summer, planting is best carried out after wetter weather begins.

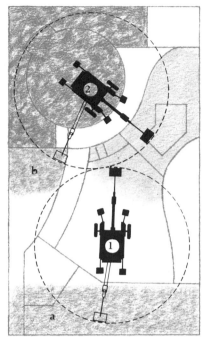

Plan of work for garden opposite

Contouring with a small backhoe *A carefully worked out plan of operation is needed when shifting soil with a small backhoe, in order that excavated soil can be dumped easily onto the raised areas. The topsoil must always be removed first.*
Backhoe strips topsoil from vicinity of station (1) and deposits it at (a). Backhoe strips topsoil from vicinity of station (2) and deposits it at (b). Backhoe excavates low level areas from vicinity of station (2) and deposits spoil in neighboring raised areas. After retaining walls are built, backhoe redistributes topsoil to planted areas, first at station (2), then at station (1).

Small-scale backhoe in operation

LEVELING THE LAND

Whether you are planning to lay a hard surface or build a terrace, the land must first be leveled, with a very slight incline to allow rainwater to run off. Although professional contractors find it easy to mold earth into accurate levels using only the minimum of reference points and a well-trained eye, amateurs do not. The problem can be overcome very simply by adopting a technique favored by the Romans. It works on the principle that water always finds its own level. All you need is a helper, a length of flexible transparent hose, a watering can and funnel, and an adequate supply of wood stakes, markers and string. The technique described below can be used wherever a level surface is needed. To make your first level, you must mark a reference point at a known distance above the final level of the terrace you are planning to create. This should ensure that you do not inadvertently cover the reference point as you alter the levels.

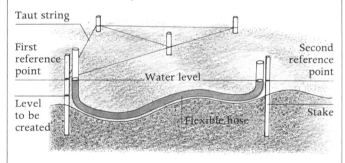

Taut string

First reference point

Second reference point

Water level

Level to be created

Flexible hose

Stake

How to level land Equipped with a watering can and funnel, you should take one end of the hose and hold it vertically beside the reference point, while your helper holds the other end vertically in the area of the site where the new level is to be established. Pour water into the hose until its level can be clearly seen in the vertical sections at both ends of the pipe. Ask your helper to slowly raise or lower his or her end of the pipe until the water level in in your vertical section stands at exactly the same level as the reference point, adding water if needed. The water level at the other end of the pipe can be marked on a stake driven into the ground at that point. Thus an accurate level will have been created and further reference points can be provided in the same way over the site; string can be stretched tautly between them to mark the levels. To check progress when excavating the site, or piling soil or rubble upon it, measurements can be made down from the reference points, or from the taut string.

It is also extremely important when moving earth around in your garden that you do not destroy the topsoil in the areas where you are planning to plant. When making the plan for your changes of contour, the planted areas should be mapped out, so that the topsoil can be scraped off them and stored to one side, while the new contours are being created. It can then be replaced afterward.

The materials for hard surfaces, building walls or making steps are all very heavy, making handling difficult. Most of them, such as sand, gravel and cement, can be supplied in bags on pallets, and a forklift truck hired to deliver them to the areas where they are going to be used.

HOLDING BACK THE EARTH

It is not enough merely to change the contours by shifting a large quantity of earth with efficient modern machines. Great thought must be given to the way it is held in place afterward. It could simply be left in flat-topped mounds with sloping sides: a pile of soil kept free from weeds and exposed to frequent downpours of rain will usually settle into a 45° slope, but this is an unpleasing angle and a difficult slope on which to work. Normally, a much more gentle gradient of about 1:3 to 1:5 is advised.

Since no low maintenance gardener would care to mow a slope covered with turf, possible solutions are to plant it with heavily mulched shrubs and ground cover plants or to top it with gravel and make a small scree garden (see p. 22). Although paving can look attractive set on a slope, large areas of inclined stonework produce an odd earthquake effect, inducing a feeling of vertigo. Such areas look fine outside public buildings, but they could be very difficult to live with in a private garden.

The best way of changing contours and holding back the earth is to create terraces. The method you use for constructing these raised areas depends on the height and volume of earth you are retaining, and whether you are going to tackle the job yourself or employ a craftsman to do the work. Provided the terraced areas are well constructed they will need little attention once built, even though considerable effort is needed initially.

Making simple terraces

If you are going to do the work yourself, there are some quick and easy methods which most do-it-yourselfers could manage. Shallow terraces, no higher than 45cm/ 18in, can be held in place quite simply with stout wooden timbers supported by strong stakes driven into the ground. Dry stone or brick retaining walls are more permanent, but take longer to construct and are more expensive.

Higher terraces, over 45cm/18in high, will need stronger retaining walls – unless you are an experienced do-it-yourselfer, seek qualified advice. Since the weight of earth they are holding back becomes infinitely greater when wet, provision must be made in the walls for drainage. Normally a series of holes is left in the foot of the retaining walls to let any water drain out, but the method will vary according to the construction of the wall. Without provision for drainage, the terrace filling, once sodden, would exert such pressure on the wall that it would rapidly cause it to collapse.

If you want to create a simple raised area no higher than 90cm/36in, the simplest method is to construct a large, very strong wooden box, to the dimensions required, as shown right. It consists of stout horizontal timber planking held in place with similarly strong vertical stanchions. Thanks to the mania of the world's railroad companies for modernizing their tracks, there is no shortage of railroad ties, which are ideal for this purpose. But if you cannot get hold of them, use hardwood timbers that have been vacuum-treated with preservative and which are at least 10cm/4in thick by 23cm/9in wide by 1.8–2.4m/6–8ft long. The construction technique shown right has the advantage that not only is it very easy to carry out, but the horizontal timbers can be slotted into place as the filling is inserted. The type of filling will be determined by the eventual use of the terrace – if a hard surface is required, then a suitably firm and level base is needed, as described on pp. 126–7. A plastic lining to the sides of the box will help to delay any rotting. Drainage holes should be cut in the horizontal timbers at intervals along the foot, and the bases of the vertical supporting timbers should be encased in polyethylene before being sunk in concrete.

MAKING A WOOD-FRAMED TERRACE

This method is quick and easy to adopt on stable, made-up land and requires neither screws nor bolts. It is suitable for a terrace up to 1.4m/4ft 6in high, using old railroad ties or similarly strong treated timber. The supporting posts should be inserted into the ground 60cm/ 24in deep at 1.8–2.2m/6–8ft intervals. As an extra precaution, the base of each post can be wrapped in a plastic bag and set in concrete. The horizontal timbers can then be slotted behind the uprights. Closely spaced drainage holes should be made in the base timbers.

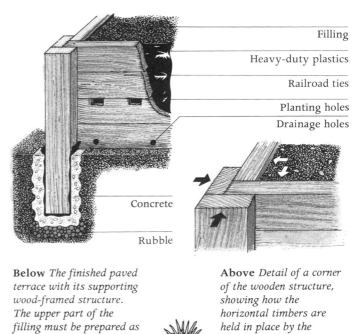

Filling

Heavy-duty plastics

Railroad ties

Planting holes

Drainage holes

Concrete

Rubble

Below *The finished paved terrace with its supporting wood-framed structure. The upper part of the filling must be prepared as for laying a hard surface (see pp. 126–7).*

Above *Detail of a corner of the wooden structure, showing how the horizontal timbers are held in place by the weight of the fill and by the supporting posts.*

Once the box has been constructed, the surface can be treated as required. A similar construction technique can be used for a higher structure using a pre-cast concrete panel box, where the panels are slotted into specially grooved concrete stanchions. If the concrete sides are faced with a veneer of brick, for example, to give the terrace a more aesthetic appearance, it is important to make sure that the drainage holes in the brick façade match those already drilled in the concrete.

If your garden has a natural slope, you may wish to construct terraces by cutting and filling the soil to create stepped areas of level ground held in place with low retaining walls of timber, masonry or concrete. However, on steeply sloping land the walls of the terraces will have to hold back a substantial weight of earth, and the job of creating them is probably best left to an expert.

Raised beds

Small raised beds are particularly useful since they not only create visual variety in the garden but help to reduce bending and stretching. (As a result, they are of particular help to the infirm or disabled.) The beds can be made quickly and easily from sheets of marine plywood, below right, but there are other more durable alternatives. Preweakened slabs can be used that crack easily into regularly shaped pieces. Piled in layers, they make very satisfactory walls for low raised beds. For those who can afford it, more aesthetically pleasing raised beds can be created from stone (either cemented or left dry) or brick. The base of the raised bed is best filled with rubble or pea gravel to make it more free-draining, covered with a final 25cm/10in layer of topsoil. Alternatively, a special planting medium can be inserted (see p. 134).

Sunken areas can be made by digging out the earth to the required depth and creating surrounding supporting walls of timber, concrete, brick or stone. Wherever you have raised terraces or sunken areas in the garden that are over 38cm/15in high, you will probably need some form of steps.

LAYING HARD SURFACES

The advantages and disadvantages of the different types of surface material have already been discussed (see pp. 26–35) but whichever type you choose, the following points must be noted.

Without a very firm, level base the hard surface so widely used in a low maintenance garden to cover the ground and reduce planting would soon become an uneven, puddled death trap. The type of base you use is normally determined by the nature of the surface and the condition of the ground on which it is laid. On recently excavated land, for example, a deeper, firmer base than usual would be needed, to avoid settlement problems later. If in any doubt about the nature of the ground, consult a professional.

To ensure good drainage, any hard surface must be laid so that it slopes almost imperceptibly (with a gradient of 1:120) toward its outside edge. If there is no natural drainage, such as a large flower bed, at the lower perimeter of the surface, then a drainage system must be incorporated.

Although pavings, bricks and log sections look attractive when grouted with coarse, sharp sand, mortar is the best choice for a low maintenance surface as weeds are less likely to grow.

SHALLOW SAND This type of base is suitable for stone slabs and for crazy paving laid in large pieces. However, on recently made up land a layer of compressed rubble should be put down below the sand base. The

Right *A low timber raised bed constructed from 2.5cm/1in thick sheets of marine plywood slotted into a frame of 7.5cm sq/ 3in sq supporting posts. The corner construction is shown above right.*

Left *Preweakened concrete slabs, cracked into regularly shaped pieces, can be piled on top of each other to make a low raised bed.*

site should be excavated evenly to within 12.5cm/5in of the desired level of the finished surface. A 5cm/2in thick layer of well-compressed coarse, sharp sand should then be spread evenly over the soil to form a suitable base for the slabs. To each slab five blobs of soft mortar, 4cm/1½in thick, should be applied – one at each corner and one in the center. The slab should be laid gently on the sand bed and tapped level. A space no wider than 12mm/½in should be left between each stone, which must be tapped level with its neighbors.

When laying crazy paving, where the stones may be of varying thickness, great care should be taken to ensure that each piece of stone is settled into the sand bed, so that the final surface is as level as possible.

RUBBLE AND SAND   A much firmer base of this type is needed both for bricks and granite setts because the bearing unit of each surface is smaller. The excavation should be deeper than for large slabs – normally 20cm/8in – and the soil well-compacted (a machine such as a vibro-roller will do this very quickly and easily). Very coarse, irregularly shaped crushed stone rubble should be spread on the compacted base and vibrated or tamped down to a 10cm/4in layer before the 5cm/2in layer of sand is laid on top. The surface units are then laid on the bed of sand and compacted down with a tamper.

Modern interlocking paving bricks, set on sand, do not require grouting: fine coarse sand, brushed over the surface, will fill the narrow gaps between them. They have the advantage that they can be removed at will to permit a terrace to be interplanted.

RUBBLE AND CONCRETE   Tiles, beach pebbles, log sections and duckboards all require an absolutely solid base. It is prepared in the same way as the sand and rubble type, except that the sand is replaced with a 5cm/2in fine concrete screed. Good provision must be made for water to drain from the final surface. Although duckboards can simply be positioned on the concrete screed log sections and pebbles must be fitted with grouting. Tiles need to be fitted with special tile cement, and the makers of good brand name products usually supply their own instructions. As tiles are relatively delicate, a raised edge may be needed at the perimeters.

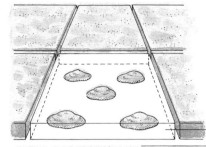

Shallow sand base *This type of base is normally used only for fairly large stones, such as rectangular slabs of concrete or natural stone, or for crazy paving.*

Paving slabs 5cm/2in
Compressed mortar 2.5cm/1in
Sand 5cm/2in
Leveled soil

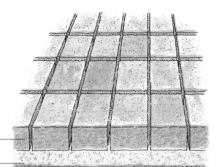

Rubble and sand base *This deeper base is used for smaller surface units such as bricks or granite setts. Both soil and base must be very well compacted.*

Bricks 7.5cm/3in
Sand 5cm/2in
Compacted rubble 10cm/4in

Rubble and concrete base *An absolutely solid base is needed for tiles, log sections, duckboard and pebbles. The rubble is laid down and compacted, and then topped with a 5cm/2in thick layer of concrete.*

Evenly cut log sections 7.5cm/3in
Soft mortar 1-2.5cm/½–1in
Concrete screed 5cm/2in
Compacted rubble 10cm/4in

Grouting with wet mortar *Joints between large stones can be grouted with wet mortar. It should be pressed down well into the joints to prevent any future cracking or shrinking, using the side of a pointing trowel or a suitably shaped piece of wood.*

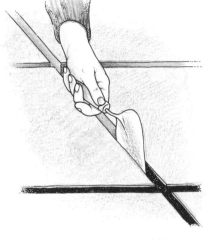

Grouting with dry cement and sand *This method is best used for thin joints between bricks or granite setts, for example. Brush the dry mixture over the stones and well down into the joints before moistening it with water, using a fine rose on a watering can.*

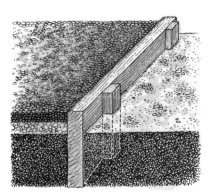

Laying gravel *When laying gravel paths or terraces, a rubble base must be provided. A firm edge is necessary to retain the gravel. Timber, held in place with wooden stakes, as here, or a row of bricks could be used.*

Grouting

The open joints between surface units are best grouted, either with wet mortar or with a dry mixture of masonry cement and sand that is subsequently moistened. When using wet mortar, trowel it well down into the joints and compress it, to prevent any shrinking or cracking later. If it does crack, weeds are likely to grow in the joints causing future maintenance problems. Any smears of wet cement should be wiped off the surface as you work.

When using a dry mixture of masonry cement and sand, brush it over the surface into the joints between the surface units. Moisten it thoroughly with water, using a watering can with a fine rose. The finished level of grouting in both methods should be just below that of the hard surface to give it a more attractive appearance.

Gravel surfacing

Gravel can be used in a number of ways in the garden – as a topping for terraces, to create a small Japanese-style garden, or for paths and driveways. When using gravel the main points to remember are that the ground must be properly prepared before the gravel is laid, that a sufficiently thick layer of gravel is used (about 5cm/2in is the minimum) and that an edging should be provided to retain the gravel. Whenever possible, unwashed gravel should be sought because the residual clay which it contains will help to bind the stones together.

To level large areas of gravel you can use a hired tractor with a scoop attachment. The heap of gravel will need to be dumped as close to the spreading area as possible. A chain or strong cable attaches the scoop to the drawbar of the tractor and scoopfuls of gravel are then pulled over the surface and allowed to spill from the scoop as the tractor moves forward.

On large sites, with unrestricted access, a family car can perform the same function. Alternatively, a modern pickup truck with an adjustable tailboard can be used, as it can control the flow of gravel, dumping it where needed. Final leveling can be done by hand with a rake.

Making easy steps

Heavy timber, such as railroad ties, makes a handsome and simple form of holding back the fill and creating

Masonry steps *When making masonry steps, a solid concrete foundation about 15cm/6in deep should be provided to prevent any settling or cracking. For the steps,* *below, a brick retaining wall holds the rubble filling, covered with a 5cm/2in concrete screed, topped with paving stones.*

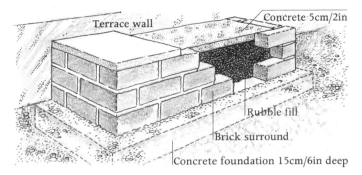

Terrace wall

Concrete 5cm/2in

Rubble fill

Brick surround

Concrete foundation 15cm/6in deep

steps between terraces where the change in level is only slight. Brick or stone terraces are more appropriately approached via masonry steps. Building these on the flanks of a terrace is easy and is similar to making small raised beds. The stone or brick risers should be set on a firm concrete foundation, at least 15cm/6in deep, to form a low surrounding wall to the step. The cavity between the walls and the terrace can then be filled with well-packed rubble, topped with a 5cm/2in layer of concrete. This ensures stability and provides a good foundation for paving the steps with stone slabs, bricks or tiles, as well as making a firm and stable base for any step above.

Decking

A strong timber frame can be used to create a raised duckboard platform. Not only does it increase the useful area of the garden, but it provides a wonderful haven for shade-loving plants, such as ferns or camellias, beneath its canopy. To avoid weed problems, it is best to cover the ground below the decking with a hard surface. If plant containers are used on the decking, they should be mounted on bricks to allow the air to circulate and to ensure good drainage, otherwise the wood beneath will remain damp, increasing the likelihood of rot. As wood hosts mosses and algae it will become dangerously slippery if not treated with a commercial algicide.

INTERPLANTING

All surfaces, whether the walls of raised beds or paved terraces, will look less forbidding when interplanted with suitable mound-forming or trailing plants (see p. 74). With some forms of walls and paving, this can be done quite easily by creating small pockets as you lay the stones or bricks, for example, and then inserting potting mix into the space. When creating a concrete base for paving, for example, you must shutter off any areas that will be required for future interplanting. Timber or concrete panel walls can be drilled or chiseled before construction to provide planting pockets.

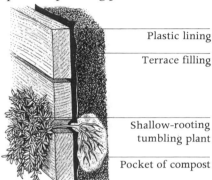

Planting in walls *Tumbling plants can be grown successfully in deep pockets of potting mix in spaces left in the wall construction. Where a plastic lining has been used, it must be cut through to scrape out the soil and insert the potting mix and plant.*

Plastic lining

Terrace filling

Shallow-rooting tumbling plant

Pocket of compost

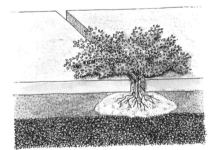

Planting into paving joints *A little of the sand in the ungrouted joints can be scraped out and replaced with potting mix before plants are inserted.*

Planting into spaces in paving *Stones or bricks can be left out, or pulled up, as required. The sand (and rubble if necessary) can be scraped away and the gap filled with suitable potting mix before planting.*

SIMPLE WATER FEATURES

If water is to make a significant contribution to the visual variety of a garden, there must be plenty of it (but consider the safety factors carefully if there are young children about). Butyl pond liners can be used but they are limiting in terms of size and shape. A better solution is to create shallow, narrow canals of thick, waterproof concrete. On level ground, a trench 80cm/32in wide by 30cm/12in deep will provide room for a canal, 60cm/24in wide and 20cm/8in deep. A concrete mixture with a waterproofing agent added should be used. It must be formed in a single operation to guarantee that it is waterproof, and requires little skill so that a competent do-it-yourselfer can easily produce long, straight or curved features, leading the eye deep into the garden, extending its vista. The sides of the canal, as with any other water feature, should be sloped, so that if ice forms in the winter, it will slide upward rather than rupturing the canal walls: the thicker the concrete, the less likely this is to happen; although a 10cm/4in thickness is adequate in most temperate climates, a minimum of 15cm/6in will be needed in very cold regions.

Shallow water canals will support a wide range of small aquatic plants, but to prevent too much green algae or

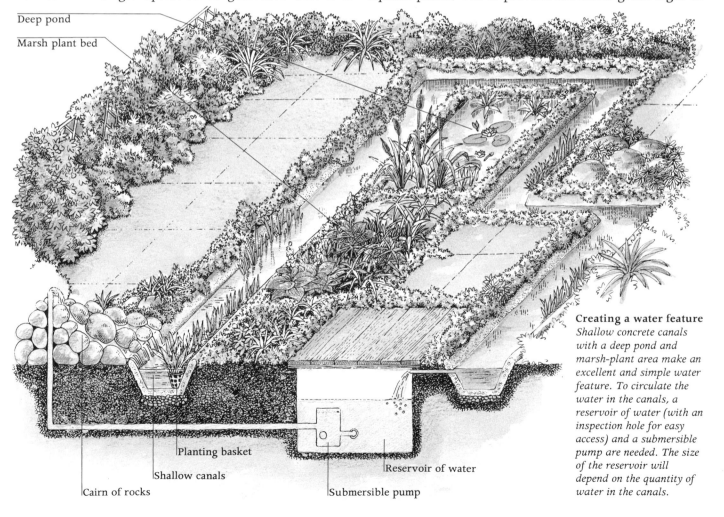

Deep pond

Marsh plant bed

Planting basket

Shallow canals

Cairn of rocks

Reservoir of water

Submersible pump

Creating a water feature
Shallow concrete canals with a deep pond and marsh-plant area make an excellent and simple water feature. To circulate the water in the canals, a reservoir of water (with an inspection hole for easy access) and a submersible pump are needed. The size of the reservoir will depend on the quantity of water in the canals.

pond weed developing, which would create more work for the gardener, it is best to make the water flow using a recirculating pump, opposite. If you provide a deep reservoir of water at one end of the system, the pump will draw the water from it, which can be returned via a splashing fountain or a cairn of rocks made to resemble a natural spring. (As vegetation builds up in the canal, the water will slow down and a reserve of water is therefore needed to prevent the pump end of the system from being sucked dry before the recirculated water arrives.)

Making ponds and marshy reservoirs

To retain plenty of reflective water surface, you can make wide ponds in the same manner as the canals. Smaller, deeper pools can be created for plants such as water lilies that are not fond of shallow or moving water. The area between the shallow and deep water system could be used to create a home for marsh-loving plants. Constructed in the same way as the deep ponds, it should be filled with a 50:50 mixture of peat and soil built up above the margin edge, as shown. As rainfall will not drain from the concrete base, it will remain to provide the reservoir of water that marsh plants need to thrive.

Planting

Open-sided baskets filled with potting mix, in which a range of easy aquatic plants can be grown, can be placed along the sides of the canals and in wider ponds. The vegetation will rapidly begin to mask the concrete, and the process can be hastened by planting creepers, such as aubrieta, in the earth just beyond the margins of the pond so that their stems tumble toward the water. Once planted, the surface of the baskets can be masked, and the potting mix held in place, with a thin layer of gravel or stones.

General maintenance

To maintain even an extended water feature takes only a few hour of intensive and messy effort in early spring, when aquatic plants that have grown too rapidly in the previous season should be taken out of the water and cut back, before being replanted.

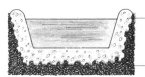

Right *A crosssection through a simple concrete canal. The trench is dug 20cm/8in wider and 10cm/4in deeper than the size of the finished canal, to allow for a layer of concrete at least 10cm/4in thick to be laid in it. The sides of the canal must slope outward to allow any ice forming in winter to slide up the sides, preventing cracking.*

Concrete 10cm/4in

Soil

Right *A marsh plant bed can be constructed as for a deep pond, but filled with a well-watered 50:50 mixture of peat and soil, the surface rising above the sides of the pond. A small drain near the rim provides drainage for the surplus water into the canal system.*

Drainage pipe
Peat and soil filling
Concrete 10cm/4in

Below left *A deep pond can be constructed in a similar way to the canal, with a trench approximately 140 × 110cm wide by 80cm deep (4ft 8in × 3ft 8in wide by 2ft 8in deep). A reinforced base, composed of a layer of rubble covered with steel mesh, will be needed to bear the extra weight of water. A concrete layer, at least 10cm/4in thick, is then used to line the trench.*

Concrete 10cm/4in
Rubble and reinforced steel mesh 10cm/4in

Left *Baskets of potting mix can be positioned on the canal base, along the side walls, to house small aquatic plants. A layer of gravel should be used to hide the basket.*

CREATING AND WORKING THE SOIL

Natural soil is a mixture of mineral particles, live and dead organic matter, dissolved salts, air and water, and its character is largely determined by the ratio in which these ingredients occur.

Since soil type has a profound effect not only upon the appearance of the garden but also upon the ease with which plants can be grown, the first task is to identify the soil in your garden and then deal with any shortcomings it may have. Although this may sound like unnecessarily hard work, the care with which you do so will determine your degree of success in keeping the garden trouble-free. The object is to create a well-nourished and free-draining soil that is neither too acid nor too alkaline, and that will, in turn, encourage vigorous plant growth. Once achieved, this balance is best kept by disturbing the soil as little as possible – a policy bound to be received as good news by people wanting to garden with minimum effort.

If you are lucky enough to have a loamy soil, there is little that you need to do to it. It is the ideal growing medium, and is very easy to work. A few very fortunate people have soil that is so high in organic matter that it

TESTING YOUR SOIL

Dig out a few trowelfuls of soil from different parts of the garden, down to a depth of about 23cm/9in. Mix them thoroughly and then put a couple of tablespoons of the mixture into a jam jar of water. Shake the jar vigorously and leave it to settle for half an hour. Any organic matter will float to the surface, leaving the minerals to settle in layers, according to size: very fine clay particles on top of sands of various sizes, with coarser stones or nodules of chalk beneath.

Clay Soil that contains a high proportion of clay feels smooth and sticky when rubbed wet between the fingers. Although it supports prolific plant growth and withstands drought well, it is often hard to handle, as well as being at times rather acid, badly aerated and poorly draining. It usually contains relatively little organic matter.

1 Organic matter
2 Clay
3 Sand
4 Gravel

Sand A predominantly sandy soil feels very gritty when rubbed wet between the fingers. Unlike clay, a ball of moist, sandy soil disintegrates rapidly as it dries. It often lacks organic matter, tending to be infertile unless treated, and usually dries out rapidly in hot weather.

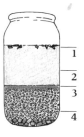

1 Organic matter
2 Clay
3 Sand
4 Gravel

Loam Loamy soils contain plenty of organic matter but vary from light to heavy, depending on the mineral ingredients. A ball of moistened loamy soil feels slightly gritty and holds its shape when it dries. The best of all soils, it supports rich plant growth and suffers longish dry periods before watering is necessary.

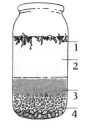

1 Organic matter
2 Clay
3 Sand
4 Gravel

Limestone This type of soil can vary from heavy to light, is often low in humus and is usually alkaline. A mainly limestone soil can be identified by the brownish-white nodules of chalk that separate out from the other ingredients in the jam jar test. Well-fertilized limestone soil will support a good growth of lime-tolerant plants, and tends to be free-draining. However, some soils with a limestone base will present considerably greater problems,

as if their bedrock lies too close to the surface, they will tend to drain poorly. Soils such as these most usually support only those plants that are lime-tolerant. The presence of lime or chalk in soil can be tested by mixing the nodules with vinegar. If the mixture froths up, then lime or chalk is present.

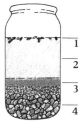

1 Organic matter
2 Clay
3 Sand
4 Chalk nodules and gravel

resembles the best of brand name potting mixes and there are few plants that will not grow successfully in it. Most soils, however, are predominantly of clay or sand or lime, and all of them need some attention to turn them into a good growing medium.

Improving drainage

One of the major obstacles to healthy plant growth is a poorly draining soil, or one that fails to hold moisture in warm weather, so in areas of the garden scheduled for planting you must make every effort to ensure that there is good drainage. If the topsoil is heavy, such as clay, it will drain better if mixed with coarse grit, in a 50:50 ratio. Small areas of both light and heavy soils can be improved if a 7.5cm/3in layer of horticultural expanded vermiculite is spread on the surface and gently forked into the topsoil to a depth of about 15cm/6in.

To find out whether the soil drains well, dig right down through the topsoil (in wet weather) to a depth of about 60cm/24in and then pour a bucket of water into the hole. If it takes more than a couple of hours for the water to vanish, some form of drainage system should be provided, as shown right.

Improving the soil balance

While some plants, such as many of the rhododendrons, like very acid conditions, and others, such as the viburnums, tolerate very alkaline situations, most plants prefer a neutral soil or one that is just slightly acid.

You can test your own soil acidity either with a commercially produced soil test kit or by using a litmus paper. If you damp the soil and touch it with the paper, the latter will turn bright red on contact with strong acids and bright blue on contact with strong alkalis. Paler shades of red or blue indicate milder acidity or alkalinity. The most useful soils are those which are just beginning to show an obvious red on the litmus paper.

It is a simple matter to correct an over-acid soil: all it needs is a once-yearly dressing of lime applied in early spring: about 750g per sq m/1½lb per sq yd for strongly acid soil, down to about 140g per sq m/4oz per sq yd for a mildly acid one. As lime contains calcium, which all plants need for healthy growth, a dressing of 200g per

MAN-MADE DRAINAGE
To improve poorly draining soil, open-jointed clay or slitted plastic pipes should be laid in trenches in the clay subsoil at least 45cm/18in below the surface, leading to a ditch or French drain at the lowest point in the garden. The trenches should be dug on a very slight incline, either parallel to each other or in a herringbone pattern, as required. The pipes should be laid on and covered with a layer of pea gravel,

before the topsoil is replaced. If a French drain is needed, it should be about 1.2cu m/ 40cu ft, filled with rubble or gravel, and covered with topsoil.

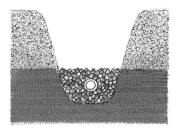

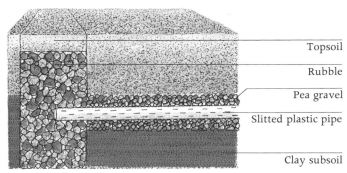

Topsoil

Rubble

Pea gravel

Slitted plastic pipe

Clay subsoil

sq m/6oz per sq yd is needed every three years for most non-alkaline types of soil.

If the soil is too alkaline, the problem is less tractable. For short periods, you can apply large doses of an acid mineral fertilizer, such as sulphate of ammonia, that will neutralize the soil. However, the effects are only transitory, since the chemical will wash away in heavy rainfall and may also upset the balance between the nitrogenous and other nutrients in the soil, doing more harm than good.

A more satisfactory solution is to plant only those species that are lime-tolerant, but if some corner of the garden simply demands a lime-hating rhododendron, for example, you can provide a satisfactory home for it by creating a raised bed or container and filling it with a suitable planting medium (see p. 124). As long as the roots are completely separated from the native soil, the plant should do very well.

CREATING YOUR OWN SOIL

Where you have a problem soil and wish to grow plants that do not fare well in it, you can create a small raised bed containing artificial growing medium. It has the undoubted advantage that all the materials used in it are sterilized before being mixed, ensuring that they are free from live weed seeds, pests, and the spores of disease. For most purposes, you need a mixture containing equal parts of coarse sand, sphagnum peat (originating from mosses, not sedges) and a good-quality sterile medium loam. Shallow rooting shrubs and perennials need a 30cm/12in layer of this medium, right, and even quite large trees can thrive on about 60cm/24in of it. Pea gravel or vermiculite can be used underneath the growing medium to provide bulk filling and to improve drainage.

The minor disadvantages of creating your own soil are firstly that it is expensive and secondly that the organic

material tends to decompose quickly, particularly in a warm climate, resulting in a loss of volume of up to 15 per cent each year. This loss can be made up by applying a 5cm/2in layer of pure organic material, such as well-rotted manure or spent tomato compost, over the surface of the bed each fall. If the soil needs liming, give the organic matter a couple of months to ferment before applying the prepared lime (see p. 133).

Improving soil nutrients

Having corrected the soil acidity balance and provided good drainage, the next step is to make sure the soil contains an adequate supply of nutrients: nitrates for good leaf growth, phosphates for root development and potash for developing flowers and fruit. Healthy plant growth occurs when the balance between the nutrients is correct. With a little forethought, you can persuade nature to do most of this work for you. All you need to do before the initial planting is spread a wheelbarrow-load of well-rotted animal manure or good compost over every square yard of soil, and mix it in well, down to a depth of about 30cm/12in. A further 5cm/2in layer of manure or other organic mulch should be applied to the surface of the beds or shrubberies each season.

A generous diet of rotting organic matter, coupled with good drainage, will provide the ideal circumstances for the microorganisms in the subsurface of the soil to do their work, and the soil structure will be greatly improved, cutting down on the need for soluble fertilizers later (see Feeding, pp. 139–40).

Having made this initial effort to improve the physical characteristics of the soil, you can sit back in your deck-chair and let nature finish off the job. In fact, too much stirring of the topsoil destroys its nice crumbly texture and drives away the earthworms and other organisms that help, by their activities, to keep it open and free-draining. Having created good planting soil, try not to trample on it, otherwise it will become compacted and poorly aerated. Annual weeds can be kept in check with mulch (see pp. 147–50) or the occasional application of weedkiller (see p. 150).

Nature's contribution

The organic matter you have laid on the surface eventually breaks down into humus – a colloidal gel much revered by traditional gardeners. The gums that humus contains help to combine tiny soil particles into larger crumbs, separating them with a jellylike substance that holds onto the soluble nutrients in the soil that would otherwise be washed away by the rain. Humus not only allows air to penetrate the soil, by changing its structure, but also provides an ideal breeding ground for the microorganisms that break down the complex chemicals in the soil into the simple nitrates, phosphates and potash salts that the plants can then absorb through the fine root hairs.

One teaspoonful of well-fertilized soil contains as many live microorganisms as there are people on earth. Look at it under a powerful microscope and you will witness a biospectacular, working for the benefit of your garden. Tiny mineral particles of soil, under magnifica-

THE NATURAL CYCLE

Nature, in the wild, provides a complete cycle of growth and decay that will normally promote healthy plant growth. In a garden, where this balance is disturbed and where rapid growth is required, a layer of organic matter with some chemical fertilizer should normally be used.

1 Organic matter carried into the soil
2 Earthworms burrowing and aerating the soil
3 Microorganisms breaking down chemicals into soluble

plant nutrients; the rotifers illustrated are very greatly magnified
4 Plant root hairs absorbing nutrients
5 Healthy plant growth

tion, assume the proportions of craters and canyons, teeming with hidden life. In a nonstop underground banquet, one tiny organism laps up and devours another almost as soon as it is formed. Jaunty whizzing rotifers power their way around with two sets of whirling, whip-like flagellae, while single-celled bacteria drift in currents of water-dissolved salts and ponderous amoebae slope along like blobs of jelly. Beside these tiny micro-organisms, earthworms assume the scale of giant anacondas, and snapping-jawed centipedes, millipedes and insect larvae that of vast Nile crocodiles, as they chew their way through the dead leaves and plant roots.

The spaces in this underground honeycomb world are filled with gases created by the feverish activity of the microorganisms, which play their part in the complex chain of action and reaction that finally provides the plants with the nutrients they need for healthy survival.

TOOLS FOR WORKING THE SOIL

The reliefs in the tombs and temples of the early Egyptians and Mesopotamians not only tell us about the lives of kings and pharaohs but are full of delightful revelations about the everyday activities of simple peasants and farmers. Time and again, they can be seen working their land with digging sticks – stout, straight tree branches fashioned to a point at one end. When plunged into the ground, the digging stick broke through the top crust of the earth and fragmented the soil below to a fine tilth. This primitive tool – the forerunner of the plow – made little impression on the early cultivators of northern Europe, presumably because the wood was not strong enough to tackle the heavier, stony or root-entangled soils of densely forested land.

Tools for heavy work

Nowadays, however, a modern version of the digging stick – the roadworker's crowbar – is an ideal tool for the gardener who wants to clear land easily and quickly or break up frost-hardened soil. Consisting of a 1.5–1.8m/5–6ft, 25mm/1in thick steel bar with a point at one

Breaking up hard ground with a crowbar
Hold the crowbar, point downward, and let it plunge into the ground. Then lever up the soil, using a block of wood to provide a fulcrum, to gain extra purchase, if needed.

Crowbar

Wrecking bar

Dividing clumps of roots with a wrecking bar *Densely rooted plants can be divided easily with a wrecking bar. Stabilize the clump with your foot, or a fork, and plunge the wrecking bar into the clump, levering out the portion required for replanting.*

Creating planting holes with a wrecking bar *Small planting holes can be created very quickly in difficult ground using a wrecking bar. Use the chisel-shaped end to loosen the soil and a long-handled trowel, opposite, to dig it out.*

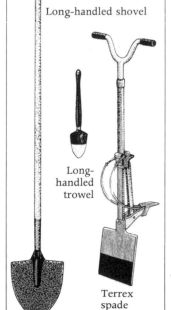

Long-handled shovel

Long-handled trowel

Terrex spade

end, it is the quintessential cultivator's tool, far superior to the standard spade. The sharp point can also be used with great success to rip out tenacious roots of matted brambles, unwanted trees or shrubs or giant clumps of weed. In the cultivated garden, it is the ideal tool for uprooting such difficult subjects as entangled clumps of iris corm, or the crowns of pampas grass or bamboo that cling so tenaciously to the ground when they need dividing and replanting.

A smaller version of the crowbar, the wrecking bar, is an equally useful digging tool. (It is popularly known as a burglar's jimmy because it can be used to open doors or windows surprisingly quickly.) The sharp point at one end can be used to break up hard ground with beguiling ease, for example when creating planting holes for small shrubs. It comes in various sizes, but one about 45cm/18in long and 18mm/$\frac{3}{4}$in thick is ideal for most purposes. The tough claw at the other end of the wrecking bar can be used for pulling unwanted nails out of walls and fence posts.

Even in the low maintenance garden there will be occasions when a spade or shovel is useful – mainly in the initial stages of creating a garden from an uncultivated plot. Having sensed the joy of using a pointed digging tool, you will find a square-bladed garden spade an outmoded and cumbersome implement. A shovel with a

Using a shovel *A shovel with an extra long handle and pointed blade makes light work of heavy digging in the garden. Left, digging the point into the ground and, above, turning the blade over to get rid of the earth.*

Using a Terrex spade *Bizarre though it looks, this spade is a great labor-saver on well cultivated soil. It is operated by pressing down on the pedal attachment with your foot, as shown.*

longer-than-average handle and a pointed blade will prove a much more satisfactory tool for initial large-scale digging and will also serve as a valuable shovel. The point ensures easy soil penetration and the long handle entails less bending.

Tests on various digging implements have proved that such a long-handled shovel puts significantly less strain on the fragile lower back than a spade does. It was beaten in this respect by one tool only, the bizarre-looking spring-assisted Terrex spade with bicycle handlebars. Invented in West Germany, it is now available internationally. Its prime use is for digging land that has been well-cultivated for a period of years; on more compacted land, its value is doubtful.

Tools for light work

Once the soil has been well loosened, you need only very light tools to maintain its condition, and to cope with any tasks such as planting new shrubs. A narrow, 15cm/6in wide, four-pronged bedding fork is useful for fluffing up soil surfaces to allow air and water to penetrate, and for loosening any weeds that may have escaped the usual control measures (see pp. 147–51). A version of the fork in which the spine is specially bent by a blacksmith has great merit for work in between closely planted perennials, and also for transplanting

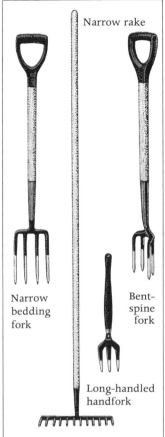

Using a narrow bedding fork *In close-planted beds of herbaceous plants, a narrow bedding fork can be used more easily to aerate the soil and remove odd weeds, without disturbing the roots of the cultivated plants themselves.*

Narrow rake

Narrow bedding fork

Bent-spine fork

Long-handled handfork

Using a long-handled trowel *A long-handled trowel demands less bending, for example when creating a planting hole after first having loosened the earth with a wrecking bar.*

Transplanting with a bent-spine fork *A fork with a specially bent spine can be used to lift the root ball of a plant in one piece, thereby causing less damage to the plant and making the gardener's work easier.*

Using a long-handled handfork *Like the long-handled trowel, this implement makes life easier as the odd weeds that grow despite the usual control measures can be teased out, without much stretching or bending.*

Wheelbarrowing *Shifting heavy material in the garden is time-consuming and hard work. The ball wheelbarrow, below, is best for soft, rough ground but the conventional single-wheeled barrow performs better on hard, even land. The type you buy will therefore depend on the design of your garden, and the work you need to do in it.*

whole plants, as it will enable you to dig underneath the entire root ball which can then be lifted from the soil without damage.

Long-handled handforks and trowels, with a 25cm/10in handle, are a much better option than their short-handled counterparts, as they entail less bending and are particularly useful, with the additional reach, for working in packed borders.

With only minimum weeding to face in the low maintenance garden, there is no need for a hoe. It is a mixed blessing even in a traditional garden, as it frequently leaves behind more half-uprooted weeds to develop than it removes from the bed. Mulching and the occasional bout of weedkilling should remove most of the weeds (provided the ground has been cleared of the perennials).

The odd weeds that continue to grow despite all your efforts can be teased out by hand with a long-handled fork. A narrow, 30cm/12in, fine-pronged rake is useful for general soil movement, and for creating a fine tilth in the seedbed for any direct-seeded annuals you may choose to plant.

Wheelbarrows

One of the most exhausting and time-consuming tasks in the garden is moving earth and carting away waste matter – whether weeds cleared from the soil, organic material to spread down as mulch, or fall leaves. The type of wheelbarrow you use can make a great difference to the effort you expend. There are three principal types of wheelbarrow: a conventional single-wheeled garden barrow with an inflatable tire, a two-wheeled cart, and a wheelbarrow with a single, large, soft ball in place of the wheel.

Scientifically approved tests have been carried out on these main types of wheelbarrow to establish which ones are the easiest to use in particular circumstances. On firm ground, the single-wheeled barrow is probably the most efficient, but on soft, rough ground the ball wheelbarrow is superior. The two-wheeled cart performs less well than the other two, but it does have more lateral stability, which might be useful for someone not very steady on their feet.

PLANT NOURISHMENT

Although the plants in a low maintenance garden are selected for their ability to thrive in most conditions, their need for regular supplies of food and water cannot be totally neglected.

FEEDING

Provided adequate light and unrestricted water are available, the most important factor determining the speed and strength of plant growth is an adequate supply of nutrients. Fast plant growth is vital to low maintenance gardeners because they rely on the coalescence of foliage of ground cover plants, close-planted perennials or the deep shadow beneath the leaf canopy of burgeoning shrubs to suppress weed competition.

But there is more to it than that. People seeking a low maintenance garden are often afflicted with an impatient temperament and want to see their gardens acquire a speedy mantle of maturity. Pottering about as their fore-fathers did, adding a drop of liquid feed here or a forkful of manure there, is not for them. While organic fertilizers are very beneficial as a mulch, their plant food content is rather low, and vast quantities are required if they are to be the sole source of plant nutrients. Unfortunately, ordinary synthetic fertilizers, although more concentrated, are immediately soluble in water and leach rapidly into the soil during rainfall or irrigation, so that frequent reapplications are necessary. Fortunately, highly concentrated slow-release fertilizers are now available that make rapid plant growth and effortless plant feeding possible.

This revolutionary concept in plant feeding came about as a direct result of escalating consumption of wood pulp to provide paper for the printed word. Conifers were being felled faster than they could be regrown and a plant food that encouraged rapid tree growth was needed.

By 1973, a Californian company had produced a marketable answer to the problem – a slow-release fertilizer which has proved extremely useful in general gardening. It consists of capsules of ordinary concentrated fertilizer wrapped in a coat of natural resin extracted from soya beans. Each capsule is about the size of a wheat grain and when moistened by natural rainfall it gradually expands. By a process similar to osmosis, dissolved nutrients move slowly out through the resinous coating into the surrounding soil, to be taken up by the fine root hairs of the plants. The rate at which nutrient release takes place accelerates as the temperature rises, so that there is happy correlation between the amount of nutrient available and the needs of the plant which increase as the temperature rises.

Nowadays, these fertilizers are prepared in a number of ways so that not only is the speed at which the granules release their contents controlled, but also the ingredients are varied to meet the requirements of particular plants – for example, high potash formulations have been developed for the tomato-growing industry.

Using slow-release fertilizers

Formulations that liberate all their nutrients in three to four months are most suitable for herbaceous plants while longer term, nine-month, formulations are splendid for feeding young trees and shrubs. In both cases, a

How a slow-release fertilizer works *The wheat-grain sized capsule, right, contains water-soluble nutrients encased in a thick organic resin coating. When the capsule is wetted, water enters it through the coating, allowing the nutrients, in turn, to dissolve, and slowly pass through the resinous coat, in a process similar to osmosis. The soluble nutrients can then be absorbed by the root hairs of the plant. The thicker the coating, the slower acting the capsule.*

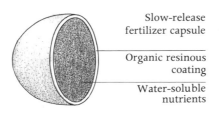

Slow-release fertilizer capsule

Organic resinous coating

Water-soluble nutrients

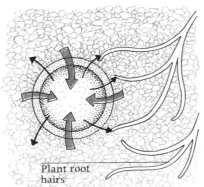

Plant root hairs

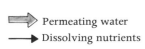

Permeating water

Dissolving nutrients

Broadcasting slow-release fertilizers *In closely planted herbaceous borders, the fertilizer capsules can be broadcast by hand. The four-month formulations are most suitable.*

Dosing trees and shrubs by volume measure *For young trees and shrubs, the nine-month formulations of slow-release fertilizers are best; they should be administered in an appropriate measure for each plant, left, as directed on the container. Once administered, the capsules should be lightly scuffled into the surface of the soil, below, with a fork or rake to ensure that they become moist.*

single application early in the season is sufficient to keep the plants well-nourished throughout the year.

Although this type of fertilizer was pioneered in the United States, similar ones are now available world-wide, and no gardener today should have much difficulty finding them, either in specially prepared retail packs in garden stores or direct from suppliers to professional horticulturists.

Slow-release fertilizers are more expensive pound for pound than conventional mineral fertilizers, but they work out less expensive in the long term, as the recommended application rates are low and a once-a-season application only is needed. Also, because the plants absorb the nutrients as they are liberated, lower quantities are lost through leaching, and water courses are not as polluted.

Foliar feeds

In periods of drought, when irrigation is not permitted by public authorities, the plants may starve. Although there are plenty of nutrients in the soil, the plant may not be transpiring sufficiently to move the nutrients up to the growth areas of the plant. As a result, the plant will yellow and wilt. Under these circumstances, first aid may be needed in the form of quick-acting liquid foliar feeds. These consist of versions of ordinary synthetic fertilizer, prepared as strong solutions that, when diluted with further water, can be sprayed directly onto foliage (but not in strong sun, or the leaves will be scorched). Although plants can receive all their food in this form, the effect of an application is short-lived and frequent doses are needed. For the low maintenance gardener, foliar feeding is best confined to emergency backup to slow-release fertilizers.

Foliar feeding *In very dry weather, when liquid foliar feed is needed, apply it directly to the leaves using a hand sprayer.*

WATERING

Once a garden is established, thorough watering in warm, dry weather will provoke abundant and satisfying plant growth. Recognizing its importance, wise nurserymen always say, send a good, patient man, not a boy, to do the watering because, done properly, it's a man's job. To a plant gasping for water, a casual splash with a hose is worse than offering a glass of vinegar to someone dying of thirst in the Sahara. If any water is provided at all, it must be copious and get well down into the root zone of the plants.

Providing this quantity of succor with a hose or watering can is a long, slow process, entailing a lot of standing about. As a result, the watering is often skimped and the plants suffer. The answer lies in installing an automatic watering system. Two principal types of system exist to do this work: sprinklers and drip irrigators. Sprinkler systems can either be of the spinning type that are attached to a hose and spray water in a circle, or they can be lengths of specially perforated irrigation pipe which send plumes of water over a rectangle of land. Drip systems, in which emitters are inserted at various points in narrow piping, allow small quantities of water to trickle slowly into the soil over long periods.

From the low maintenance point of view, the drip system is the more successful option. Sprinklers are bothersome to lay out, look ugly if left in place and have to be moved about to make sure that the whole garden is evenly watered. In these days when water is becoming costly, the disadvantage of sprinkler systems is that a lot of water is wasted, owing to evaporation of the spray droplets as they fly through the air. The drip system uses up less water, because it is applied where the plants need it most – in the region of the root hairs.

For low maintenance gardens, a drip system based on flexible plastic tubing, into which emitters are fitted at the planting positions, is hard to beat. It is easy and cheap to install, can be modified endlessly to cope with the changing needs of a developing garden and is economical to run, placing the water exactly where it is needed – at the plant roots. Best of all, for those with little time to spare, the garden can be watered at the twist of a tap. In fact, even this work can be done automatically using an electric clock mechanism linked to an electronically controlled valve on the pipe.

A drip irrigation system can be used in the ornamental and vegetable gardens with equal success. With good planning, it can be just as permanent in both locations. Since the system is lightweight, a section can be lifted

HOW A DRIP SYSTEM WORKS

A system of plastic pipes of various diameters can be linked together via special connectors to make T-shaped and L-shaped joints, in order to form a grid of pipes in any pattern required. Normally, wider-diameter piping is used for the main line and narrower-diameter piping for any branch lines leading from it. A filter connector joins the drip-system piping to a garden hose. Drip emitters can be push-fitted into the piping at any point, to provide water where required. A corkscrew-shaped channel is incorporated in each emitter to slow down the rate of water supply to a

thin trickle. Very fine flexible 'spaghetti' piping can be run from the drip emitters to reach awkwardly placed container plants, for example. A specimen layout for this type of system is shown overleaf.

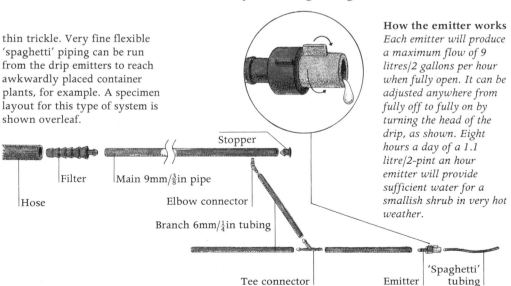

Stopper

Hose

Filter

Main 9mm/$\frac{3}{8}$in pipe

Elbow connector

Branch 6mm/$\frac{1}{4}$in tubing

Tee connector

Emitter

'Spaghetti' tubing

How the emitter works
Each emitter will produce a maximum flow of 9 litres/2 gallons per hour when fully open. It can be adjusted anywhere from fully off to fully on by turning the head of the drip, as shown. Eight hours a day of a 1.1 litre/2-pint an hour emitter will provide sufficient water for a smallish shrub in very hot weather.

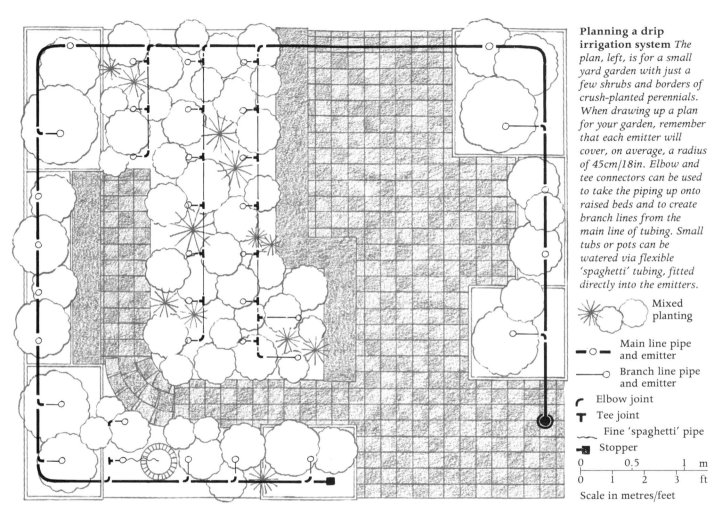

Planning a drip irrigation system *The plan, left, is for a small yard garden with just a few shrubs and borders of crush-planted perennials. When drawing up a plan for your garden, remember that each emitter will cover, on average, a radius of 45cm/18in. Elbow and tee connectors can be used to take the piping up onto raised beds and to create branch lines from the main line of tubing. Small tubs or pots can be watered via flexible 'spaghetti' tubing, fitted directly into the emitters.*

Mixed planting

Main line pipe and emitter

Branch line pipe and emitter

Elbow joint

Tee joint

Fine 'spaghetti' pipe

Stopper

Scale in metres/feet

and moved aside to enable the vegetable plot, for example, to be prepared for planting at the beginning of each season. If you should decide to redesign a planting plan, any drip emitters not required can be removed and the small holes plugged with 'stoppers'; new emitters can be push-fitted where needed. Where required, the system can be buried beneath the soil or hidden below a layer of mulch without any impairment of efficiency, or carried up onto raised beds or containers.

New technology has allowed for an alternative form of drip irrigation, consisting of piping designed to leak water very slowly along its length through thousands of tiny pores which penetrate its walls. In use, it is made up into kits that fit onto a standard 12mm/½in garden hose, with a pressure regulator and a very fine filter built into the hose connector. The pipe is laid in parallel rows across the garden at 45cm/18in intervals and can be hidden by burying it below the surface. The soil between the lines of pipe will become thoroughly damp after it has been fed with water for a few hours.

Automatic sensors can be fitted to the system which, if stationed in the soil at strategic places, will gauge its degree of dampness and open valves that allow water into the drip system, as required.

SIMPLE PROPAGATION

Just because someone is busy and has little free time for gardening, it does not mean that they must forgo all its pleasures. And undoubtedly one of the most rewarding gardening activities is to grow a few plants from seed or start some shrubs from cuttings. Watching their miracle of development induces a profound feeling of wonder and provides a sense of fulfillment that is easily obtained and demands little time if it is carefully planned.

Encouraged by success in propagating annual plants from seed and shrubs from rooted cuttings using the quick and simple methods described here, it is almost inevitable that even the low maintenance gardener will wish to indulge in more ambitious propagation. But by that time he will have become as hooked on gardening as the rest of us, realized how cheap homegrown plants can be and will have discovered more profound books on propagation to consult!

Propagation should never be approached too casually as nature has a nasty habit of snatching away her blessings as readily as she prepares them. Seeds will fail to germinate or their scant crop of seedlings will rot; cuttings will dawdle endlessly in pots making no attempt to make roots. You must marshal the right equipment, deploy it like a prudent general and carry out each operation with military precision and clinical hygiene.

The economy and value of raising a few annual flowering plants from seed each year has been mentioned previously (see p. 83) because they will provide color during times when shrubs or perennials are not in flower. Being easy to grow from seed, they provide excellent subjects for debutant propagators to practice on while developing skills in the art.

Propagation equipment

The equipment required is rudimentary and fairly inexpensive; the only major requirement is for some method of heating the potting mix in which the seeds are sown. A low voltage electric heating element, right, performs this function admirably. It consists of two sheets of tough plastic resin (impervious to water or chemicals) between which is sandwiched a thin metal-foil element. The element is usually connected by cable to a normal household power point using a small transformer to reduce the electric current to a safe 24 volts, in case an exceptionally robust gardener with perverted ingenuity manages to puncture the plastic resin and make contact with the electric element. It is very cheap to run – the element only consumes 14 watts of electricity for every 930 sq cm/1 sq ft of surface – and can be rolled up and stored away when not in use.

To get the best from the element, it should be laid on an insulating sheet of wood or polystyrene to prevent any heat loss below. It will normally warm the potting mix to an even temperature of 25°C (77°F).

The constant even warmth allows germination to take place in about a third to half of the time normally taken, which helps to guard the seedlings from fungus attack. The potting mix itself must remain in contact with the heated surface and it is therefore best to use open-bottomed polystyrene propagation flats, peat cylinders

Flexible heating element *An electric heating element, insulated by a sheet of wood to prevent heat loss, will ensure success when propagating seeds,* *by keeping the potting mix container on it at an even warmth. As a result, it will cut germination time down by approximately half to one third.*

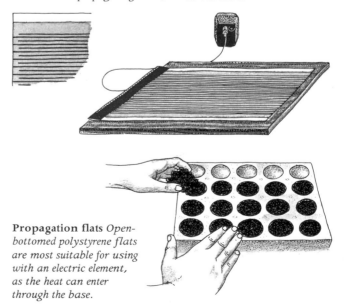

Propagation flats *Open-bottomed polystyrene flats are most suitable for using with an electric element, as the heat can enter through the base.*

or blocks. Of these, the flats are the most efficient because there is no heat loss through the sides of the potting mix.

Sowing seeds

Whichever potting mix container you use, sow three well-separated large seeds (or a pinch, if they are fine) near the middle of the surface of each one. When germination is complete, the weaker-looking seedlings can be thinned out, leaving only the strongest to grow. In this way, the gardener is guaranteed at least one good plant per potting mix unit, and does not waste the heating area.

After sowing seed, the surface of the potting mix must be sprayed with a liquid fungicide to prevent damping-off fungi from attacking the seedlings. And from the

SOWING SEEDS
To ensure germination, and to prevent root disturbance, the seeds should be sown in individual containers in an open-bottomed flat. The flat should be placed on a sheet of plastic on the heating element. Wooden supports can be provided to hold a sheet of glass over the flat, so that the potting mix stays moist.

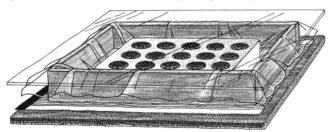

Right *Three large seeds sown in each container, in the center of the surface of the potting mix.*

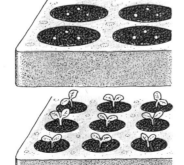

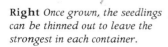

Right *Once grown, the seedlings can be thinned out to leave the strongest in each container.*

moment the seeds are sown, the potting mix must never dry out. The whole area should be covered with a sheet of glass or clear plastic, held well clear of the potting mix on a simple wooden frame, or it should be dampened frequently with a fine mist of water from a hand sprayer.

Although rearing individual plants in their own units of potting mix, rather than in a seed flat, is wasteful of space, it does save the bother of potting on and guarantees that the roots are not disturbed. If annual plants are to flower abundantly on time, their growth must not stop accelerating from the time they are sown.

Sowing seeds out of doors

Some annual seeds can be successfully sown directly into well-cultivated fine soil in borders where they will ultimately flower. More seeds than are needed should be sown, and when the young seedlings are growing strongly they can be thinned out by hand to leave sufficient strong plants to provide a good show. The intervals between the seedlings left to grow on will vary from 5cm/2in to 15cm/6in, depending upon the expected spread of the mature plant.

However, a major snag with direct sowing out of doors is that in many seasons germination will be slowed down because the soil is unsuitable or the weather is too hot, too cold, too wet or too dry to initiate the process.

One solution is to sow pregerminated seeds using a technique known as fluid drilling, above right. The seeds will begin to root and grow immediately if kept well-watered in dry weather.

Taking cuttings

Apart from wanting to grow a few annuals from seed, the low maintenance gardener may well wish to propagate a few shrubs from cuttings. Shrubs are often very expensive to buy from a nursery, and if you already have an established shrub that is particularly attractive, why not propagate a few cuttings from it?

There are various methods for propagating plants from cuttings, but in general it is easiest to take cuttings from semimature branches in the summer. They should not, however, be in flower or in bud when you take the

FLUID DRILLING

Seed sown directly out of doors often fails to germinate. Success is more certain if the seed is pregerminated indoors and then sown in a prepared seed-bed using the fluid drilling technique, right. To germinate the seed, scatter it over moist blotting paper in a plastic sandwich box and store it, covered, in a warm place such as an airing cabinet for 48–96 hours until the germinated seed is showing about 3mm/⅛in of embryo root.

1 Wash the germinated seed off the blotting paper into a sieve. Mix up some non-fungicidal cellulose wallpaper paste to half normal strength.

2 Transfer the seed into a half-filled bowl of the prepared fluid, and fill the bowl with the remainder of it. Stir the seeds well into the mixture.

3 Transfer the mixture into a clear plastic bag with a corner cut off to make a nozzle. 'Spot' sow the seeds in a prepared seedbed, each in a gobbet of fluid.

cuttings, or rooting will be delayed. To take a good cutting, pull one of the side shoots from a semimature branch by tearing it away from the mainstem so that a heel of bark and flesh from the branch comes with it. The base should then be trimmed to remove the scrappy, torn edges, dipped in rooting hormone, and plunged into a moist cuttings mixture of two parts of sharp sand and one of peat. If the potting mix is held in a 15cm/6in pot, several regularly spaced cuttings (up to four) can be set just inside its perimeter. The whole pot should be sealed in a polyethylene bag, supported as shown right, and placed in a warm but shaded spot outdoors. After six weeks, many of the cuttings should have rooted (pull one up to check) and the polyethylene can be removed and the pot transferred to full sunshine. Six weeks later, the cuttings should be growing on strongly enough to pot on into a large container of shrub potting mix (John Innes No. 3) where they can remain until they are planted out.

Layering

This technique is bound to appeal to the carefree gardener since it requires very little effort. There are two types of layering: air and ground.

PROPAGATING SHRUBS FROM CUTTINGS

Most shrubs can be propagated easily from semimature branches in summer, provided the shrub is not bearing flowers or buds at the time. If you trim the lower leaves from each 15cm/6in shoot and dip the base of it in rooting powder, you will improve the chances of rooting.

Above *Testing the shoot to see if it is suitable – it should be flexible but not too soft.*

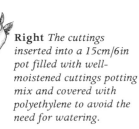

Left *Tearing the cutting away from the mainstem, leaving a heel of bark at the base.*

Right *The cuttings inserted into a 15cm/6in pot filled with well-moistened cuttings potting mix and covered with polyethylene to avoid the need for watering.*

AIR LAYERING   This method involves fastening moist potting mix onto a semimature portion of shrub stem while still attached to the plant. A shallow-angled cut is made in the stem, held open with a twist of newspaper, and a sheet of clear polyethylene, into which the potting mix is inserted, is tied around the cut stem, below. After some months, the rooted stem can be cut from the parent plant, the polyethylene removed and the rooted stem transferred to a shrub potting mix in a pot.

AIR LAYERING
Air layering is usually carried out on semimature shoots of shrubs that do not have flexible branches, provided the shrub is not in an exposed situation where the branch might snap off. The rooting process will take several months. Once rooted, the shoot can be cut off with sharp hand pruners and transferred to a pot of potting mix until ready for planting.

Above *A portion of the stem, with the shallow-angled cut in it held open with a twist of newspaper. Rooting hormone can be applied to the cut part of the stem with a fine paint brush.*

Right *When the polyethylene is tied below the cut, the potting mix can be inserted, and the polyethylene then closed with string.*

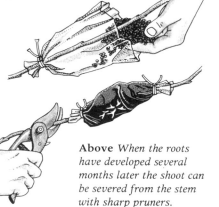

Above *When the roots have developed several months later the shoot can be severed from the stem with sharp pruners.*

GROUND LAYERING This consists of pulling down one of the outer one- or two-year-old stems of a shrub, cutting it as for air layering, and then holding the cut portion on the soil surface with a strong, hooked wire staple. Left in this position for about six to 12 months, the buried portion of the stem will put out roots and can then be severed from the stem with sharp pruners, and planted in a pot.

GROUND LAYERING
The young non-flowering shoots of soft- or hardwood shrubs can be used for simple propagation in this way, provided they are sufficiently flexible to reach the ground without splitting or snapping. Early spring is a good time to choose, but no particular season is best. The ground under the layered part of the shoot should be prepared with a mixture of coarse sand and peat, and the layered shoot should be pinned down securely into this mixture. Rooting will normally take place in about three months with fairly soft wood, longer with hard wood.

Above *A cut should be made in the shoot at a point where it will reach down to the ground easily. The cut part should be held open, with a twist of newspaper, for example, to prevent the wound closing up again.*

Left *The layered shoot secured in prepared soil by a strong wire staple.*

Division

Many tubers and corms can be propagated very easily by division; the large clumps of roots are simply lifted and divided (see p. 136), after the foliage has died down, into appropriate sized pieces and replanted. Bulbs will acquire small new bulblets that can be removed every two or three years or so, after the flowering season, and replanted to provide a better spread of colour throughout the garden.

Dividing bulbs *Dig up the bulb carefully, and gently separate any new bulblets from the main bulb, taking care not to damage the roots. Replant in the usual way.*

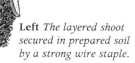

WEED CLEARANCE AND CONTROL

Weeds are the scourge of all gardens, but particularly where the gardener's time is strictly limited. The first task for any low maintenance gardener is to clear the ground of any perennial and annual weeds, the second to prevent their regrowth.

Few gardeners who have ever planted on land inadequately cleared of an infestation of deep-rooted perennial weeds can claim not to have regretted their early idleness. For the low maintenance gardener, a clean start is mandatory. It involves digging over the plot to a depth of at least 30cm/12in, using a crowbar when necessary to loosen the soil and to remove weed roots, and a long-handled shovel or a fork to sift through it. Every scrap of plant root that can be seen must be removed, since any fragments of weed carelessly left in the cultivated soil will profit mercilessly from the improved growing conditions. If you do not have time to do the job yourself, hire someone who is completely trustworthy. If it is tackled casually and accomplished too quickly, it will do more harm than good. However, if you spray the ground with a total weedkiller (see p. 150) before it is dug, you will eliminate the likelihood of reinfestation through carelessness.

Weed seeds, unfortunately, are ubiquitous and their arrival in your garden inevitable. No matter how scrupulously you clear the land, birds, wind, pets and people will introduce new weed seed to contaminate your borders and beds unless you take preventive action by creating circumstances that deter such seeds from germinating and growing. For example, you can cover large areas of the garden with a hard surface; you coulc close-plant perennials (see p. 42) so that any weed seeds are denied access to light; or you can cover areas of exposed soil with a thick blanket of mulch. Finally, if all these measures fail, you can use chemical weedkillers (see p. 150).

MULCHING

Apart from suppressing weeds, or making their removal easy, mulches benefit the plants they surround by allowing moisture to penetrate the soil while limiting its evaporation by providing a barrier between the soil and the atmosphere. The increased soil moisture level that results provides, in turn, ideal conditions for earthworm activity, so the plants enjoy the extra benefits of improved root aeration and better drainage.

The material you use for mulching can vary from pure minerals, such as gravel, crushed stone chippings or black plastic for example, to organic substances like peat or ground tree bark. Your choice will be governed by a number of factors, such as local availability, price, and the aesthetic or practical effects desired.

Organic mulch

If an organic mulch is used, the gardener usually gains an added bonus since soil organisms break it down gradually, carrying it into the soil and initiating the process that gradually transforms it into valuable humus. The type of organic mulch you choose will probably be dictated by local circumstance. If you lived near a brewery, for example, you would be almost bound to use spent hops. In general, though, the most satisfactory and pleasing mulch is coarsely ground tree bark. This is becoming increasingly popular, and has the advantage that it breaks down slowly, does not blow about and has a very attractive, natural appearance. Equally, any well-fermented compost made from non-

Clearing the ground
After loosening the soil, use a fork to sift out every scrap of weed. Arduous though this is initially, it will save a lot of work in the future.

CHOOSING AN ORGANIC MULCH

	AVAILABILITY	COST	APPLICATION	DURABILITY	ADVANTAGES	DISADVANTAGES
PEAT	Available in many places	Moderately cheap	In shrubberies and on beds	Loses roughly 15 per cent of its volume every year – more in a hot climate	Has a very natural appearance and improves soil structure	If allowed to dry out completely, it blows about and prevents light rain from reaching the soil
STRAW	Easily obtainable in rural areas	Very cheap	Most suited to vegetable gardens	Must be renewed annually	Cheap enough to use copiously	Looks messy, may carry weed seed and can only be used if supplementary nitrogenous fertilizer is added
COMPOST	Can be made in any garden	Cheapest of all mulches	Can be used anywhere	Must be renewed annually	Improves both the fertility of the soil and its structure	The average household can only provide a limited quantity
WELL-ROTTED MANURE	Freely available in rural areas	Very cheap	Useful anywhere	Dissipates quickly	Improves and enriches the soil	If not well-rotted, it can be acid and smelly; it introduces weed seeds into the garden
SAWDUST	Easy to obtain from sawmills or planing mills	Very cheap	Looks good in herbaceous beds and shrubberies	Must be topped up annually	Very easy to spread	Can be used only if it has been fermented for 12 months. Blows away easily from a windy site, and needs supplementing with nitrogenous fertilizer
COARSE TREE BARK	Becoming available in many garden stores or direct from mills	Reasonably cheap	Shrubberies and borders	Must be topped up every 2 years	Looks attractive and improves the structure of the soil	Must be well-fermented and needs supplementary nitrogenous fertilizer
SEAWEED	Available only near the sea	Free	Can be used anywhere	Lasts only a season	Good source of humus and trace elements	Must be well-composted before use or it will remain on the ground and look unsightly
SPENT MUSHROOM COMPOST	Easily obtainable from mushroom farms	Very cheap	Can be used anywhere	Must be renewed annually	Fine source of humus	Very short duration; only suitable for lime-tolerant plants.
SPENT TOMATO COMPOST	Easily obtainable from professional growers	Very cheap	Can be used anywhere	Must be renewed annually	Improves soil texture	Blows about when it dries out and can then prevent light rain from reaching the soil
SPENT HOPS	Available from breweries	Moderately cheap	Can be used anywhere	Must be renewed annually	Has an attractive texture and quickly improves soil structure	Tends to blow about on windy sites
CREEPING PLANTS	Universal	Expensive initially	Beneath trees and shrubs	Long term, but can be wiped out rapidly by pests or disease	The most attractive weed suppressant	Take a long time to become really effective

woody vegetable waste from either the kitchen or the garden provides a splendid mulch. It can be simply made in a stout plastic fertilizer bag, for example, into which are packed 10cm/4in layers of vegetable matter, alternating with 5cm/2in layers of sedge peat, mixed with 10 per cent of soil. When it is full, the bag should be tightly fastened and punctured all over with a fork, to provide ventilation and drainage. After six to eight months, the bag will contain a rich, dry sweet-smelling friable mass, ready to spread on the soil.

Whatever type of mulch you choose, it must be fully fermented before it is applied to the garden, otherwise continued fermentation will generate heat, possibly damaging your plants.

The table opposite shows the main types of organic mulch available, their relative cost, and their advantages and disadvantages.

Inorganic mulch

While these do not bestow any benefits on the soil apart from helping to conserve moisture, they have the advantage of permanence, requiring no annual renewal.

TREE SPATS   Young trees and shrubs can be protected effectively with squares of bituminous felt, known as tree spats. They were invented to suppress weeds likely to develop above the root zone of young trees. Some-

thing similar could be constructed very easily at home out of builders' roofing felt, if the spats are not commercially available in your area. The tree spats not only provide protection from weeds, they conserve vital moisture in warm weather. Although they decompose in time (about three to five years), by then they will have done their job. To improve their appearance, cover them with a thin sprinkling of gravel or soil.

GRAVEL   If you decide to use gravel, it should be put down only where it is unlikely to be distributed by people, children or animals. (Crushed limestone must not be used to mulch acid-loving plants.) It must be well-washed to free it from the tiny soil and clay particles that would bind the pebbles together, hosting weeds and making them hard to remove, and preventing rainwater from reaching the soil surface. The pebbles must pack snugly together to prevent any light reaching the soil surface, and individual stones must be small enough to pass through a 1cm/½in diameter mesh sieve. The gravel should be laid fairly thickly – a minimum depth of 5cm/2in – to keep weeds at bay. The odd few that appear can be removed with a once-yearly application of total weedkiller.

BLACK PLASTIC   This makes an excellent weed suppressor, but can only be used on level ground, since any slope will cause rainwater to collect at the lower edge of

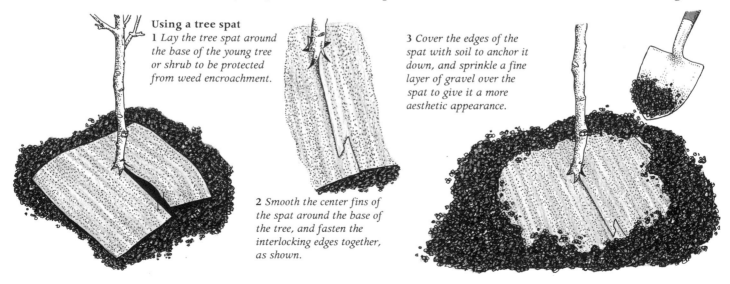

Using a tree spat
1 Lay the tree spat around the base of the young tree or shrub to be protected from weed encroachment.

2 Smooth the center fins of the spat around the base of the tree, and fasten the interlocking edges together, as shown.

3 Cover the edges of the spat with soil to anchor it down, and sprinkle a fine layer of gravel over the spat to give it a more aesthetic appearance.

Right *Thick black plastic sheeting used as a weed suppressant in a vegetable plot. Cross-shaped planting holes are cut in the plastic, which is anchored at the edges with soil, and the young plants inserted through the holes at the appropriate planting distances.*

the black plastic sheeting, depriving the plants above of vital moisture. The best application for black plastic is in the vegetable plot. A covering of soil at the outer margins will hold the sheets in place, and the seeds or young plants can then be sown or planted through small crosses cut in the plastic. The holes will stretch and widen as the young plants develop.

Black plastic can also be used in a shrubbery, for example, but it will need to be covered with a thin layer of gravel, soil or ground bark to improve its appearance.

WEEDKILLERS

When handling weedkillers of any type, care must be taken to avoid contaminating susceptible, cultivated plants, domestic animals and people. The golden rule is to obey the instructions on the container to the letter and to keep the products under lock and key.

There are two basic types of weedkiller: total and selective. Total weedkillers, based on chemicals such as sodium chlorate, aminotriazole, paraquat or glyphosate, can destroy any plants, cultivated or wild, that they make contact with. Extreme care is needed when handling them if a prized plant is not to perish along with an unwelcome thistle. Selective weedkillers based on alloxydim sodium, for example, will kill only narrow-leaved plants such as grasses, leaving broad-leaved plants unscathed. Those based on MCPA and MCPB mixtures, on the other hand, will affect broad-leaved plants like dandelions and daisies while leaving narrow-leaved plants, like grasses, undamaged, and are therefore good for controlling lawn weeds.

While the above types of weedkiller act on the plant foliage, a third type, known as preemergent, acts on bare ground, suppressing any weeds attempting to break through the soil surface. Simazine is a well-known type in this category. Since different chemicals will act for varying periods of time, always check the manufacturer's instructions before use.

Applying weedkillers

One of the problems with weedkillers has always been how to apply them without splashing and injuring the plants you are trying to save from weed competition.

Some progress was made with the introduction of a highly effective total weedkiller called glyphosate, which can be prepared in a nondrip jelly form for direct application to weeds that grow in awkward places. A special 'Weedwiper' applicator for ordinary liquid glyphosate, right, developed in the United States, is now available internationally. All you have to do is brush the moistened wick of the applicator over the leaf surface of the weed, without any danger of contaminating neighboring cultivated plants. However, the Weedwiper requires stronger-than-normal concentrations of glyphosate to be effective, and you will probably have to purchase the chemical direct from a supplier to professional growers.

Clearing the ground

Where you are clearing neglected ground of perennial and annual weeds, and there is no danger to cultivated plants, you can use glyphosate in a knapsack sprayer. Woody weeds, such as prickly shrubs or brambles, will respond better to an ammonium sulphamate spray. Follow the instructions on the container for making up the spray, and leave the ground for at least 12 weeks after spraying to give the chemical time to act. If the climate is dry, and the regulations permit, you can set light to the dried-up weed fragments, before digging it over. HERBACEOUS BORDERS If your plants are too close together to allow the Weedwiper access, you will have

Right *A knapsack sprayer being used to kill weeds on a neglected plot. The right hand is used to pump the liquid into the nozzle, which is directed down toward the area to be treated.*

Right *A roller applicator used to treat lawns. The chemical drips from the tank on the handle onto the surface of the roller, which spreads it evenly over the grass.*

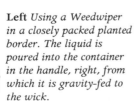

Left *Using a Weedwiper in a closely packed planted border. The liquid is poured into the container in the handle, right, from which it is gravity-fed to the wick.*

to remove any broad-leaved weeds by hand. Narrow-leaved grasses can be destroyed with an overall spray of selective weedkiller based on alloxydim sodium, provided there are no cultivated grasses nearby.

LAWNS   Although many people these days are happy to see the tinier, less harmful types of weeds, such as daisies, stud their grass, if they prosper too well it may be necessary to keep them in check. A selective weedkiller such as an ioxynil/mecoprop mixture can be applied once a season. If you use a knapsack sprayer for the job, the chemical may drift from the nozzle onto the nearby flower beds. A solution is to hire a roller applicator, such as the Driftmaster. It consists of a large plastic reservoir for the weedkiller, mounted above a perforated tube which, at the touch of a lever, dribbles the chemical onto the top surface of the roller. Since no attempt is made to break the liquid down into spray, there is no risk of damage from drift. For very small lawns you could use a sprinkler bar attachment on a watering can, but it is not as safe or as effective as the Driftmaster.

HARD SURFACES   Weeds on gravel paths or paved terraces can easily be kept in check by a once-a-season application of a nonselective weedkiller such as paraquat, applied with a watering can with a fine rose. The particular advantage of paraquat is that its ability to kill plants vanishes once it has made contact with the soil, so even after heavy rain the chemical cannot do any damage to nearby garden plants, if it is washed off the terrace. It is, however, extremely toxic to humans. Where there is a great deal of interplanting, attack the weeds with glyphosate, using a Weedwiper, to avoid killing the cultivated plants.

WILD GARDEN   Wild flowers that are regarded as weeds in a cultivated garden can be a source of great joy in a wild meadow. If you have planted shrubs or trees in a wild-flower meadow, you will probably need to use a selective weedkiller to keep weeds at bay in the early stages of their development. An area round their stems can be kept weedless by a single application, in early spring, of a preemergent weedkiller such as simazine, spread over the appropriate surfaces with a watering can or knapsack sprayer.

CONTROLLING PESTS AND DISEASES

If you grew only those plants which are highly resistant to all the common pests and diseases, you would have a very small number to choose from, and your garden would be a drab place indeed. Inevitably, if you are looking for joy from foliage and flowers, your garden will occasionally play host to active insect invaders or to parasitic fungi.

Conservationists full of heady goodwill and understandable anxiety about contaminating the environment will bid you to let nature do whatever is necessary to control pests and diseases. Sadly, by gardening at all you interfere with the natural balance and as you and your neighbors plant a number of similar shrubs and perennials, for example, any insects or diseases that occur will prosper extraordinarily well on the unexpected banquet provided. Nature will be unable to respond quickly enough to correct the balance, and circumstances will be ripe for total disaster.

The munching insects, such as moth and butterfly caterpillars, sawfly larvae and plant bugs, can strip a whole garden in a few days, if left to chew unbridled. Sucking bugs, like froghoppers or aphids, can multiply with alarming profligacy, insidiously draining the sap from a whole fresh green shoot in hours, leaving it withered and a prey to mold infection. Root eaters, like wireworms and root weevils, do their damage unseen and undetected until the plant withers and dies. Although, given time, nature would undoubtedly redress the balance, the garden will, in the meantime, have become irretrievably damaged, with all the appeal of a busy mortuary.

Although nature can keep insects at bay by eventually providing her own brigades of parasites and predators, she seems reluctant to interfere with the processes that cause plant disease. Roses and fruit trees, in particular, are prone to contract black spot, apple scab, downy and powdery mildews. These can defoliate and even kill plants very rapidly if conditions favor their development. For this reason, low maintenance gardeners are advised to limit the number of such trees and shrubs in their garden.

Faced with these challenges to the health of their plants, most gardeners conclude that they must take defensive action by applying chemical pesticides and fungicides. There are so many different preparations available that no attempt is made here to give specific recommendations about the rates of application, only the types of chemical most suitable. The safest approach to the quantity to apply is to comply exactly with the instructions on the container.

Once you have taken the decision to apply insecticides, it would be irresponsible not to try to reduce the

RECOGNIZING PEST AND DISEASE DAMAGE
The range of pests and diseases that can attack your plants is enormous. There is no short cut to complete control. The main task is to identify the problem and treat it as rapidly as possible. The method of treatment will depend broadly on the type of pest or disease. The main categories are shown right, but you will need to consult an appropriate authority for precise information.

Right *Chewed leaves and petals are usually the result of attacks by munching insects, such as caterpillars, and resmethrin can be used as a control measure.*

Left *Withered leaves and shoots are often caused by sucking bugs, such as green or black aphids. Systemic insecticides, such as dimethoate methyl, can be used to control most insects in this group.*

Right *Wilting plants are often the first sign of root damage by soil pests, such as root weevils. A soil insecticide such as phoxim should be used as a preventative measure.*

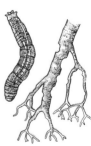

Left *Discolored, spotted, damaged and mildewy leaves are usually caused by a fungus infection. The choice of chemical depends on the nature of the disease (see p. 154).*

environmental contamination as much as possible, in an effort to prevent the less pestilential species of insect from dying as well. This can be achieved in two ways: by using sprayers that are effective when greatly reduced quantities of pesticides are applied and by choosing, wherever possible, chemicals that are scarcely toxic to humans and animals. If they are active for just long enough to carry out their specialist task, they will pose less of a threat to harmless (or even beneficial) insects that arrive later.

Foliage pesticides

Over recent years, research has been carried out in developing effective and less pernicious insecticides. Resmethrin and permethrin (synthetic relatives of pyrethrin, used to control household flies) are effective out of doors for controlling a wide range of chewing pests, such as caterpillars, beetles, crickets and earwigs, that are active on the buds and foliage of plants.

Sucking pests, like aphids, are most effectively controlled by spraying plants with a systemic insecticide, which is absorbed into the sap. The safest systemic chemical to use on most plants is probably dimethoate methyl. Once applied, it is rapidly absorbed and only insects sucking the plant juice are affected.

Applying foliage pesticides

The conventional sprayers normally used for applying foliage pesticides are not suitable for the low maintenance garden. Operating the traditional pump-handle or pressure-retaining type of applicator is almost as hard work as mixing wet cement, not to speak of the effort of carrying a large quantity of liquid around on your back on a hot day. As a result, you shirk the work until the situation becomes desperate, by which time it is already too late.

To be effective, insecticides must be applied at the first sign of an invasion. A controlled droplet application (CDA) sprayer, such as the Micro Ulva, will make this more likely, as it is particularly easy to use. Although less common than conventional sprayers, it is well worth seeking out. Supplies of the sprayers, and the pesticides specially prepared for use with them, can usually be located at suppliers of products to professional growers.

SPRAYING BUSHES AND PERENNIALS
A controlled droplet application (CDA) sprayer is less harmful, more effective and easier to use than the conventional type of sprayer as smaller quantities of chemical are used. Choose a fairly calm day and do not spray directly onto the plants. Stand about 1.8m/6ft upwind of the area to be sprayed.

Reservoir of chemical

Bottle holder

Feed nozzle

Battery housing

Spinning disk

How the CDA sprayer works (above) The chemical is gravity fed from the reservoir to a spinning disk atomizer which is operated by a battery, converting the liquid into a fine mist.

The CDA machine, above, is a typical example, powered by eight $1\frac{1}{2}$-volt batteries, and light enough to be carried easily in one hand. It creates such a fine spray that the skeptic may doubt that the work is being done at all. But if you suspend a pair of glasses in the foliage of the area to be sprayed, and then hold it up to the light after the passage of the machine, you will see that the surface is covered with thousands of tiny active particles of chemical. This intense level of protection is obtained when as little as 0.3 litres per hectare (1/5th of a pint per acre) of spray liquid is applied, compared with, say, 450 litres per hectare (40 gallons per acre) used by an ordinary sprayer.

For taller trees a CDA fan-sprayer, like the Turbair, may be needed, below. Lightweight even when charged with spray, it can protect even quite large gardens in less than ten minutes. Both types of CDA sprayer are particularly valuable for treating obdurate pests, such as whitefly, which fill the air with clouds of tiny white particles when foliage is shaken. Frequent spraying at short intervals is required since a single application of pesticide would be as useless as a man trying to stem a forest fire with a glass of water. The CDA-type sprayers make this a less time-consuming and exhausting chore. When operating any kind of chemical sprayers, protective clothing and face shields should be worn.

Controlling soil pests
Insecticides to control soil pests, such as wireworm, cutworm and root weevils, whose presence is not generally noticed until the plants collapse, are normally applied at the beginning of the growing season, either in powder or granular form. They are spread on the soil surface, scuffed into the top few inches of soil with a light fork and then watered heavily. A supplementary application is usually needed in midsummer to catch any larvae hatching from eggs laid by pests that invaded the garden after the first application. One of the most effective, and least toxic, of these chemicals is phoxim.

Controlling foliage diseases
While good timing is important in reducing the ravages of insect pests, it is absolutely critical in the prevention of diseases that attack susceptible plants such as roses or apple trees. Many of the fungicides available, such as bupirimate and those based on copper or zinc salts (for the control of downy mildews) or on dinocap (for the control of powdery mildews), are only really effective if they are applied to protect leaf surfaces or developing buds and fruit before the disease spores arrive on the wind. Since plants develop through the season, creating new foliage as they grow, this too has to be protected as it emerges. In practice, therefore, antifungus spraying must become a regular routine, carried out at 10–14 day intervals. Happily the fungicides are relatively harmless to man provided the manufacturer's instructions are well observed. If a regular fungicidal program becomes disrupted and disease takes hold, there are several eradicant fungicides like benomyl that can be applied to clear up infections, but a number of applications at short intervals may be necessary in order to eradicate a really bad attack.

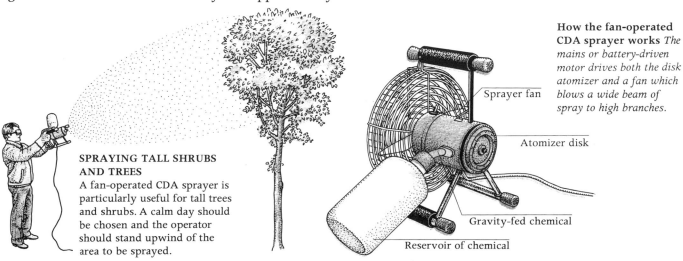

SPRAYING TALL SHRUBS AND TREES
A fan-operated CDA sprayer is particularly useful for tall trees and shrubs. A calm day should be chosen and the operator should stand upwind of the area to be sprayed.

How the fan-operated CDA sprayer works *The mains or battery-driven motor drives both the disk atomizer and a fan which blows a wide beam of spray to high branches.*

Sprayer fan

Atomizer disk

Gravity-fed chemical

Reservoir of chemical

GENERAL GARDEN CARE

Although many gardens can lose their feeling of naturalness if they are too tidy (a phenomenon known as the 'park-keeper syndrome'), general neglect will induce an unwelcome feeling of desolation. Even the most casual of gardeners should make a modicum of effort to keep the garden presentable, but, provided the original planning has been sound, little time need be spent on such work, particularly if modern aids are used.

The type of equipment you require depends to some extent on the design of your garden. If you have a traditional lawn, you will need a good electric rotary mower. Large-scale equipment used on a once-a-season basis only is probably best hired. All garden tools should be kept well-oiled and the blades, where appropriate, must be sharp. They should be sharpened once a year, either in the fall or before the start of the growing season. You will save a lot of time if you keep the equipment handily stored in a dry place, and make sure it is clean before it is put away.

Keeping hard surfaces tidy

Although terraces and paths can be kept weedless (see pp. 150–51), you will still have to clear away general debris, fall leaves and soil, if only to prevent it being trampled into the house. Possibly the easiest way of doing so is by directing a high-pressure water supply onto it, via a hose. If you confine the water pressure with an adjustable nozzle on the hose, you can create a water-jet sweeper that will be effective on any hard surface. After preliminary spraying to loosen any debris, you should move the head of the hose slowly from the high to the low edge of the area to sweep the water and debris away.

An alternative solution is to use one of the small-scale sweeper-blowers that can be hired fairly easily. They do raise prodigious quantities of dust, so you must keep any windows and doors closed when using it, and warn your neighbors in advance, so that they can do the same (and take in their wash – they will cease to become very neighborly if it becomes surfaced with a fine rime of dust). Yet another option is a really strong industrial vacuum cleaner. Many of them can tolerate

Sweeping debris with a hose *Debris can be removed easily from a paved terrace, for example, using an ordinary garden hose with a very fine nozzle to create a powerful jet of water. Aim the jet to sweep the water from the higher to the lower levels.*

Blow-sweeping leaves *A backpack blower can be used to get rid of leaves and debris from hard surfaces and lawns, for example. It will sweep the leaves into a heap on a strong beam of air. They can then be collected and made into leaf compost, or burned, as appropriate.*

Vacuum-cleaning terraces and paths *Some industrial models will sweep water safely, and if the nozzle is held above the ground, can even be used to rid gravel-clad areas of light debris without picking up stones.*

Using a rotary mower *A rotary mower needs no basket – the clippings can simply be left on the surface of the grass, where they will break down to provide an enriching mulch. Similarly, fall leaves can be chopped up using the rotary mower.*

sucking in water without endangering the operator or the engine, which makes them safe to use out-of-doors on terraces and paths.

Gravel

Areas of gravel can also be swept with an industrial vacuum cleaner. With practice, if you hold the nozzle a little distance above the surface, you will be able to pick up leaves, for example, without filling the cleaner with gravel. An occasional raking over may be needed to keep the surface of the gravel level, and a once-yearly application of a total weedkiller (see p. 150) will help to keep weeds at bay.

Lawns

Fall leaves lying in wind-formed drifts on a small area of mown lawn can be dispersed using a technique adopted by the custodians of country houses where there is a large expanse of turf. You can run a rotary mower over the lawn, cutting the leaves into small fragments. They are then quickly broken down, enriching the soil. If the discharge shoot is blocked, it will grind leaves smaller. Since the mown lawn in a low maintenance garden should only be large enough to make a

sitting area, even the smallest electric rotary mower will keep it trimmed and tidied in a few minutes.

Wild gardens

Gardeners who have created a wild area with a meadow lawn on a larger plot need only top it to a height of about 25cm/10in once or twice a year (once in midsummer will normally suffice in a temperate climate), to keep it open to access and to encourage wild flowers that develop late in the season to seed themselves.

The most suitable type of machine for the work is a portable string trimmer, opposite, which can usually be hired. When the motor is running, the operator suffers surprisingly little vibration although the noise can be irritating. Any bystanders should be kept well out of range of the whirling saw, but experience with a string trimmer soon dispels any fears the operator might have of falling onto the saw blade. The harness keeps the shaft attached to the operator's body and even if he or she should fall, the cutting head will be held rigidly several feet away. Goggles must always be worn when operating a string trimmer, to protect the eyes from flying fragments of hard twigs and the juices of soft vegetation, which could be blinding.

Using a portable string trimmer *A portable string trimmer can be hired once a season to top a meadow lawn. Various models and types of blades are available to deal with different types of vegetation, from grasses to woody shrubs. Safety goggles must be worn, and the trimmer strapped on with a harness.*

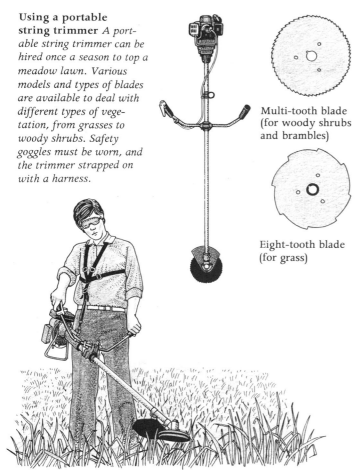

Multi-tooth blade (for woody shrubs and brambles)

Eight-tooth blade (for grass)

Hedges

While some power trimmers can be used to trim hedges, a neater, more controlled finish is obtained with an electric hedge trimmer, which can also be hired. No dedicated low maintenance gardener would want to spend too long operating a hedge cutter (when planting a new hedge, slow-growing species are best used, as the need for trimming is reduced). Hedge trimming becomes easier each season as the hedge mats together, presenting a smoother surface. The process will be hastened if, in the early years, great care is taken to prune out any strong, woody branches that grow out horizontally from the body of the hedge. These should be amputated with sharp pruners at a point well within the overall canopy of the hedge, below left. (It is worth paying a lot for good-quality, heavy-duty pruners that will slice off thumb-thick branches like a good kitchen knife beheading a carrot.) Treated in this way, the cutting surface of the hedge should ultimately consist only of fleshy young shoots, which are very easy to sever without the trimmer blade being deflected.

Once a hedge has achieved this degree of finish, a light trim is normally needed only once a year, particularly if the hedge is sprayed afterward with a growth suppressant based on the chemical dikegulac sodium. Although this cannot be used on certain species, such as *Euonymus*, it is very effective in suppressing the growth of vigorous common hedging plants like hawthorn and privet.

Using an electric hedge trimmer *An electric hedge trimmer makes short work of hedge clipping (far right). Tough horizontal branches should first be cut back within the canopy of the hedge with a pair of heavy-duty pruners (near right). A conical profile should be aimed at when clipping the hedge, to keep it solid at the base (center right).*

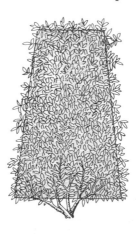

Trees and shrubs

Provided you choose your trees and shrubs from the relatively compact species in the recommended lists (see pp. 46–66) you will have little maintenance to undertake on them. From time to time, dead or wind-damaged branches may need to be removed, as will straggling new shoots that obtrude over paths or windows, for example.

For climbers and tall shrubs, long-handled pruners are best used because they will reach many branches from the ground, which makes the gardener's work easier. The main purpose of pruning, apart from general tidying, is to help the tree or shrub to develop a more attractive shape or to flower more vigorously. Such pruning can be a complicated art and before it is attempted the advice of an expert should be sought. Normally, the nurseryman supplying your trees or shrubs should be able to advise you. Alternatively, consult a good reference manual on the subject. If in doubt, do not prune at all – inexpert pruning can lead to misshapen branches or to loss of the tree or shrub.

In areas where a wheelbarrow cannot be used to cart away clippings, a woven polypropylene bag with metal handles, below, is a useful aid. Otherwise, a lightweight canvas bag, supported on a metal frame with wheels, may be helpful.

Pruning tall branches
Long-handled pruners or pole pruners can be used to lop off overhanging branches of tall climbing shrubs. The blades must be kept sharp to ensure a clean cut. Damaged torn branches will lead to disease.

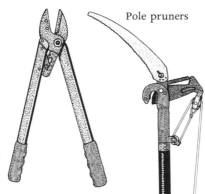

Pole pruners

Long-handled pruners

Removing dead wood
When removing broken or unwanted branches, do not cut them flush with the main stem or branch from which they emerge. Cut just outside the slight collar that always exists at the junction between the main stem and branch. Never apply any form of wound dressing, despite advice to the contrary, because it may even lead to the tree or shrub being damaged by rot.

Trimming unwanted shoots with long-handled pruners.

Collecting clippings and garden waste *For areas of garden where a wheelbarrow would be impractical, a woven polypropylene bag with carrying handles at the four corners is a useful aid.*

CHOOSING THE RIGHT PLANTS FOR YOUR SITE

In the wild, plants have become adapted to all sorts of environment and there are few places where some plants, at least, will not grow. Since man-made habitats often have similar conditions to natural ones, you should have no difficulty in choosing suitable plants for practically any site.

The map below is divided into zones that show minimum temperatures. It should be consulted when deciding which plants to grow. However, although the information is helpful, other factors must be taken into consideration. The effect of an absolute low temperature varies both with its duration and with wind conditions (whether still or blowy). Steadily falling temperatures over a period of several weeks or months allow plants a certain amount of acclimatization but a sudden cold spell in the winter does the most damage. Plants thoroughly ripened by plenty of sun and warmth in the previous season are more resistant to cold, while growth made in cool, sunless summers is soft and prone to frost.

Do bear in mind the following points when making your selection. Which way does your garden face? If it is due south, there will be plenty of winter light and summer warmth. East- and west-facing sites will be shaded in the morning and afternoon respectively, but should otherwise provide enough light for most plants. North-facing areas or walls will be fully shaded for much of the year and can be colder in winter. However, circumstances may cause these effects to vary – a south-facing wall might be shaded by a taller building and an exposed north-facing wall given some protection by a taller structure. Exposure to wind is another factor to consider, and a wall that offers protection from a prevailing north wind, for example, will give your plants a great deal of protection. An exposed site will need to have some kind of shelter provided along its boundaries, to cut down the damaging effects of cold, strong winds.

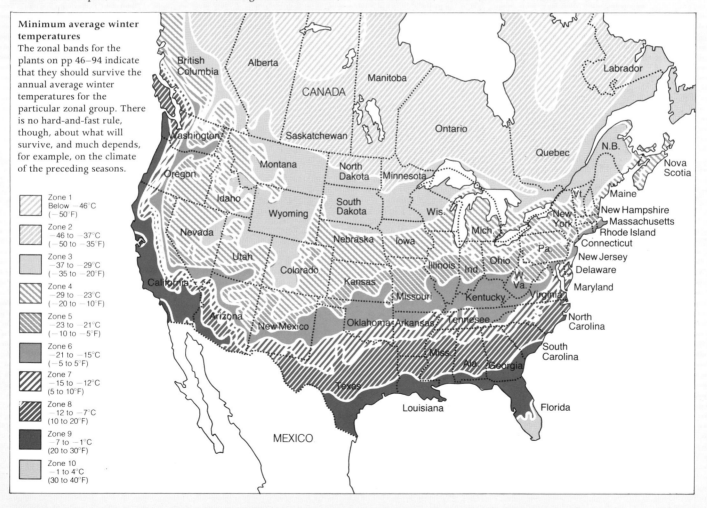

Minimum average winter temperatures
The zonal bands for the plants on pp 46–94 indicate that they should survive the annual average winter temperatures for the particular zonal group. There is no hard-and-fast rule, though, about what will survive, and much depends, for example, on the climate of the preceding seasons.

Zone 1
Below −46°C
(−50°F)

Zone 2
−46 to −37°C
(−50 to −35°F)

Zone 3
−37 to −29°C
(−35 to −20°F)

Zone 4
−29 to −23°C
(−20 to −10°F)

Zone 5
−23 to −21°C
(−10 to −5°F)

Zone 6
−21 to −15°C
(−5 to 5°F)

Zone 7
−15 to −12°C
(5 to 10°F)

Zone 8
−12 to −7°C
(10 to 20°F)

Zone 9
−7 to −1°C
(20 to 30°F)

Zone 10
−1 to 4°C
(30 to 40°F)

The following list comprises those plants that require, or do well in, special conditions, such as full sun or heavy shade and those that do not tolerate an alkaline soil. A list of good ground-covering plants is also included, as these are likely to play an important role in the low maintenance garden.

SUN-LOVING PLANTS
Trees
Acacia baileyana
Citrus maxima
Cornus florida
Eriobotrya japonica
Eucalyptus niphophila
Lagerstroemia indica
Pinus mugo
P. thunbergii
Prunus subhirtella
Thuja plicata 'Fastigiata'
Shrubs
Abelia × grandiflora
Berberis thunbergii
Cassia corymbosa
Ceanothus dentatus
C. thyrsiflorus 'Repens'
Chimonanthus praecox
Cistus 'Silver Pink'
Convolvulus cneorum
Hebe 'Edinensis'
Hebe 'Great Orme'
Kolkwitzia amabilis
Lavandula angustifolia
Nandina domestica
Nerium oleander
Paeonia lutea
Rosa × cantabrigiensis
Santolina neapolitana
Senecio greyi
Spiraea thunbergii
Syringa microphylla
Yucca recurvifolia
Climbers and wall shrubs
Actinidia kolomikta
Clematis flammula
C. macropetala
Fremontodendron californicum
Hedera helix 'Buttercup'
Jasminum officinale
Lonicera hildebrandiana
Plumbago capensis
Teucrium fruticans
Trachelospermum jasminoides
Perennials
Agapanthus 'Headbourne Hybrids'
Aubrieta deltoidea
Ballota pseudodictamnus
Chrysanthemum parthenium
Dianthus × allwoodii
Gypsophila paniculata 'Rosy Veil'
Hypericum olympicum
Hyssopus officinalis
Iris pumila
Meconopsis cambrica
Nepeta × faassenii
Paeonia mlokosewitschii
Pelargonium × hortorum
Salvia officinalis
Solidago hybrida 'Golden Thumb'
Thymus serpyllum
Annuals
Anchusa capensis
Arctotis stoechadifolia
Calendula officinalis
Dianthus barbatus
Dimorphotheca aurantiaca
Eschscholzia caespitosa
Helichrysum bracteatum
Bulbs, corms and tubers
Blandfordia nobilis
Camassia cusickii
Eremurus × 'Shelford'
Muscari armeniacum 'Blue Spike'
Aquatics
Iris kaempferi

SHADE-TOLERANT PLANTS
Shrubs
Aucuba japonica
Kalmia latifolia
Magnolia wilsonii (semi-shade)
Mahonia × media 'Charity'
Pieris 'Forest Flame'
P. japonica
Rhododendron augustinii
Rosa 'Canary Bird'
Climbers and wall shrubs
Camellia 'Inspiration'
Clematis montana
Hedera helix
H.h. 'Sagittifolia'
Hydrangea petiolaris
Parthenocissus henryana
P. tricuspidata 'Veitchii'
Perennials
Adiantum pedatum
Ajuga reptans
Arenaria balearica
Athyrium filix-femina
Bergenia cordifolia
Digitalis grandiflora
Dryopteris dilatata
Epimedium × youngianum
Euphorbia griffithii
Hosta tardiflora
H. 'Thomas Hogg'
Lamium maculatum
Lysimachia nummularia
Mentha requienii
Mitella breweri
Pachysandra terminalis
Primula denticulata
Saxifraga × urbium
Tiarella cordifolia
Bulbs, corms and tubers
Anemone nemorosa
Cyclamen coum
C. persicum
Dodecatheon media
Eranthis hyemalis
Galanthus nivalis
Leucojum aestivum
Aquatic and marsh plants
Astilbe chinensis 'Pumila' (semi-shade)
Caltha palustris (semi-shade)

GROUND COVERS
Shrubs
Cotoneaster horizontalis
Euonymus fortunei 'Emerald 'n' Gold'
Hypericum patulum
H. 'Rowallane'
Juniperus horizontalis
Rosa x 'Swany'
Vinca major
V. minor
Climbers
Clematis tangutica
Genista lydia
Hedera helix 'Buttercup' (sun only)
H. h. 'Hibernica'
Perennials
Ajuga reptans
Arenaria balearica
A. montana
Arundinaria variegata
A. viridistriata
Aubrieta deltoidea
Bergenia cordifolia
Bolax gummifera
Campanula carpatica
Epimedium × youngianum
Geranium renardii
G. 'Russell Prichard'
Hosta tardiflora
H. 'Thomas Hogg'
Hypericum olympicum
Lamium maculatum
Lysimachia nummularia
Mentha requienii
Minuartia verna
Mitella breweri
Nepeta × faassenii
Pachysandra terminalis
Sedum spurium
Tiarella cordifolia

LIME-HATING PLANTS
Trees
Cornus florida
Eucryphia cordifolia
Magnolia × loebneri 'Leonard Messel'
M. virginiana
Shrubs
Callistemon viridiflorus
Camellia japonica
C. sasanqua 'Fragrant Pink Improved'
C. × williamsii 'J.C. Williams'
Ceanothus dentatus
C. thyrsiflorus 'Repens'
Comptonia peregrina
Kalmia latifolia
Pieris 'Forest Flame'
P. japonica
Pittosporum tobira
Rhododendron augustinii
R. catawbiense
Tamarix chinensis
Climbers and wall shrubs
Ceanothus 'Edinburgh'
Perennials
Iris pumila

GLOSSARY

Acid (soil) Deficient in lime; most peaty and some very sandy soils come into this category.

Air layering Method of layering (q.v.) in which the stem is slit and the cut area kept moist until roots are formed. Once rooted, the shoot can be cut off and transferred to a pot of potting mix until ready for transplanting. See also **Ground layering**.

Alkaline (soil) Having a high lime content.

Annual Plant that grows from seed and completes its lifecycle in less than 12 months.

Aquatic Plants living wholly or partly in water. They may be submerged, floating, oxygenating or marginal.

Bedding plant Plant used for short-term display, then removed, e.g. wallflowers in spring.

Biennial Plant whose lifecycle spans two years. The seed germinates and grows into a leafy tuft or rosette the first year, elongates, flowers, seeds and dies in the following one.

Bonemeal Type of fertilizer made up from ground animal bones. It is available in different grades according to requirements. Finely ground bonemeal is quick-acting while coarser grains act more slowly and are therefore best used as long-term feeds.

Bract Modified leaf, sometimes small and scale-like and either green or brown, or large and brightly colored. In the latter case it takes over the job of attracting pollinating insects, and helps to shelter the insignificant flowers.

Broadcasting Method of sowing in which seeds, fertilizers or pesticide powders are scattered all over the soil rather than in the straight rows.

Bulb/bulblet Storage organ, usually underground, composed of short, thick, fleshy white leaves or leaf bases (scales) which store food reserves. A bulblet is a small bulb formed at the base of, or on the stem above, a mature bulb. See also **Corm** and **Tuber**.

Chalk A soft, white, gray or buff stone.

Clay Stiff earth, largely composed of aluminium silicate and the basis of which is fine particles of sand. Soil with a high proportion of clay is often rather acid, badly aerated and poorly draining.

Close-planting Method of growing plants closer together than usual to suppress weeds in the vicinity.

Colonizing Plants with vigorous rhizomes of suckering roots that spread sideways and soon invade adjacent plants or territory.

Conifer Class of primitive plants, mainly trees, that bear woody seed clusters known as cones, e.g. pine, fir, spruce.

Containerized plants Plants not grown directly in the soil but in containers such as pots or tubs.

Corm Storage organ, usually underground, formed of a short, thick, fleshy, often rounded, stem covered with a fibrous sheath.

Crown (1) Top of the root system of a herbaceous perennial plant. (2) Head and branches of a tree above the trunk or main stem.

Cultivar Short for cultivated variety and referring to a distinct variant of a species (q.v.) maintained in cultivation. Such a plant does not usually come true from seed and is maintained only by vegetative propagation (cuttings, division, layering or grafting).

Cutting Severed piece of stem, leaf or root used for propagation.

Deadheading Removing spent blossom to prevent seed formation, to prolong flowering, or to improve the appearance of a plant.

Deciduous Used mainly of trees and shrubs that are leafless for part of each year, usually from autumn to spring.

Division A method of propagation in which the roots of the plant are cut or pulled apart. It is particularly suitable for bushy plants.

Dormant period Resting stage in the annual cycle of a plant's growth, e.g. leafless trees and shrubs in winter, rootless and leafless bulbs in summer.

Double Flowers with extra petals derived from stamens and sometimes also from pistils.

Drip irrigation An irrigation system that supplies water to individual plants in small drops from emitters fitted into a system of plastic piping.

Evergreen Plants that retain their leaves for at least one whole year.

Floating Aquatic plants whose roots are not lodged in soil.

Floret Very small flowers borne in large or dense clusters.

Fluid-drilling A method of sowing in which the seed is pregerminated indoors before being sown in a specially prepared fluid, made of non-fungicidal cellulose wallpaper paste and water.

Foliar feeding A method of feeding whereby the plants are made to absorb nutrients through their foliage rather than their roots, by the application of a liquid fertilizer to the leaves, using a hand-sprayer.

French drain A pit filled with rubble or stones which receives water from a garden drainage system.

Genus (pl. **genera**) Category of plant classification in which are placed all species with characters in common. See also **Species**.

Grafting Method of propagation used for plants that either do not come true from seed or are difficult to root or establish from cuttings. A piece of the plant to be increased is severed and united to a vigorously rooted plant raised from seed or a cutting (the rootstock).

Gravel/pea gravel Smallish, rounded, waterworn stones widely used in gardens. Pea gravel is a particularly small variety.

Ground cover Plants that cover the surface of the soil so completely that they smother weeds.

Ground layering A method of layering (q.v.) used mainly for shrubs. One of the outer one- or two-year-old stems is pulled down and slit as for air layering, and the cut portion is then held down on the soil surface with a strong, hooked wire staple for several months. When the buried portion of the stem has rooted, it can be severed from the stem and planted in a pot.

Growing-on Used particularly of biennials, perennials and shrubs raised from seeds or cuttings that have to be grown for a period indoors or in a glasshouse before they are ready for their flowering quarters.

Harden-off Gradual acclimatization to the open air of plants grown in warmth.

Hardwood Fully mature stem at the end of its first growing season; a propagation term used when taking cuttings.

Hardy/half-hardy In the temperate zone, used of plants that live outside from year to year without any kind of protection. Half-hardy plants can survive only limited cold and need either a sheltered or protected site or removal to a more or less frost-free place for the winter.

Herbaceous Used of perennial plants that die back to ground level at the end of the growing season.

Humus In a garden sense, well-decayed manure, garden compost, peat and similar providers of organic matter. Technically, humus is the dark, colloidal substance clinging to the particles of inorganic matter in the soil. Humus is a soil conditioner, enabling it to hold more water and dissolved mineral salts.

Hybrid Plant resulting from crossing two distinct parents. There are three main levels of hybridity: members of two distinct genera (bigeneric hybrids), species within a genus, and forms or varieties within a species. To denote hybrid origin a multiplication sign is used. Before the Latin name, this means it is a bigeneric, e.g. × *Fatshedera*. Before the species name, this denotes that two species were crossed, e.g. *Abelia* × *grandiflora*. Hybrids between distinct forms or varieties of species are not designated in this way, but the word hybrid may be used in the name.

Inflorescence The flowering part of a plant.

Lanceolate (literally 'lance-shaped') Term applied to leaves which are a good deal longer than they are wide and taper to a point.

Layering Method of propagation whereby a shoot is made to form roots while still attached to the parent plant. See also **Air layering** and **Ground layering**.

Leaching Used of soluble fertilizers and such substances as lime that are washed deep into the soil out of the reach of roots or out of the bottom of containers by rain or continual watering.

Lime/lime hater Vernacular name for various compounds of calcium, an essential element for all plant life. Certain plants, e.g. rhododendrons and heather, require minute amounts, and an excess brings about leaf yellowing and ultimately death.

Limestone Soil that can vary from light to heavy and is usually neutral to alkaline in pH.

Loam Ideal soil type, blending particles of clay or silt with sand and organic matter (humus).

Marginal Plants which grow either in moist soil or shallow water (their roots are often partly above water level).

Mulching Application of a layer of material (mulch) that may feed the plant, condition the soil, or conserve moisture, or do all three. In the latter category it is an organic substance, such as decayed manure, garden compost, or leaf mold.

Naturalize To establish a group of plants in a naturalistic setting, such as grassland like a meadow, allowing them to grow and increase without attention.

Offset In the strict sense, plantlets borne at the tip of short, usually horizontal stems. Also used for the small bulbs that form at the base of larger ones. Offsets can be removed for propagation purposes.

Oxygenating plants Plants grown submerged in water to produce oxygen for plant and animal welfare.

Palmate Leaves with spreading finger-like lobes.

Peat Dead plant-remains in a state of arrested decay that form, due to a lack of oxygen, in the waterlogged conditions of bogs and fens. Peat is a valuable supplier of humus to the soil and, with mineral additives, makes an excellent compost or mix for container plants.

Perennial Non-woody plant that lives for several years, often called a border or a herbaceous perennial.

Pistil Female organ of a flower.

Pollarding Regular cutting back of trees or vigorous shrubs to a given point above ground level. Pollarding is carried out on plants with colourful winter stems and is usually done annually or every two or three years.

Potting Placing of a plant in a flower pot or similar rooting container with a suitable soil or potting mix. Potting-on is the moving of an established pot-grown plant into a larger container. Repotting involves taking a well-rooted or pot-bound plant into a larger container, removing some of the soil and outer roots and returning it to the same (cleaned) pot or another of the same size with some fresh potting mix.

Potting mix or soil Rooting medium containing minerals essential for growth, formulated for growing plants in pots and other containers. Loam-based mixes have always been popular, but nowadays moss peat with or without sand or grit, plus fertilizer, is more common.

Rhizome Below or partially below ground, usually horizontal stem that bears erect aerial shoots.

Root ball The thickly matted roots and soil surrounding a plant growing in the ground, or in a pot or container.

Runner Long, more or less prostrate slender stem, each leaf node rooting quickly and forming a new plant, e.g. strawberry.

Sand Gritty soil often lacking in organic matter, it usually dries out rapidly in hot weather.

Scree Natural screes are slopes made up of loose rock fragments. In a garden, it is of stone chippings, mixed with a small amount of loam.

Screed A thin, accurately levelled layer of cement, used to provide an even base for a ground covering.

Semihardwood Partially mature stem a bit more than halfway through its first growing season, distinguished by its firm woody base and soft, sometimes still-growing tip; a propagation term used when taking cuttings.

Shrub Plant formed of woody persistent stems, usually with most of the main branches arising near to or below ground level, and not much above 4m/13ft tall.

Shutter A movable partition used in concreting to direct the path or form of the concrete.

Single Opposite of double (q.v.); used in plant groups such as roses where most cultivars have double flowers.

Slow-release fertilizers Fertilizers that are specially formulated to release their nutrients over a long period of time.

Softwood Soft, sappy, actively growing stem near the start of the first season's growth; a propagation term used when taking cuttings.

Species Plant type within a genus with distinct characteristics which breed true from seeds or spores.

Sphagnum peat A type of peat made from decomposed sphagnum moss. It is extremely absorbent.

Stamen Male organ of a flower.

Subsoil The layer below the topsoil. Often used to imply a layer which is inferior.

Sucker Stem arising from below ground level, mainly from the base of a tree or shrub, or from its roots nearby, e.g. roses. See also **Offset**.

Tender Used of plants that can be grown outside during the summer only in the temperate zone, or that must be kept indoors all the time.

Tilth A 'good' tilth refers to a soil surface that has been finely broken down and is suitable for seed sowing.

Topsoil (the opposite of **Subsoil**) The uppermost layer of soil. Under normal conditions, it is reasonably fertile.

Tree spats Squares of bituminous felt used to protect the bases of young trees and shrubs from weed competition.

Tuber Enlarged root or stem that functions as a storage organ and is usually, but not invariably, underground. The potato provides the best known example of a stem tuber, bearing buds (eyes) on its surface.

Variegated Mainly used of leaves that are variously patterned, spotted or blotched with white, cream or yellow, or sometimes also with pink, red or purple.

Variety Distinct form of a species that occurs as a true breeding entity in the wild. See also **Cultivar**.

Vermiculite A substance made up of cellular flakes that will retain air and absorb water without ever becoming waterlogged. Often added to seed and potting mixtures to increase their porosity, it is used mainly by gardeners, either alone or mixed with sand or peat, as a medium in which to grow seeds and especially to root cuttings. It can be obtained in many grades, ranging from fine to coarse.

GENERAL INDEX

Bold type denotes illustration

PLANT INDEX

Bold type denotes illustration
Italic type denotes major plant entry

ACKNOWLEDGMENTS

The publishers would like to thank the many organizations and people who gave valuable advice and assistance in the production of this book, including: Robin Williams for designing the gardens on pp. 18–25 (using the author's plant lists) and for his general advice on garden design; Don Evemy and Leo Pemberton for checking horticultural information; David Carr for his advice on the practical text; Miren Lopategui and Anna Selby for editorial work; Valerie Winter, Helen and Robert Rummey and Mrs J. Woolf for allowing photographs to be taken of their gardens, and Deborah Thompson for her help with photography; C. Rassell Limited, the Camden Garden Centre and Neal's Garden Centre for lending plants and equipment for photography; Ann Smalley for providing information on digging machinery; Bulldog Tools, and Spear and Jackson Limited, for lending tools for photography; Mr M. K. Sylvester of Turbair Limited for demonstrating equipment for photography; Anne Hardy for compiling the index.

Thanks are also extended to Paul Meyer and Bill Graham of the Morris Arboretum for acting as horticultural consultants, and to Joanna Chisholm for her editorial work on this edition.

Photography

B = bottom, T = top, R = right, L = left
Karl-Dietrich Bühler: 8, 10, 13, 15, 27, 31, 34(L), 36, 39, 43, 70, 79, 82, 100, 101, 108, 109, 116, 117, 120 and front cover
Linda Burgess: 28, 38(R), 83
Camerapress: 33(L)
Geoff Dann: 92
Arnaud Descat: 1, 110, 111
Pamela J. Harper: 11(T)
Jerry Harpur: 9, 12, 14, 29, 32, 38(L), 40 (B), 80, 89
Pat Hunt: 17(B and T), 34(R), 37, 60, 85, 114, 115
Willem Kleppe: 105
Tania Midgley: 2, 11(B), 33(R), 63, 66, 103, 106, 107, 112, 113(T and B), 118, 119
Harry Smith (Horticultural Photographic Collection): 50, 52, 56, 65, 68, 72, 74, 78, 91
Michael Warren: 40(T), 86

Illustrations

Style of four-colour illustrations set by Andrew Macdonald, style of two-colour illustrations set by Jane Cradock-Watson
Russell Barnett: 122, 125–131
Jane Cradock-Watson: 48(B), 63(B), 67, 81(B), 96, 97, 123, 124, 132–158
Christine Howes: 69(BR), 71–3, 76(BR), 93, 94
Andrew Macdonald: 4, 5, 19, 21, 23, 25, 46, 47, 48(T), 49–64, 69(T and BL), 70, 87–90, 95
Sue Wickison: 75, 76(T and BL), 77–80, 81(TL and TR), 82–4
Robin Williams: 102–120
Steven Wooster: 18, 20, 22, 24
David Worth: 159

Garden designers

Tim Abrahams: 17(B); Michael Bellham: 15; Gilles Clément: 110, 111; Dick Huigens: 31, 34(L), 120 and front cover; Svend Kierkegaard: 13, 27; Ian Mylles: 103; Piet Oudolf: 100, 101; Stuart Pittendrigh: 17(T), 114, 115; Niek Roozen: 105; Robert Rummey: 106, 107; Vic Shanley: 32; John Vellam: 9; Valtin von Delius: 108, 109; Henk Weijers: 8, 43, 116, 117; Robin Williams: 112, 113(T and B); Valerie Winter: 2, 118, 119

Editor Susan Berry
Art Editor Caroline Hillier
Designers Louise Tucker, Polly Dawes

Art director Debbie MacKinnon